FOREIGN LANGUAGE LEARNING

A RESEARCH PERSPECTIVE

Bill VanPatten
*University of Illinois
at Urbana-Champaign*

Trisha R. Dvorak
University of Michigan

James F. Lee
*University of Illinois
at Urbana-Champaign*

NEWBURY HOUSE PUBLISHERS, Cambridge
A division of Harper & Row, Publishers, Inc.

*New York, Philadelphia, San Francisco, Washington, D.C.
London, Mexico City, São Paulo, Singapore, Sydney*

Library of Congress Cataloging-in-Publication Data
Foreign Language Learning.
   (Cross-linguistic series on second language research)
   Includes bibliographies.
   1. Language and languages—Study and teaching—Research. 2. Second language acquisition—Research. 3. Interlanguage (Language learning)—Research. I. VanPatten, Bill. II. Dvorak, Trisha. R. III. Lee, James F. IV. Series;
P53.F594   1987   418'.007   86-21772
ISBN 0-06-632558-7

Sponsoring Editor: Leslie Berriman
Project Editor: Basiliola Cascella
Text Composition: Desktop Publishing, Consultation & Services
Tabular Composition: Williams Graphics
Printer: McNaughton & Gunn

NEWBURY HOUSE PUBLISHERS
A division of Harper & Row, Publishers, Inc.

Language Science
Language Teaching
Language Training

Copyright © 1987 by Newbury House Publishers, A division of Harper & Row, Publishers, Inc. All rights reserved. No part of this book may be reproduced or transmitted in any form or by any means, electronic or mechanical, including photocopying, recording, or by any information storage and retrieval system, without permission in writing from the Publisher.

Printed in the U.S.A.   First Printing: February 1987
63 25583   2 4 6 8 10 9 7 5 3

CROSS-LINGUISTIC SERIES
ON SECOND LANGUAGE RESEARCH

Roger W. Andersen, Editor

Second language research within the United States has tended historically to focus on the acquisition of English as a second language. The purpose of this series is to expand the focus of second language research to include a wider variety of languages, and to approach such research from a more inter-disciplinary perspective. In addition to language acquisition, the series will deal with second language use and its related psychological, social and anthropological concerns. Other volumes in the series include *Second Language Acquisition by Adult Immigrants: A Field Manual,* Clive Perdue, Editor; *First and Second Language Acquisition Processes,* Carol W. Pfaff, Editor; and *Second Language Acquisition by Adult Immigrants,* Clive Perdue, Editor.

CONTENTS

Foreword vii

INTRODUCTION 1

PART I: INTERLANGUAGE STUDIES 17

Chapter 1: The subjunctive in Spanish Interlanguage: accuracy and comprehensibility (Tracy D. Terrell, Bernard Baycroft, Charles Perrone) 19

Chapter 2: The acquisition of German negation by formal language learners (Lynn Eubank) 33

Chapter 3: Developmental patterns of past tense acquisition among foreign language learners of French (Marsha A. Kaplan) 52

Chapter 4: Classroom learners' acquisition of *ser* and *estar*: accounting for developmental patterns (Bill VanPatten) 61

PART II: SKILLS AND STRATEGIES 77

Chapter 5: Is written FL like oral FL? (Trisha R. Dvorak) 79

Chapter 6: Learner self-correction of written compositions: what does it show us? (Diana Frantzen, Dorothy Rissel) 92

Chapter 7: FL learners' ability to recall and rate the important ideas of an expository text (James F. Lee, Terry Lynn Ballman) 108

Chapter 8: Learner comprehension of oral and written sentences in German and Spanish: the importance of word order (Veronica LoCoco) 119

PART III: FACTORS AFFECTING FL DEVELOPMENT   **131**

Chapter 9: Differentiated cognitive style and oral performance   133
(Susan Cameron Bacon)

Chapter 10: Linguistic and communicative competence: reassessing   146
foreign language aptitude (Elaine K. Horwitz)

Chapter 11: The linguistic and communicative functions of foreign   158
language teacher talk (Barbara H. Wing)

CLOSING REMARKS   **175**

Foreword

Foreign language learning (FLL) as a field of inquiry has suffered until now from disciplinary dispersion and a lack of research identity. If its purpose is to shed light on the way in which most learners across the world acquire foreign languages, namely under classroom conditions and under the guidance of a teacher, it should strive to integrate the knowledge acquired in various disciplines and encompass both the cognitive and the social dimensions of language learning. And indeed, FLL research builds on insights gained in such broad fields as linguistics, psychology and sociology, philosophy of language, artificial intelligence, conversation and discourse analysis, cultural anthropology. More specifically, it draws on but is in no way exhausted by such directly relevant fields of inquiry as linguistic theory, second language acquisition, psycho- and sociolinguistics and foreign language education.

Whereas linguistic theory is only concerned with the nature of language, second language acquisition (SLA) research elucidates some of the processes at work in learning a second language as compared with the acquisition of a first language. It examines, for example, the sequence in which structures are mastered, the universal grammar principles that govern both first and second language acquisition, and phenomena of transfer from the native into the second language. SLA research was originally the study of how learners of English formally learn and informally acquire a second language in English-speaking environments; it has now been extended to include the acquisition of all second and foreign languages. However, its research focus is almost exclusively psycholinguistic/cognitive and it rarely deals with the social conditions of the classroom. It tends to use a generally quantitative experimental approach that dissociates the phenomena observed from their interactional social context.

Work done in sociolinguistics and pragmatics does help clarify the interactional aspects of speech, such as why one says what to whom, but this research is done mostly in nonclassroom environments. There are two exceptions: *Ethnomethodology*, a branch of sociolinguistics concerned with elucidating the social norms that control the way people of a given group or culture communicate with one another, brings light to the ecology of the classroom, but is has focused until now on classes where the subject matter, but not the language, was the object of study. *Classroom-oriented research*, a recent offshoot of SLA research, does take into account the social environment of the language classroom, but it holds a noncognitive view of learner comprehension and reconstruction of input and remains typically at the surface level of the utterances observed.

Research in foreign language education consists generally of materials development and curriculum design, guided very often by specific methodologies. These are built around certain hypotheses generated by research but they cannot do justice to the enormous complexity of the language learning process. They are ultimately unsatisfactory as tools of inquiry as they try to systematize the unsystematizable, namely the learners' acquisition of a foreign mode of expression, their critical perception of self and of their surrounding world.

Thus within the general field of applied linguistics FLL research occupies a very distinct place that is in dire need of self-definition and of experimental data. This field of investigation is interdisciplinary by nature; it is predicated upon and justified by classroom learning and teaching. Most current teaching practices derive from observations of language acquisition in natural settings; for instance, the audio-lingual method was based on the mimetic way in which children were presumed to learn their first language. Krashen's natural method emerged from the observation of the way in which foreigners pick up or "acquire" English as a second language when living in the United States. However, if the main purpose of learning a foreign language in an institutional setting is to become communicatively proficient in the language, to gain insights into the symbolic and the communicative functions of language, and to develop cultural awareness and cross-cultural understanding, then we are dealing with an extremely complex phenomenon composed both of classroom and language-specific, and of universal learning processes, that integrates individual and group learning, conscious and unconscious acquisition of knowledge, secondary socialization and conceptualization, and that serves both special and general educational purposes through the guidance of a teacher in an institutional setting.

This volume represents a first attempt to stake the field of foreign language learning through original experimental research conducted with American classroom learners. It uses a variety of experimental designs and methods of data collection, both quantitative and qualitative, both with and without participants' involvement in the observation, collection and interpretation of these data. The purpose of these studies is to generate hypotheses which could eventually lead to a comprehensive theory of FL acquisition. While the individual papers focus on different linguistic, psycholinguistic, pragmatic and attitudinal aspects of the learning process, the volume itself offers a broad integrated view of language learning both as a cognitive and as a socially mediated process. It presents language not only as a system of formal properties and structures, but as a means for expressing and communicating meaning in oral and written speech, within a sociocultural environment which it both reflects and creates.

While FLL research is not in the service of any particular pedagogy, its general goal is to improve language learning conditions by advancing our knowledge and understanding of these conditions. Thus its findings should be of interest to foreign language teachers and researchers alike and to all those who are responsible for mediating the mastery of a foreign language and the sensitization to a foreign culture in institutional settings. The national interest in foreign languages aroused anew by the 1978 President's Commission Report has drawn the attention of teachers and methodologists to research done in SLA. They hope to find there the ultimate answers to the complex question: How can I best help learners become more proficient in their use of a foreign language? The emergence of the field of FLL research, as distinct from but complementary to SLA research, is a timely reminder of the need for an interdisciplinary approach and a warning against too hasty applications of hypotheses generated by individual disciplines. For the first time American research dares address the complexity of the total foreign language learner, thus echoing the efforts done abroad, for example, in the Federal Republic of Germany, where the *Sprachlehr- und lernforschung* or Foreign Language Learning and Teaching research address issues similar to those raised in this volume.

Current language research tends to examine psychological change divorced from its social context or social phenomena separated from their cognitive underpinnings. FLL research strives to integrate both and sets itself an ambitious agenda for the years to come. Three main future directions can already be detected. First, an increase in action-oriented research with methods of investigation similar to those of the social sciences: interviews, questionnaires, group discussions, participatory observation, sociometric procedures. Strong arguments are being made for involving the participants in the interpretation of the data, in order to reach a multiple perspective on the phenomena observed and to examine them from learner and teacher points of view. In answer to questions concerning the ethics of classroom-centered research, FLL research advocates increased sensitivity on the part of researchers to the interactional aspects of classroom realities. By making the participants both practitioners and researchers of the classroom, FLL research will not only elucidate the processes under study but also bring about changes in the unique communicative potential of the classroom and its own authentic metacommunicative purpose.

The second area in need of FLL research is the cultural/conceptual development of the learner. This line of inquiry has long been neglected in this country and has never found a home in language learning research. Yet, as the learner acquires with a foreign language not only a new mode of communication but a new way of conceptualizing reality, we need to investigate both the interlanguage and the interculture of foreign language learners. Related questions to be explored are, for example, foreign language textbooks' representation of foreign reality and its impact on the development of foreign concepts, or the cultural relativity of learning and teaching styles and its effect on the learning process.

A third field of study in need of FLL experimental data is the evaluation of learning outcomes. Much of the current evaluation procedures are pre-theoretical and are not supported by research. They account for only a small portion of the language learning process and thus their reliability has been put in question. Through its broad perspective on the multiple uses of language and its symbolic, phatic and communicative functions, FLL research can start investigating how to evaluate not only the development of proficiency or communicative competence, but also that of literacy in a foreign language — the ability to manipulate contexts and to create new ones.

Such a research agenda can certainly not be satisfied by isolated findings and short-term answers. It will demand both perseverance and humility, but at least FLL research is heading in the right direction and asking the right questions about its object of study.

Claire J. Kramsch
Massachusetts Institute of Technology

FOREIGN LANGUAGE LEARNING

Introduction: An Overview of Foreign Language Learning

Bill VanPatten, Trisha R. Dvorak, James F. Lee

What is foreign language (FL) learning research? For many years in this country research in the context of FL study has been directed almost exclusively at investigating methodology. The research question that has dominated the field has been how to manipulate teaching so that students would learn faster and retain longer. Not without reason, it has been likened to the "search for the Holy Grail" (Higgs 1984). Underlying this emphasis on methodology has been the basic assumption that classroom language learning, like a clear plastic bag, reveals the nature of the instruction that is poured into it but is without shape or color of its own. What students learn and how well they learn was assumed to be primarily a result of how they were taught. To a certain extent, the methods research did in fact support the idea that students tend to learn what they practice. Audiolingual methods generally proved superior to more grammar-centered methods at producing students who could speak and listen (cf. Scherer and Wertheimer 1964; Smith 1970), while students taught by communicative methods were more competent in language interactions than those taught by mimicry and memorization (cf. Savignon 1972) or by an eclectic approach (cf. Dvorak forthcoming).

On the other hand, researchers who were investigating such factors as individual differences and cognitive style (Doty and Doty 1964; Cronbach and Snow 1969; Alvord 1969; Wachtel 1971, among others) were gradually accumulating evidence that classroom learning, like any other human learning, has a character quite its own. Learning a FL has proved to be no exception. The work of Asher (1965, 1969) and Postovsky (1974), for example, indicated that students can apparently learn certain skills even when they do not practice them. Gardner and Lambert's work on attitude and motivation (1972) and Stevick's discussion of the relationships between meaning and memory (1976) addressed the issue of why some students learn what they are taught and others do not, concluding that learning does not so much result from, as interacts with, teaching.

Even more persuasive evidence of the need to examine foreign language learning as a process, rather than as essentially the more or less flawed product of instruction, has come from research in the field of second language (L2) learning. Since Krashen (1978, 1982, and elsewhere) has heightened awareness of the terms "learning" and "acquisition," a note on terminology might be appropriate here. In the context of this introduction, these two terms will be used interchangeably to refer to the process — for the most part subconscious — involved in the internalization of language.

Since the 1967 publication of Corder's article on the significance of learners' errors and Selinker's 1972 article on interlanguage, L2 research has largely been focused not on the manipulation of methodology but on the observation of learning. During this time observations of L2 learners in both classroom and naturalistic settings have resulted in important new insights about the way in which individuals go about developing competence in another language and the factors that affect that development. Perhaps one of the most significant discoveries has been the realization that at least some of the processes that allow children to acquire language are available to adults as well. This is evidenced by L2 learners of different backgrounds, who make similar errors, pass through similar transitional stages, and follow similar orders of structure acquisition regardless of their first language (L1) backgrounds or of the particular methodology to which they have been exposed.

Can the same be assumed for FL learners? Is there an identifiable process (or set of processes) that guides their development of language competences? Are these fundamentally the same processes as those underlying the development of competences by L2 learners? The importance of the differences between the contexts of FL and L2 learning should not be underestimated. With respect to attitudes and motivations toward learning another language — two factors that are crucially important to language acquisition — FL learners, as a group, are qualitatively different from L2 learners. Most of them have not chosen to study another language because they are interested in the target language or culture, and many of them do not consider language learning a particularly valuable or enjoyable experience and are often resentful of the time and energy demanded to master a skill they do not want and never intend to use. L2 learning, by definition, takes place within the environment of the target language, while FL learning is essentially limited to a classroom within the L1 environment. That means that the quality and amount of input available to the L2 learner is much richer than that available to the FL learner. For the same reason, the kind and quantity of opportunities for real language use are considerably greater for the L2 learner. Each of these differences helps to explain the difference in outcome between L2 and FL learning: the former tends to result in higher levels of proficiency than does the latter. However, these distinctions trigger a number of other important questions:

1. Do the contextual differences between FL learning and L2 learning somehow result in changes in the learning process itself or merely in changes in the product?
2. Is there an identifiable process (or set of processes) that guides FL learners' development of language competence? Are these processes fundamentally the same as those underlying the development of competences by L2 learners? What would a comparison of FL and L2 learning processes reveal?
3. Are there patterns or sequences of acquisition common to all classroom learning of the same language?
4. Does the observation of learners in contact with a variety of different languages reveal the development and use of universal strategies?
5. How restrictive is the formal environment in terms of providing input for acquisition?
6. What is the impact of the academic setting (as opposed to a Berlitz or other private language institute) on language learning?
7. To what extent can acquisition take place within a strictly formal environment?
8. How do FL learners develop listening, reading, and writing skills?
9. What happens to FL development in learners after the first two years of study? To what extent is conscious learning necessary or beneficial for continued language development?
10. What characteristics of FL learners might account for potential differences in development?

In moving beyond concerns for methodology, FL research is attempting to answer these and other questions. While the research in this volume alone does not address all of these questions, it does provide important pieces to the puzzle by focusing on the learner, the process, and the context of learning. It is our hope that it will also contribute to an eventual clarification of the relationship between L2 acquisition and FL learning at the theoretical level. At the same time, the reader may gain a better understanding of the limits or boundaries of formal language instruction.

At this juncture, several other issues central to any volume about FL (or L2 acquisition for that matter) need discussion. One issue concerns theories of language. It will be clear to the reader that the authors who have contributed to this volume approach language-oriented research from a variety of different perspectives. On the one hand, that can be considered a weakness in that the papers collected here do not contribute to an evaluation of any particular aspect of linguistic theory. Some researchers in L2 acquisition (see Flynn 1985, for example) are calling for a more "principled" approach to research involving a specific theory of language to be considered a priori. However, one could argue that construction of an adequate theory of language might follow rather than precede advances in our understanding of how natural languages are acquired. Indeed, the absence of any one approach to language research can be considered an asset for FL research. In a certain sense, the researcher is not bound by any particular research methodology or methodologies and is not predisposed toward any specific outcome, with the danger of ignoring possibly important data. The editors, then, in assembling this collection, did not impose or restrict views of language, nor did they impose any restrictions on research methodology. A perusal of this volume indicates that FL researchers are indeed investigating a myriad of aspects of FL learning, ranging from how learners construct grammatical systems (using oral and metalinguistic data) to how learners process incoming information (using text as well as isolated sentences during experimentation) to what factors contribute to eventual outcome (using constructs from educational research and L2 acquisition studies).

Regarding theories of language learning, this collection of studies again reflects a variety of different approaches. Some papers reflect the impact that Krashen (1978, 1981, 1982) has had on the FL professionals by referring to acquisition and learning as separate constructs, by restricting the use of the term "input" to mean only language that is used for information exchange, or by researching some aspect of Monitor Theory. On the other hand, some papers seemingly ignore Krashen's Monitor Theory by using acquisition and learning as interchangeable terms or by addressing issues to which Monitor Theory is at best tangential. By admitting these diverse approaches to investigating the classroom learner, the volume provides at least an overview of the multifaceted and diverse opinions that exist among those concerned with FL learning. Nevertheless, there is one underlying thread concerning language learning which does connect all of the studies: classroom learners, like their naturalistic counterparts, are viewed as individuals who interact with the language in the specific environment in which it exists and internalize at least some of the language from this interaction. In other words, while certain aspects of formal instruction may be necessary or at least beneficial to language learners, language development involves factors independent of the classroom. One goal of FL research is to discover the parameters of the effects of classroom instruction, a search that is already underway in L2 investigations (e.g., Ellis 1984; Seliger and Long 1983; Hyltenstam and Pienemann 1985).

Foreign Language Learning: A Research Perspective is divided into three major sections. Part I presents data relating to the emergence of interlanguage patterns or transitional structures in classroom learners of several different languages. The research in Part II investigates learner use of particular skills and strategies during FL development. Part III examines the impact of various factors characteristic of FL learners and their environment on the language learning process.

PART I: INTERLANGUAGE STUDIES

For learners of English as a second language (ESL), there is ample documentation not only of errors and error types (see, for example, Burt and Kiparsky 1972; Richards 1974), but also of the development of learner language over time. There are, for example, numerous studies that document the acquisition of certain morphemes (e.g., Dulay and Burt 1974; Bailey, Madden and Krashen 1974; Larsen-Freeman 1975), studies that document transitional stages in the acquisition of one structure, such as negation (e.g., Cazden et al. 1975; Wode 1978), the auxiliary (e.g., Cancino et al. 1975), Wh- question formation (e.g., Ravem 1974) and plural formation (e.g., Natalicio and Natalicio 1971). There are also studies treating communication strategies in ESL interlanguage (e.g., Tarone 1980, 1981; Faerch and Kasper 1983) and the acquisition of phonology (e.g., Dulay, Hernández-Chávez and Burt 1978; Eckman 1977, 1985; Broselow 1983; Flege 1981; Flege and Davidian 1984; Sato 1984).

Compared with the vast amount of data collected on learners of ESL, research in FL acquisition in the United States has produced only a few studies that document actual interlanguage development. To be sure, important studies that investigate major issues in L2 acquisition theory have been carried out using FL learners as a data source. LoCoco (1975), for instance, used learners of Spanish and German to examine the proportion of error types in interlanguage (e.g., intralingual versus interlingual errors) and Holley and King (1974) used learners of German to investigate the effect of certain types of error correction. But few studies using FL learners have been published which are comparable to the ESL studies on acquisition orders, transitional stages, performance, or the acquisition of phonology.

The question, of course, can be raised, Why investigate FL learners' speech when already-existing studies deal with the key issues in L2 acquisition theory? The answer is twofold. On the one hand, cross-linguistic research is invaluable to second language acquisition theory, for it either helps to support existing hypotheses or it helps to suggest alternative explanations for hypotheses based on data from ESL learners (see Andersen 1984 and VanPatten, this volume, for examples). Futhermore, the knowledge of what learners of ESL do does not provide an appropriate set of expectations for the teacher of French, for example, who wishes to know how the typical learner of French goes about internalizing rules for past tense usage. Aside from satisfying intellectual curiosity, then, well-documented accounts of the emergence of language structure over time in FL learners can be of great service to both L2 researchers (for purposes of cross-linguistic comparison) and classroom teachers (for the purpose of understanding the learner in greater detail).

Terrell, Perrone, and Baycroft, in "The Subjunctive in Spanish Interlanguage: Accuracy and Comprehensibility", examine the acquisition and use of Spanish subjunctive constructions by a group of first year college learners. Although the learners' overt knowledge of the subjunctive mood seemed complete on a written grammatical task, Terrell et al. found that in an interview learners' speech contained few correct uses of the subjunctive forms even though class time had been largely devoted to practice of this structure. While this documents the informal observations of many frustrated language teachers, Terrell et al. go on to show that beginning learners' speech also contains very few constructions actually requiring the use of the subjunctive and that only a few learner errors result in misunderstanding of the message by native speakers. Without denying the morphological problem represented by the subjunctive, Terrell et al. suggest that these last two factors—communicative value (usefulness and communicative impact of error—play a major role in learner acquisition of this structure.

Eubank, "The Acquisition of German Negation by Formal Language Learners", compares the development of negation in classroom learners' speech with the development of negation in the speech of learners acquiring German as a L2. While the two developmental sequences are comparable, Eubank notes several important differences between them. Rejecting the instructional sequence as the principal source of such differences, Eubank accounts for them by positing different production strategies for L2 and FL learners. The development of negation in L2 learners conforms to the use of a production strategy appropriate to a concern for expressiveness; the transitional negative structures of the FL learners, on the other hand, suggest the use of a strategy principally concerned with conservation of formal sentence structure. Eubank notes that, in this case, the classroom emphasis on use of complete sentences has moved the learners toward error instead of accuracy, a phenomenon that has been described elsewhere in the literature on classroom learner error. Stenson (1974) discusses "induced errors," those that would not occur as a result of general acquisitional principles, but rather are a result of teacher explanation, textbook presentation, drilling techniques or classroom-management techniques. Newmark (1966), Taylor (1975) and Krashen (1982) have suggested that L2 learners, particularly when forced to perform beyond their competence, will fall back on their L1 and make errors not attributed to those who perform "naturally" in the second language. Eubank's work is provocative in that the negative constructions of his FL learners do not show L1 influence but must still be considered "unnatural" in that they involve the use of strategies peculiar to the classroom.

Kaplan, "Developmental Patterns of Past Tense Acquisition among Foreign Language Learners of French", continues the discussion of the factors that affect the order of acquisition of foreign language structures. In her study of the use of the French *imparfait* and *passé-composé* among beginning and intermediate university students, Kaplan observes several important similarities to their use by children acquiring French as L1 and adult learners of French as a L2: despite being morphologically more complex, the *passé-composé* emerges first, and the *imparfait* is usually replaced by the present tense rather than the *passé-composé*. She argues that accounting for these patterns involves an interaction of factors: frequency in input (which is related to semantic usefulness) and semantic complexity. Even more important, possibly, is the connection that Kaplan makes to Bickerton (1981). Kaplan finds that Bickerton's model for the dynamic evolution of tense-aspect systems in creoles and other languages accounts for her FL data as well. This link adds to the evidence for universal properties underlying all kinds of language acquisition.

VanPatten, "Classroom Learners' Acquisition of *Ser* and *Estar*: Accounting for Developmental Patterns", identifies five stages through which FL learners of Spanish pass as they acquire the Spanish copula. As in the Terrell and Eubank studies, VanPatten concludes that these stages cannot be the result of formal presentation, explanation, and practice, but are, rather, evidence of the interaction of a number of other factors. VanPatten proposes that learner performance with *ser* and *estar* is attributable to a hierarchical interaction of three different factors, each previously documented by L2 research— simplification, frequency in input, and L1 transfer—with a fourth, communicative value. The communicative value or usefulness of a structure is a factor whether one addresses how learners make sense of input, as in VanPatten, or how learners process output as in Terrell et al., and in Eubank.

PART II. SKILLS AND STRATEGIES

In this section, the focus of research is not on the development of language forms per se but rather on the emergence of skills and strategies for language use: comprehension (in both reading and listening), writing, self-correction.

We now have evidence from other language acquisition studies that comprehension may be an important predecessor of production. That is, in natural language learning contexts and even for classroom learners, language comprehension generally precedes language production (see Winitz 1981 for a useful collection of articles on this topic and Sheldon and Strange 1982, who present some counterevidence involving the acquisition of certain phonological features). Many believe that learners build up some sort of linguistic competence via the processing of incoming language data, but one of the questions that has not yet been answered is just what stategies are involved in the comprehension of language and how a passive competence ever becomes active. What learners actually hear or see and how that information is understood or perceived are areas that need much investigation.

One of the central constructs of any classroom instruction is that clear and accurate explanations are helpful to learners. Krashen's Monitor Theory (1978,

1982) has modified this assumption with respect to the language classroom. Arguing that grammar instruction is only marginally important to language learners and does not lead to acquisition, Krashen claims that the domain of conscious grammar use is necessarily limited to simple rules applied in unhurried, form-focused situations. Seliger (1979), on the other hand, has suggested that the relationship between rule learning and rule usefulness may be even more tenuous because learners' verbalization of rules may in some instances have little to do with the linguistic structures they are attempting to manipulate. While studies of FL composition correction abound (see Hendrickson 1980 for a review of this research), little is known about the types of rules that FL learners use in self-correction or their strategies for analyzing and revising possible errors.

The development of written language and writing skill is another area needing investigation. Written language has often been used by both L2 and FL researchers as a source of data for revealing lexical and grammatical development, as well as for examining the operation of the monitor. However, the processes involved in learning how to use written language to effectively communicate a message or a point of view are only beginning to be identified in L1 language research. Considerably less is known about the development of writing skills in a FL or a L2. Since effective writing involves much more than the mere ability to produce grammatically correct utterances, such as the correct use of rhetorical devices and adherence to appropriate discourse constraints, it would seem that the development of writing might involve at least some processes that are different from those used in the acquisition of linguistic structure. When and how does the FL learner develop such abilities? What is the relationship between oral and written language development? Traditionally, skill in written language has been assumed to depend on the development of oral language ability; Krashen (1984), however, has suggested that the development of writing skill depends on extensive exposure to written input: the more learners read, the better their chances of developing effective written communication abilities. While Krashen cites evidence from L1 studies to support his hypothesis, his hypothesis has yet to be critically tested in the FL or L2 contexts.

Dvorak, "Is Written FL Like Oral FL?", compares the written and oral language of FL learners at several levels of proficiency across two modes of discourse: narration and argumentation. The results indicate important similarities and differences between oral and written language. On the other hand, written language is more similar to oral language within the same discourse mode than it is to written language in a different discourse mode. On the other hand, students who were even at fairly low levels of proficiency tended to write more elaborately than they spoke regardless of whether they were narrating or arguing, which suggests that written language begins to diverge somewhat from oral language fairly early in the learning of another language. Since the beginning students in Dvorak's study were minimally exposed to FL, it is likely that they, if not the more advanced students, may have been drawing on their experience with written English rather than on their experience with written Spanish as a model for their written language.

"Learner Self-Correction of Written Compositions: What Does it Show Us?", by Frantzen and Rissel, is concerned with how learners apply the Monitor (see Krashen 1982) to written language. Frantzen and Rissel examine the strategies that learners use to analyze and repair language when they are informed that an unspecified error is present. These researchers argue that learners correct errors according to a binary-option strategy: an error in X needs a correction of Y, where X and Y are typical instructional pairs. That is, an error with the Spanish verb *ser* will usually provoke substitution of *estar* rather than a change in verb tense or mood. Frantzen and Rissel also establish an "order of correctability," in an attempt to see which structures the learners have more success in correcting. Their results are comparable to those reported for L2 learners investigated under similar conditions (cf. Krashen and Pon 1975; White 1977): individual correction rates averaged around 70 percent, and many of the most easily corrected rules tended to be simple ones (article and adjective agreement). Frantzen and Rissel note that cases where complex rules appeared easier to correct than simpler ones (e.g., preterit verb forms were corrected with greater accuracy than was the use of the feminine plural article) could be explained as a result of the use of the binary-correction strategy.

Lee and Ballman, in "FL Learners' Ability to Recall and Rate the Important Ideas of an Expository Text", compare first and second language readers in terms of their ability to rate and recall the important information from an essay-like passage. Of these two abilities, rating importance has been shown to be maturational in L1 speakers (adults have the ability while children do not); whereas the recall of important ideas has been related to reading skill and progressively improves as linguistic and reading skills develop. For FL readers in this study, length of FL study was unrelated to the learners' ability to recall and rate the important units of a passage; this ability was one that all of the adult L1 readers were able to transfer to the FL reading task. Although the learners did differ from the researchers in their rating of the important units, these differences were attributable to the different perspectives that each had in performing this type of task.

LoCoco in "Learner Comprehension of Oral and Written Sentences in German and Spanish: The Importance of Word Order", presents the findings of an experiment to determine how early-stage FL learners interpret sentences of differing word orders. Her results support the findings of other researchers in second language acquisition (e.g., Ervin-Tripp 1974; Nam 1975; VanPatten 1984) that learners apparently apply non-language specific-word-order comprehension strategies in order to make sense of incoming language. Learners seemingly rely on a comprehension strategy that interprets noun-verb-noun sequences as agent-action-object, a strategy that is similar to, if not the same as, that observed in child L1 learners (Bever 1970; Schlesinger 1971; Sinclair-deZwart 1973). Studies such as LoCoco's help to explain learner difficulty in the acquisition of FL structures whose surface order does not conform to this pattern, for example, Spanish *gustar*, French *plaire*, and object pronouns in many languages. In relying upon the agent-action-object strategy to get at the meaning of an utterance, learners may skip over and ignore many inflections, functors, and other devices. These grammatical items may only become available for processing in the input as the learner progresses in acquisition and this early-stage comprehension strategy is joined by other language-specific strategies.

PART III. FACTORS AFFECTING FL DEVELOPMENT

Early accounts of FL learning assumed that the interaction between the L1 of the learner and the process of acquiring the FL was the major factor in accounting for the development of learner language. As Lado (1957), Stockwell, Bowen, and Martin (1965), and others claimed, problems in the acquisition of a FL revolved around the tendency for learners to transfer the structures (or "habits") of their L1 to the L2 or FL. According to these early hypotheses, it was the conflict between linguistic systems that caused learners their principal difficulty in mastering the L2.

Research began to surface, however, as early as the fifties (Gardner and Lambert 1959) which documented that a number of nonlinguistic variables are also important in accounting for eventual success or failure in L2 acquisition. When we say nonlinguistic, we refer to variables other than the linguistic systems themselves and to variables other than the rules or discrete points that comprise these linguistic systems. One set of nonlinguistic variables has been labeled "affective." Affective variables, in the simplest terms, are those related to learner personality, motivation, emotion, and anxiety. Research in the seventies with FL learners and students of ESL has indicated that different types of motivation (integrative and instrumental, Gardner and Lambert 1972) and anxiety (facilitating and debilitating, Scovel 1978), along with personality factors such as self-esteem (Heyde 1979) and empathy (Guiora, Beit-Hallami, Brannon, Dull, and Scovel 1972; Guiora, Brannon, and Dull 1972) are important shapers of learner language success. Another subset of nonlinguistic variables are those that come into play as language learners find themselves in contact, and sometimes in conflict, with another culture. Research has identified the importance of such sociocultural variables as anomie (Lambert 1967), attitudes toward native and target language groups (Teitelbaum, Edwards, and Hudson 1975; Oller, Hudson, and Liu 1977; Chihara and Oller 1978; Oller, Baca, and Vigil 1978; Pierson, Fu, and Lee 1980), social and psychological distance (Schumann 1976, 1978; Acton 1979), intergroup support (Genesse, Rogers, and Holobow 1983), and a number of others (see Wolfson and Judd 1983 for a discussion of variables affecting the acquisition of sociolinguistic competences).

Cognitive variables must also be considered. These subconscious and conscious processes, which enable the learner to abstract and to organize information, to see patterns where they exist, and to make sense of the environment, also affect the learner's use of a number of production and comprehension strategies (see

Brown 1980 for a brief discussion of the most well documented of these strategies). Another cognitive variable is FL aptitude. While the importance of this construct has come under recent fire (the reader may wish to see Carroll 1963 and 1973 for a discussion of language aptitude and then compare his discussion with Schumann 1978 and Krashen 1982), research on this and other cognitive variables (see, for example, Naiman, Fröhlich, and Stern's 1975 study of field dependence and field independence, and Brown's 1977 discussion of both cognitive and affective variables) have helped to clarify the extent to which the task of the language learner is influenced by factors beyond the nature of the target language itself. Implicit in this discussion, of course, is that the impact of affective and cognitive variables is not limited to language learning: they bear upon many other facets of human learning as well.

Another area for research in FL learning concerns the importance of a meaningful language environment. Research to date (Carroll 1967; Plann 1979; Hatch 1983; Peck 1978; and especially the volume by Gass and Madden 1985) has addressed type, amount, and quality of real-life, meaningful interaction in the target language. It has been suggested that while grammatical and phonological instruction is insufficient for developing proficiency in the FL, communicative interaction is absolutely essential. Other research makes even stronger claims: that interaction with native-speaking peers is what is valuable in second language acquisition and that interaction with teachers or other authority figures does not promote success to the same degree (see, for example, Plann 1979). Krashen (1978, 1982) and others (Wagner-Gough and Hatch 1975; Larsen-Freeman 1976) make different claims about language environment. Common to these researchers is the hypothesis that input data, what the language learner hears or reads, is just as important — if not more so — for language development as the practice the learner receives in oral or written language production. (See, however, Day 1986 for a collection of papers that treats the issue of "talking to learn," as well as Swain 1985 who argues for some important roles of output in language learning.)

In short, variables unrelated to language structure are now seen as playing fundamental roles in successful language development. No longer is the L1 viewed as the only important factor in language learning. Nor is it viewed as the most important. To be sure, the L1 is still considered an important variable, and recent research has been done in order to pinpoint exactly how, when, and to what degree the L1 plays a role (see Gass and Selinker 1983 for an important collection of papers treating traditional and current approaches to L1 transfer). But in the end, any theory that attempts to account for FL learning must consider much more than differences and similarities between two languages.

Bacon, in "Differentiated Cognitive Style and Oral Performance", investigates the role that field dependence and field independence may play in learners' ability to use a FL. Borrowing both theoretical constructs and methodological procedure used in psychological research, Bacon finds no support for the claim that field dependence and field independence affect language learning in different ways. Her results indicate that beginning language learners' ability to use the FL to communicate information (assessed by both quantity and quality of speech) is not affected by whether the other interlocutor is "supportive" or "nonsupportive" during an interview. This is particularly interesting given that research in which the L1 was the medium of interaction has suggested that field-dependent individuals perform much better (talk more) when there is a supportive linguistic environment. Bacon attributes her different findings for FL to the level of language possessed by the learner. Perhaps with more advanced FL learners for whom fluency is not a problem, field dependence and field independence may very well play a role in communicative interaction, thus causing differences in output and perhaps differences in advancement toward native-like ability.

Horwitz, in "Linguistic and Communicative Competence: Reassessing Foreign Language Aptitude", examines the importance of conceptual level in facilitating the development of FL linguistic and communicative competence. As Horwitz describes it, conceptual level places an individual along two developmental dimensions: cognitive complexity and interpersonal maturity. The results of her study of high school French learners suggest that linguistic and communicative competence derive from different sources: the cognitive abilities associated with conceptual level contribute to linguistic competence; interpersonal factors, such as empathy and low ethnocentrism, contribute to communicative competence.

Wing, in "The Linguistic and Communicative Functions of Foreign Language Teacher Talk", characterizes the teacher talk of fifteen high school teachers of Spanish. Gathering data at three different class meetings across a four-month period, Wing's analysis indicates that the average FL classroom is relatively input poor. Teachers use the target language only about half the time and are more likely to use English when talking about "real things" than when conducting formal language practice. Leeman (1984) has also examined FL teacher talk. In her study she finds that teachers switch back and forth between linguistic use and communicative use of language in such a way that learners are often not able to follow the teacher. That is, learners are confused about what is conversation, what is directive language, what is a correction of grammatical error, and in general whether they should be focused on content, on form, or on both. Thus, target-language use cannot automatically be considered input available for internal processing. The absence of intensive meaningful input in the FL class can be regarded, then, as a significant constraint on language development in the learner.

REFERENCES

Acton, W. 1979. Second language learning and perception of difference in attitude. Ph.D. dissertation, University of Michigan.
Alvord, R. W. 1969. Learning and transfer in a concept attainment task: a study of individual differences. Technical Report No. 4. Project on instructional variables. Standord: Stanford University Press.
Andersen, R. (ed.) 1984. *Second Languages: A Cross-Linguistic Perspective*. Rowley, MA: Newbury House Publishers.

Asher, J. J. 1965. The strategy of total physical response: an application to learning Russian. *International Review of Applied Linguistics* 3:291-300.
Asher, J. J. 1969. The total physical response approach to second language learning. *Modern Language Journal* 53(1):1-17.
Bailey, N., C. Madden, and S. Krashen. 1974. Is there a "natural sequence" in adult second language learning? *Language Learning* 24(2):235-243.
Bever, T. G. 1970. The cognitive basis for linguistic structures. In *Cognition and Development of Language*, J. Hayes (ed.), 279-352. New York: John Wiley & Sons.
Bickerton, D. 1981. *Roots of Language*. Ann Arbor: Karoma.
Broselow, E. 1983. Nonobvious transfer: on predicting epenthesis errors. In *Language Transfer in Language Learning*, S. Gass and L. Selinker (eds.), 269-280. Rowley, MA: Newbury House.
Brown, H. D. 1977. Cognitive and affective characteristics of good language learners. In *Proceedings of the Los Angeles Second Language Research Forum*, C. Henning (ed.). Los Angeles: University of California at Los Angeles.
Brown. H. D. 1980. *Principles of Second Language Learning and Teaching*. Englewood Cliffs, NJ: Prentice-Hall.
Burt, M., and C. Kiparsky. 1972. *The Gooficon: A Repair Manual for English*. Rowley, MA: Newbury House.
Cancino, H., E. Rosansky, and J. Schumann. 1975. The acquisition of English auxiliary by native Spanish speakers. *TESOL Quarterly* 9:421-430.
Carroll, J. B. 1963. The prediction of success in foreign language training. In *Training Research, and Education*, R. Glazer (eds.), 245-256. Pittsburgh: University of Pittsburgh Press.
Carroll, J. B. 1967. Foreign language proficiency levels attained by language majors near graduation from college. *Foreign Language Annals* 1:131-151.
Carroll, J. B. 1973. Implications of aptitude test research and psycholinguistic theory for foreign language teaching. *Linguistics* 112:5-13.
Cazden, C. B., H. Cancino, E. Rosansky, and J. Schumann, 1975. *Second Language Acquisition Sequences in Children, Adolescents, and Adults*. Final report to the National Institute of Education.
Chihara, T., and J. Oller. 1978. Attitudes and attained proficiency in EFL: a sociolinguistic study of adult Japanese speakers. *Language Learning* 28:55-68.
Corder, S. P. 1967. The significance of learners' errors. *International Review of Applied Linguistics* 5:161-170.
Cronbach, L. J., and R. E. Snow. 1969. Individual differences in learning ability as a function of instructional variables. ERIC ED 009 001.
Day, R. R. (ed.). 1986. *Talking to Learn: Conversation in Second Language Acquisition*. Rowley, MA: Newbury House.
Doty, B. A., and L. A. Doty. 1964. Instructional effectiveness in relation to certain student characteristics. *Journal of Educational Psychology* 54:334-338.
Dulay, H., and M. Burt. 1974. Natural sequences in child second language acquisition. *Language Learning* 24:37-53.
Dulay, H., E. Hernández-Chávez, and M. Burt. 1978. The process of becoming bilingual. In *Diagnostic Procedures in Hearing, Speech, and Language*, S. Singh and J. Lynch (eds.), 251-303. Baltimore, MD: University Park Press.
Dvorak, T. R. Forthcoming. *The Effects of Communicative Practice on Second Language Acquisition in the Classroom*. Report to the U.S. Office of Education.
Eckman, F. 1977. Markedness and the Contrastive Analysis Hypothesis. *Language Learning* 27:315-330.
Eckman, F. 1985. Some theoretical and pedagogical implications of the Markedness Differential Hypothesis. *Studies in Second Language Acquisition* 7:289-307.
Ellis, R. 1984. *Classroom Second Language Development*. Oxford: Pergamon Press.

Ervin-Tripp, S. 1974. Is second language learning like the first? *TESOL Quarterly* 8:111-127.
Faerch, C., and G. Kasper. 1983. *Strategies in Interlanguage Communication*. London: Longman.
Flege, J. E. 1981. The phonological basis of foreign accent. *TESOL Quarterly* 15:443-455.
Flege, J. E., and R. D. Davidian. 1984. Transfer and developmental processes in adult FL speech production. *Applied Psycholinguistics* 5:323-342.
Flynn, S. 1985. Principled theories of L2 acquisition. *Studies in Second Language Acquisition* 7:99-107.
Gardner, R. C., and W. E. Lambert. 1959. Motivational variables in second language acquisition. *Canadian Journal of Psychology* 13:266-272.
Gardner, R. C., and W. E. Lambert. 1972. *Attitudes and Motivation in Second-Languge Learning*. Rowley, MA: Newbury House.
Gass, S., and C. Madden (eds.). 1985. *Input in Second Language Acquisition*. Rowley, MA: Newbury House.
Gass, S., and L. Selinker (eds.). 1983. *Language Transfer in Language Learning*. Rowley, MA: Newbury House.
Genesee, F., P. Rogers, and N. Holobow. 1983. The social psychology of second language learning: another point of view. *Language Learning* 33:209-224.
Guiora, A. Z., B. Beit-Hallami, R. C. L. Brannon, C. Y. Dull, and T. Scovel. 1972. The effects of experimentally induced changes in ego states on pronunciation ability in second language: an exploratory study. *Comprehensive Psychiatry* 13:421-428.
Guiora, A. Z., R. C. L. Brannon, C. Y. Dull. 1972. Empathy and second language learning. *Language Learning* 22:111-130.
Hatch, E. M. 1983. Simplified input and second language acquisition. In *Pidginization and Creolization As Language Acquisition*, R. W. Andersen (ed.), 64-86. Rowley, MA: Newbury House.
Hendrickson, J. 1980. The treatment of error in written work. *Modern Language Journal* 64:216-221.
Heyde, A. 1979. The relationship between self-esteem and the oral production of a second language. Ph.D. dissertation, University of Michigan.
Higgs, T. V. 1984. Language teaching and the quest for the Holy Grail. In *Teaching for proficiency, the organizing principle*, T. V. Higgs (ed.), 1-9. Skokie, IL: National Textbook Company and ACTFL.
Holley, F., and J. King. 1974. Imitation and correction in foreign language learning. In *New Frontiers in Second Language Learning*, J. H. Schumann and N. Stenson (eds.), 81-89. Rowley, MA: Newbury House.
Hyltenstam, K., and M. Pienemann. 1985. *Modelling and Assessing Second Language Acquisition*. San Diego: College Hill Press.
Krashen, S. D. 1978. The monitor model for second language acquisition. In *Second-Language Acquisition and Foreign Language Teaching*, R. Gringas (ed.), 1-26. Washington, D. C.: Center for Applied Linguistics.
Krashen, S. D. 1981. *Second Language Acquisition and Second Language Learning*. Oxford: Pergamon.
Krashen, S. D. 1982. *Principles and Practice in Second Language Acquisition*. Oxford: Pergamon Institute of English.
Krashen, S. D. 1984. *Writing: Research, Theory and Application*. New York: Pergamon Press.
Krashen, S. D., and P. Pon. 1975. An error analysis of an advanced ESL learner. *Working Papers on Bilingualism* 7:125-129.
Lado, R. 1957. *Linguistics Across Cultures*. Ann Arbor: University of Michigan Press.
Lambert, W. E. 1967. A social psychology of bilingualism. *Journal of Social Issues* 23:91-109.

Larsen-Freeman, D. 1975. The acquisition of grammatical morphemes by adult ESL students. Paper presented at the annual TESOL Convention, Los Angeles.
Larsen-Freeman, D. 1976. An explanation of the morpheme accuracy order by learners of English as a second language. *Language Learning* 26(1):125-135.
Leeman, E. 1984. Intake, communication, and second-language teaching. In *Initiatives in Communicative Language Teaching: A Book of Readings,* S. J. Savignon and M. S. Berns (eds.), 35-54. Reading, MA: Addison-Wesley.
LoCoco, V. 1975. An analysis of Spanish and German learners' errors. *Working Papers on Bilingualism* 7:96-124.
Naiman, N., M. Fröhlich, H. H. Stern, and A. Todesco. 1978. *The Good Language Learner.* Toronto: The Ontario Institute for Studies in Education.
Nam, E. 1975. Child and adult perceptual strategies in second language acquisition. Paper presented at the annual TESOL Convention, Los Angeles.
Natalicio, D., and L. Natalicio. 1971. A comparative study of English plural formation by native and non-native English speakers. *Child Development* 42:1302-1306.
Newmark, L. 1966. How not to interfere with language learning. *International Journal of American Linguistics* 40:77-83.
Oller, J. W., L. Baca, and A. Vigil. 1978. Attitudes and attained proficiency in ESL: a sociolinguistic study of native speakers of Chinese in the United States. *Language Learning* 27:1-27
Oller, J. W., A. Hudson, and P. Liu. 1977. Attitudes and attained proficiency in ESL: a sociolinguistic study of Mexican-Americans in the Southwest. *TESOL Quarterly* 11:173-183.
Peck, S. 1978. Child-child discourse in second language acquisition. In *Second Language Acquisition: A Book of Readings,* E. M. Hatch (ed.), 383-400. Rowley, MA: Newbury House.
Pierson, H., G. Fu, and S. Lee. 1980. An analysis of the relationship between language attitudes and English attainment of secondary students in Hong Kong. *Language Learning* 30:289-316.
Plann, S. 1979. Morphological problems in the acquisition of Spanish in an immersion classroom. In *The Acquisition and Use of Spanish and English as First and Second Languages,* R. W. Andersen (ed.), 119-132. Washington, D.C.: TESOL.
Postovsky, V. A. 1974. Effects of delay in oral practice at the beginning of second language learning. *Modern Language Journal* 58: 229-239.
Ravem, R. 1974. The development of wh-questions in first and second language learners. In *Error Analysis: Perspectives on Second Language Learning,* J. C. Richards (ed.), 134-155. London: Longman.
Richards, J. C. 1974. Error analysis in second language strategies. In *New Frontiers in Second Language Learning,* J. H. Schumann and N. Stetson (eds.), 32-53. Rowley, MA: Newbury House.
Sato, C. J. 1984. Phonological processes in second language acquisition: another look at interlanguage. *Language Learning* 34:43-57.
Savignon, S. J. 1972. *Communicative Competence: An Experiment in Foreign Language Teaching.* Philadelphia: Center for Curriculum Development.
Scherer, G. A. C., and M. Wertheimer. 1964. *A Psycholinguistic Experiment in Foreign Language Teaching.* New York: McGraw-Hill.
Schlesinger, I. M. 1971. Production of utterances and language acquisition. *In the Ontogenesis of Grammar.* D. I. Slobin (ed.), 63-101. New York: Academic Press.
Schumann, J. H. 1976. Social distance as a factor in second language acquisition. *Language Learning* 26:135-143.
Schumann, J. H. 1978. Second language acquisition: the pidginization hypothesis. In *Second Language Acquisition,* E. Hatch (ed.), 256-271. Rowley, MA: Newbury House.

Scovel, T. 1978. The effect of affect on foreign language learning: a review of the anxiety research. *Language Learning* 28:129-142.

Seliger, H. 1979. On the nature and function of language rules in language teaching. *TESOL Quarterly* 13:359-369.

Seliger, H., and M. Long (eds.). 1983. *Classroom Oriented Research in Second Language Acquisition.* Rowley, MA: Newbury House.

Selinker, L. 1972. Interlanguage. *International Review of Applied Linguistics* 10:201-231.

Sheldon, A., and W. Strange. 1982. The acquisition of /r/ and /l/ by Japanese learners of English: evidence that speech production can precede speech perception. *Applied Psycholinguistics* 3: 243-261.

Sinclair-deZwart, H. 1973. Language acquisition and cognitive development. In *Cognitive Development and the Acquisition of Language,* T. E. Moore (ed.), 9-25. New York: Academic Press.

Smith, P. 1970. *A Comparison of the Cognitive and Audiolingual Approaches to Foreign Language Instruction.* Philadelphia: Center for Curriculum Development.

Stenson, N. 1974. Induced errors. In *New Frontiers in Second Language Learning,* J. H. Schumann, and N. Stenson (eds.), 54-70. Rowley, MA: Newbury House.

Stevick, E. W. 1976. *Memory, Meaning, and Method.* Rowley, MA: Newbury House.

Stockwell, R., J. D. Bowen, and J. W. Martin. 1965. *The Grammatical Structures of English and Spanish.* Chicago: University of Chicago Press.

Swain, M. 1985. Communicative competence: some roles of comprehensible input and comprehensible output in its development. In *Input in Second Language Acquisition,* S. Gass and C. Madden (eds.), 235-256. Rowley, MA: Newbury House.

Swain, M., G. Dumas, and N. Naiman, 1974. Alternatives to spontaneous speech: elicitation and imitation as indicators of second language competence. *Working Papers on Bilingualism* 3:68-79.

Tarone, E. 1980. Communication strategies, foreigner talk, and repair in interlanguage. *Language Learning* 30:417-431.

Tarone, E. 1981. Some thoughts on the notion of communication strategy. *TESOL Quarterly* 15:285-295.

Taylor, B. 1975. The use of overgeneralization and transfer learning strategies by elementary and intermediate university students learning ESL. In *New Directions in Second Language Learning, Teaching, and Bilingual Education,* M. Burt and H. Dulay (eds.) 55-69. Washington, D. C.: TESOL.

Teitelbaum, H., A. Edwards, and A. Hudson. 1975. Ethnic attitudes and the acquisition of Spanish as a second language. *Language Learning* 25:255-266.

VanPatten, B. 1984. Learner's comprehension of clitic pronouns: more evidence for a word order strategy. *Hispanic Linguistics* 1:88-98.

Wachtel, P. L. 1971. Cognitive style, attention and learning. *Perceptual and Motor Skills* 32:315-318.

Wagner-Gough, J., and E. Hatch. 1975. The importance of input data in second language acquisition studies. *Language Learning* 25:297-308.

White, L. 1977. Error analysis and error correction in adult learners of English as a second language. *Working Papers on Bilingualism* 13:42-58.

Winitz, H. (ed.). 1981. *The Comprehension Approach to Foreign Language Teaching.* Rowley, MA: Newbury House.

Wode, H. 1978. Developmental sequences in naturalistic L2 acquisition. In *Second Language Acquisition,* E. Hatch (ed.), 101-117. Rowley, MA: Newbury House.

Wolfson, N., and E. Judd (eds.). 1983. *Sociolinguistics and Language Acquisition.* Rowley, MA: Newbury House.

PART ONE
Interlanguage Studies

CHAPTER 1
The Subjunctive in Spanish Interlanguage: Accuracy and Comprehensibility

Tracy D. Terrell
University of California at San Diego

Bernard Baycroft
Stanford University

Charles Perrone
University of Florida

INTRODUCTION

One of the problems that a teacher of a second (L2) or foreign language (FL) faces is how to use the time in a course so that it may be profitably spent on developing communication and literacy skills. For the most part this has traditionally meant that the instructor should focus the students on various facets of the language itself, such as vocabulary, pronunciation, syntax, and morphology. The usual practice is to introduce the entire grammar of the target language in the first year course and then to review it in the second year. Since no one has written, much less taught, the entire grammar of any language, the use of the word entire is somewhat exaggerated. Nevertheless, because this system is followed by virtually all colleges and universities in the United States, most introductory texts are written with this sort of "complete" grammatical syllabus in mind. In support of this approach, it is often asserted that it is difficult to engage in any sort of conversation or discussion, much less in the reading of interesting material, unless the student has been introduced to the main structures of the language. As far as we are aware, there has never been any empirical evidence to support the view that all of the syntax and morphology presented in introductory courses is necessary for basic communication of ideas in the languages most commonly studied. Because of the strength of the tradition, it is almost impossible to institute any program or to write materials that break radically with the standard approach, in which morphology and syntax are central. It is interesting to note that this teach-the-entire-grammar-in-the-first-year tactic in American colleges and universities is not often followed in other countries. Courses in English as a second language (ESL) and English as a foreign language (EFL) have traditionally been divided into several levels, with syntax and morphology spread out over a long period of study.

One of the areas of Spanish grammar that is considered to be difficult for students of Spanish, or of any Romance language for that matter, is the subjunctive mood. Unlike its English counterpart, the Spanish subjunctive is used in normal conversation by all native speakers, including children. Instructors of Spanish have not been in agreement about the specific analysis of the semantic and syntactic functions of the subjunctive paradigm or about the most efficient way to teach the use of the subjunctive mood. (See, for example, Hooper and Terrell 1975.) In most texts the presentation of the subjunctive paradigms and the syntactic and semantic rules of distribution are usually presented at the end of the introductory course. There are several arguments that are often given to justify late introduction of the subjunctive. First, the subjunctive is mostly a phenomenon of dependent clauses; since it is assumed that the students will not use complex sentences until the end of the course, it follows that the subjunctive is not as necessary at the beginning. Furthermore, the subjunctive forms are not as common as indicative verb forms, and many instructors argue that the indicative forms should be thoroughly mastered first in order to avoid confusion when the subjunctive forms are finally introduced. Bull (1947) did an extensive study of written Spanish from a variety of sources and concluded that the present subjunctive forms make up about 3 percent of all verb forms used. The other subjunctive tenses add another 2 percent or so to this total. Although we know of no similar study for speech, there is no reason to believe that these figures would be any different; they would certainly not be higher.

This paper represents the results of one experiment in which the following questions were asked:

1. What does first year learners' interlanguage reveal about learner strategies in the use of the subjunctive? How accurate are learners in the use of this particular morphosyntactic feature? Furthermore, if we consider the subjunctive an advanced structure, what is the effectiveness of teaching it to beginning learners?
2. How does learner use or non-use of the subjunctive affect others' comprehension of his or her speech?

In short, we are investigating the relative short-term effects or non-effects of instruction on one particular grammatical structure. The various aspects of question 1 were investigated using an error analysis of the tape-recorded speech of students of first year Spanish. Question 2 was researched by submitting learners' utterances to native speakers of Spanish for intelligibility assessment.

PART I: LEARNER ERRORS

SUBJECTS AND METHOD

The subjects for this experiment were students in the third quarter of the first year course which, in the fall quarter, is designed as a review course for students who have studied Spanish for at least two years in high school before enrolling at the University of California-Irvine. In this particular class, the approach was cognitive; i.e., the class periods consisted of a presentation of a series of grammar points that were first explained (usually in Spanish), practiced (by means of audiolingual drills or cognitive grammar exercises), and then applied in guided conversations. The teaching of the subjunctive was scheduled for the last four weeks of this ten-week course.

The written exams revealed that the students had satisfactorily comprehended the topics covered. On this exam students successfully performed exercises asking them to choose the subjunctive or indicative forms. For example,

Juan José quiere que su hermana _____ en casa esta tarde. (quedarse)
Juan José wants his sister _____ at home this afternoon. (to stay)

The class average on this grammar exam was 23 out of 25. Furthermore, in the written evaluations, the students judged the course in general to be a success. Although the course was cognitively oriented in terms of grammar presentation and practice, we emphasized the development of spontaneous oral skills as well, and the students were overwhelmingly pleased to have learned to communicate as well as they did. Because of this oral emphasis, in addition to the written final exam, an oral final exam was administered. Sitting before a tape recorder, students were expected to engage in spontaneous conversation with their instructor on one of twenty topics. Although the students knew the topic possibilities in advance, they had no way of knowing which of the twenty would be selected for their particular oral exam. In addition, the instructors were asked to include certain questions in the conversation as naturally as possible. These questions included two that were specifically aimed at giving the students an opportunity to use the subjunctive:

> What sort of person would you like to marry?
> What are your plans for this summer? After you graduate?

The corpus of raw data for this study consisted of approximately six hours of these recorded oral examinations from seventy students. All cases were noted in which the subjunctive was used (1) correctly, (2) incorrectly, and (3) required but not used. The substitutions for the subjunctive in this last case were incorrect tense forms or other inappropriate structures.

In the six hours of recorded conversations there were only eighty one sentences that fell into one of these categories (see Appendix One for a complete list). That is only about one sentence per student, although some students used no subjunctive sentences and others used several. This is not an unreasonably low figure of usage since, as pointed out earlier, the relative frequency of use of the subjunctive mood by native speakers is also quite low.

RESULTS AND DISCUSSION

There were only 10 sentences of the 81 (12 percent) in which the subjunctive mood was used correctly. Of these, two were so reduced in structure that they were incomprehensible to native speakers (see Part II). (The numbers in parentheses refer to the appendices at the end of this paper.)

> [I-A.(6)] *Mis padres quieren mí venga aquí.
>   My parents want me to come here.
> [I-A.(7)] * ¿Qué quieres mí diga?
>   What do you want me to say?

The correct versions should have included the relator *que*, and the pronoun that is the subject of the verb in the dependent clauses should be nominative in form:

> [I-A.(6)] Mis padres quieren que yo venga aquí.
> [I-A.(7)] ¿Qué quieres que yo diga

Only 8 of the 81 sentences were both correct and comprehensible to native speakers. That is only a 10 percent yield for conversational production in classes in which the norm for correct answers on the sections of the written final exam which dealt with the subjunctive was approximately 92 percent. In the terminology of Krashen's Monitor Theory of second language acquisition (Krashen 1982), these students have learned the rules, they have not yet acquired them. Although they apparently had learned the forms and rules, they were unable to monitor with them effectively during the oral examination. It should be noted that the low level of monitoring occurred even though the students were in an exam situation. Thus, it appears that motivation for correctness is not sufficient to guarantee success in monitoring with learned rules even in testing situations.

It is of interest to inquire whether a reduction in correctness from 92 percent in written work to 10 percent in coversation in unusually high or whether it is the norm for beginners in a FL classroom. Is it that most of the rules that are learned are indeed not acquired and in addition are not available for monitoring in spontaneous conversation? We know of no studies that address this question directly, but preliminary work with rules such as person-number agreement in the present indicative, gender agreement, number agreement, and so forth (rules that are expected to be acquired intuitively before the subjunctive), shows that they are used in spontaneous speech at much higher levels of accuracy than 10 percent.

It appears doubtful that any beginning learner of Spanish ever acquires subjunctive usage in a single year of study, although many do indeed learn the principal rules of formation and distribution, as the results of the written exam data demonstrate. No data are available showing how much input and interaction in a natural environment are required for the acquisition of the subjunctive. Informal reports indicate that even an entire year of residence in a Spanish-speaking country may not be sufficient input for the acquisition of the subjunctive.

Unfortunately, there are considerations that lead us to believe that even the 10 percent figure is too high as a measure of actual ability to use the subjunctive forms correctly in speech. The regular subjunctive verb forms are generally taught as a vowel quality switch rule: /a/ for first conjugation verbs such as *hablar* (to speak) is replaced by /e/, i.e., the indicative *habla* becomes the subjunctive *hable*; /e/ and /i/ of second and third conjugation verbs such as *comer* (to eat) and *vivir* (to live) are replaced by /a/, i.e., indicative *come* and *vive* become subjunctive *coma* and *viva*. Since the conjugation classification of a particular verb is arbitrary, and since mood is not associated with a single phoneme consistently (indeed, what is indicative for one conjugation is subjunctive for the other and vice versa), it is not always possible to determine whether the student was purposely using the subjunctive or indicative forms. In the following sentences, for example, the subjunctive forms, although used correctly, may have been chosen randomly:

[I-A.(5)] Yo creo que es muy necesario que nosotros hablemos español.
I believe it is very necessary for us to speak Spanish.

[I-B.(8)] Tiene que tener un apartamento que cueste menos.
He has to have an apartment that costs less.

Confusions caused by the vowel switch rule may also account, at least in part, for many of the examples in which the subjunctive mood was used in simple independent sentences, a context that for all practical purposes never requires the subjunctive:

[II-A.(1)] *En México si no hablan correcto, ellos entiendan (entienden).
In Mexico, if they don't speak correctly, they understand.
[II-A.(2)] *Cuando es enojado, no me escuche (escucha).
When she's mad, she doesn't listen to me.

The same is true for sentences [II-A.(3)], [II-A.(4)], and [II-A.(5)] (see Appendix One). It is questionable that the students consciously intended to use the subjunctive mood in these sentences, i.e., that their use was the result of monitoring. Nor could the students have acquired such use since the subjunctive forms would never occur in the input in these sorts of independent clauses. One possible explanation is that students have heard and stored both forms, i.e., *entienden* and *entiendan*, as "they understand" and simply access one of the two at random. Another possibility is that they have stored a single form with randomly alternating thematic vowels.

The situation is only slightly less complex in the case of the irregular forms of very common verbs. Most of these irregular verbs have a subjunctive stem identical to the stem of the first person singular present indicative forms. For example, the verb *decir* (to say, tell) is *digo* for the first person singular present indicative, and the subjunctive form is *diga*. Because of the high frequency of the first person singular forms, these irregular indicatives are generally well known. In addition, the command forms, which also use the same stem, are also common in teacher-talk. Thus, in sentences [II-A.(6)] and [II-A.(7)], these forms may be the result of incorrect extensions of the first person singular indicative stem, or they may be simple repetitions of command forms the students have heard frequently:

[II-A.(6)] *No más hagas (haces) lo que tú quieres.
  You should only do what you want.
[II-A.(7)] *Pregunta y yo diga (digo).
  Ask and I'll say.

It is also possible that students confuse the irregular subjunctive stems with the past (preterit) irregular stems:

[II-A.(8)] *El verano pasado yo miro este escuela y dígales (les dije) a mis padres...
  Last summer I saw this school and I told my parents...
[II-A.(9)] *'Customs' nos diga (digo) que hay una plaga.
  Customs told us that there was a plague.

However one analyzes these errors with subjunctive forms used in noun clauses, the fact remains that in more sentences the subjunctive forms were used incorrectly than correctly.

Of the remaining 52 sentences in which the subjunctive is required but not used, 35 are in noun clauses (III-A.), 13 in adverbial clauses (III-B.), and only 4 in adjectival clauses (III-C.). The frequency of adverbial and adjectival clauses in which the subjunctive is required is extremely low in the speech of first year students.

There were 27 noun clauses produced that may be classified semantically as volition [III-A.(1)]. Eight more were of the doubt category [III-A.(2)], and no examples appeared in the emotive category. (See Hooper and Terrell 1975 for a discussion of these terms.) Within the category of volition, a single predicate, *querer* (to want), was the governing matrix for the embedded noun clause in 16 of the 27 cases. That is, a single verb accounts for 46 percent of all of the subjunctive use in noun clauses and 31 percent for the entire corpus.

[III-A.(1)] *Quiero que él tiene muchos intereses.
  I want him to have many interests.

Of the 13 adverbial clauses used by these students, 12 were examples in which the subordinator is *cuando* (when, whenever), followed by some kind of anticipated or projected proposition. There were no examples of this sort of construction used correctly in the corpus.

[III-B.(42)] *Yo les visitaré cuando tendré dinero.
I will visit them when I have money.

If one considers that the mistakes in sentences with *querer* and *cuando* account for 54 percent (28/52) of all of the omissions of the subjunctive in this corpus, one is led to the conclusion that the teaching strategies did not match the communicative needs of the students of this study. If, for example, in this corpus the students had been able to restrict their use of the subjunctive to only these two contexts, they would have made only 24 errors instead of 71, a reduction of over one-half.

PART II: INTELLIGIBILITY OF ERRORS TO NATIVE SPEAKERS

A number of investigators have looked at the effects of errors on native speakers. There have been essentially two kinds of studies. One kind looks at the subjective effect of errors on native speakers, while the other looks at the comprehensibility or intelligibility of these errors. Politzer (1978), for example, looked at the reaction of native German teenagers to errors committed in German by English speakers. The German speakers were asked to judge the relative seriousness of errors in sentence pairs. Politzer found that "vocabulary errors are definitely considered as the most serious" (257).

Chastain (1980) did a similar study for Spanish but asked native speakers to classify errors as comprehensible and acceptable, comprehensible but unacceptable, or as incomprehensible. Chastain tested only two sentences with subjunctive errors:

*Quiero (a) ustedes me llamen esta noche.
I want you to call me tonight.
*Me pide que le presto mi raqueta de tenis.
He asks me to lend him my tennis racquet.

Both sentences were judged by all but one native speaker as comprehensible. A majority claimed the sentences to be unacceptable as well, while a minority judged them acceptable.

Galloway (1980) examined the "effectiveness of message transmission and reception" (428) in her subjects. Using videotapes, Galloway investigated the following parameters: (1) amount of communication, (2) efforts to communicate comprehensibility, (3) paralanguage, and (4) overall impression made by the students on the video viewers. These viewers consisted of non-native Spanish-speaking teachers, native Spanish-speaking teachers, native speakers of Spanish living in the United States, and native speakers of Spanish living in Spain. The main response from all groups indicated that "errors did not seriously impede overall comprehension" (431), and Galloway concluded that the absence of grammatical accuracy in learner speech may not produce negative reactions in native speakers if the learner's desire and urgency to communicate are evident. It is also interesting to note that the native group living in Spain rated the students higher in every category (except paralanguage) than did the other three groups of raters.

Guntermann's (1978) study of speech errors of Peace Corps volunteers in El Salvador is most like the present study in that it looked at comprehensibility. Native speakers were asked to listen to sentences and then to restate them "according to what they the volunteers had intended to say" (251). Of the 1290 interpretations given, only 22 percent were inaccurate. She concluded that "for comprehensibility, grammar errors were not serious impediments even though no situational context for the sentence was provided to the informants" (251). Regarding mood, only 10 percent of the sentences was misinterpreted.

The research to date, then, indicates that grammatical errors are not usually barriers to the communication of messages. However, it is clear that certain kinds of grammatical mistakes could lead to confusion. For this reason, it was decided that errors related to the use of the subjunctive should be tested for native-speaker intelligibility.

PROCEDURE

Representative sentences with errors were culled from the corpus produced by the students. These were mixed with invented sentences containing other error types in order to avoid any learning effect on the part of the native-speaker judges. This list of forty sentences was submitted to twenty native speakers from Latin America. Specifically, the native speakers were asked in Spanish (1) to tell what they thought the sentence meant, or (2) to explain in their own words the intent of the speaker, or (3) to translate the sentence into English. Most of the responses were simple paraphrases in Spanish of the test sentences since the English of this particular group was minimal.

RESULTS AND DISCUSSION

The results are striking. (See Appendix Two.) No verb form, however great the formal error, was misunderstood by more than 30 percent of the natives. Severe problems with comprehension arose only when the syntactic frame of the dependent clauses was greatly changed from the norm. This was especially true if the syntactic pattern had been reduced and pronouns were involved. For example, five of the six most frequently misunderstood sentences resulted from the reduction of the pattern "main verb + *que* (relator) + dependent clause."

[A.(1)] *¿Nos quiere ir al laboratorio usted?
(¿Quiere Ud. que vayamos al laboratorio?)
Do you want us to go to the lab?

Sentences containing these sorts of errors are especially difficult to process since the two clauses involve different subjects or objects or both in pronominal form. The result is that native speakers have difficulty in assigning the pronouns to the verbs of the two clauses. For example, see Appendix Two sentences [A.(1)], [A.(2)], [A.(4)], [A.(5)], and [A.(6)]. On the other hand, whenever the relator *que* was preserved with a conjugated verb, the sentence was usually interpreted correctly regardless of verb form.

[C.(18)] *Quiero que el será un buen jugador.
I want him to be a good player.

Errors in the use of pronouns were especially problematic. Sentence [A.(1)] in Appendix Two, which appears above with its correct gloss, was interpreted by native speakers as "Do you want to take us to the lab?" or "Do you want to go with us to the lab?"

One could attribute these particular student errors partially to the copying of English syntax and partially to developmental errors resulting from the simplification of the system of Spanish complementation. However, in either case, the fact remains that the key items to be acquired (learned) are (1) syntax (i.e., main verb + relator + conjugated verb) and (2) pronoun use (form and placement). The choice of the verb form appears to be quite secondary to clause marking insofar as comprehension by native speakers is concerned. That is not surprising since this appears to be precisely the same strategy our students use in comprehension of sentences that contain subjunctive forms. That is, before (and perhaps after!) they have formally studied the subjunctive, students may simply ignore the verb forms, concentrating on context for the necessary semantic cues for comprehension. Students seemingly do not have to have studied the use of the subjunctive in order to comprehend sentences in which these uses are present. (See VanPatten 1985 for a discussion of communicative value and information processing.)

SUMMARY AND CONCLUSIONS

The Spanish system of subjunctive and indicative verb morphology is extremely difficult to acquire (or learn) and is subject to reduction and simplification at all stages of the acquisition or learning process. The data indicate that at the end of a single year of college-level study, most students have not acquired the rules for the use of the subjunctive paradigm sufficiently to be able to produce them correctly in speech. Futhermore, students do not seem to be able to monitor their conversational output by using learned rules in order to increase accurate use of the subjunctive.

There is, of course, some evidence that certain morphemes and structures are acquired in specific orders and that age, language background, and the nature of the learner's exposure to the language have little effect on this sequence (Dulay and Burt 1974: Larsen-Freeman 1975; Bailey, Madden, and Krashen 1974; Fathman 1975; and others). Although the relevant research has not been conducted on learners of Spanish, it is suggested here that future research will reveal that the subjunctive is acquired in stages (cf. VanPatten and Eubank, this volume), all of which may be late in the overall picture of the acquisition of syntax. The data in this study lead one to the conclusion that these developmental stages in the acquisition of the subjunctive occur after the first year of language study for most, if not all, college-level students.

One might ask a priori why 40 percent of course time would be spent on a paradigm that is used in only about 5 percent of normal speech. One possible answer is that most instructors believe that the subjunctive is indeed quite common in ordinary speech, which is contrary to what is known about written Spanish and what has been suggested for spoken Spanish as well. However, in certain situations or for certain speech events, the subjunctive might appear with more frequency than usual, for example, in conversations between parents and children where directives with volition might abound. On the other hand, for all situations, subjunctive verb forms are clearly redundant and do not add significantly to message content in most cases (e.g., the subjunctive of doubt where the doubt is expressed in the matrix clause). In a certain sense, then, neither frequency nor function is a good reason to devote so much time to the subjunctive in a beginning Spanish course.

There is a different reason, however, that one might offer for including the subjunctive in a first year course. If the learning of a form is an aid in its eventual acquisition, then it is logical to teach it, keeping in mind that immediate acquisition is certainly not expected. However, there is a caveat to this position. The data in this study show that when beginning students converse freely, they will frequently use two constructions involving the subjunctive: *querer que* and *cuando*. The following recommendation is made, then, for curriculum decisions: the students should concentrate on learning the subjunctive for use in just these two contexts, with less emphasis on other uses. It is hypothesized that perhaps with a "smaller baggage" of use to master, learners could more effectively monitor in these frequent contexts and thus boost their accuracy. Also, if frequency of need for communication has anything to do with how grammatical structure is acquired, then it may well be that these two contexts are where the acquisition of the subjunctive is begun. Thus, the grammar curriculum would not be in conflict with the tendencies in acquisition and use of language.

The experiment with native-speaker intelligibility of learner errors, however, may lead one to modify slightly the recommendation just made. In that part of the study, problems in interpretation of the verb form were not problematic, whereas problems in comprehension did arise due to syntactic or sentence-level errors involving omission of the relator and incorrect use of pronouns (form and placement) in subjunctive use where *querer* was the matrix verb. These results suggest that the teaching of the subjunctive would be more profitable for students if the curriculum not only limited teaching to two specific contexts for the subjunctive, but also concentrated on syntax (relator and pronoun use) rather than morphology.

REFERENCES

Bailey, N., C. Madden, and S. Krashen. 1974. Is there a "natural sequence" in adult language learning? *Language Learning* 24:235-243.
Bull, W.E. 1947. Modern Spanish verb form frequencies. *Hispania* 30:451-466.
Chastain, K. 1980. Native speaker reaction to instructor-identified students' second-language errors. *Modern Language Journal* 64:210-215.
Dulay, H., and M. Burt. 1974. Natural sequences in child second language acquisition. *Language Learning* 24:37-53.
Fathman, A. 1975. The relationship between age and second language productive ability. *Language Learning* 25:245-253.
Galloway, V. 1980. Perceptions of the communicative efforts of American students of Spanish. *Modern Language Journal* 64:428-433.
Guntermann, G. 1978. A study of the frequency and communicative effects of errors in Spanish. *Modern Language Journal* 62:249-253
Hooper, J. B., and T. D. Terrell. 1975. A semantically based analysis of mood in Spanish. *Hispania* 57:484-494.
Krashen, S. D. 1982. *Principles and Practice in Second Language Acquisition.* Oxford: Pergamon Institute of English.
Larsen-Freeman, D. 1975. The acquisition of grammatical morphemes by adult ESL students. Paper presented at the annual TESOL meeting, Los Angeles.
Politzer, R. 1978. Errors of English speakers of German as perceived and evaluated by German natives. *Modern Language Journal* 62):253-261.
VanPatten, B. 1985. Communicative value and information processing in second language acquisition. In *ON TESOL '84: A Brave New World for TESOL,* P. Larson, E. L. Judd, and D. S. Messerschmitt (ds.), 89-99. Washington, D.C.: TESOL.

APPENDIX ONE

I. Sentences in which the subjunctive forms are used correctly
  A. Noun clauses
    1. Correct Structure
      (1) Quieren que yo venga aquí.
      (2) El quiere que lo mantenga...
      (3) Es importante que él sea inteligente.
      (4) Es importante que él no tenga las tendencias del machismo.
      (5) Yo creo que es muy necesario que nosotros hablemos español.
    2. Incorrect Structure
      (6) *Mis padres quieren mí venga aquí.
      (7) *¿Qué quieres mí diga?
  B. Adjective clauses
      (8) Tiene que tener un apartamento que cueste menos.
  C. Adverbial clauses
      (10) Si tuviera accidente, no podía hacer nada.

II. Sentences in which the subjunctive forms are used erroneously
   A. Independent clauses
   (1) *En México si ho hablan correcto, ellos entiendan.
   (2) *Cuando es enojado no me escuche.
   (3) *...no se entre en casa...
   (4) *...no hable...
   (5) *Los negros estudiantes piensen que cosas es malo.
   (6) *No más hagas lo que tú quieres.
   (7) *Pregunta y yo diga.
   (8) *El verano pasado yo miro este escuela y dígales a mis padres.
   (9) *'Customs' nos diga que hay una plaga.
   (10) *Mi mama se muera el verano pasado.
   (11) *Ellos planearan casarse el verano pasado.
   (12) *Para muchos años yo vuelva a California.
   B. Noun clauses
   (13) *Pienso que sea un problema importante.
   (14) *Creo que trabaje mucho.
   C. Adjective clauses
   (15) *Tengo muchos amigos que hablen...
   (16) *Es mis abuelos que estén italianos.
   D. Conditional sentences
   (17) *Si vaya a una escuela, yo puedo trabajar.
   (18) *Si quiera asistir en una gran universidad, tiene que.
   (19) *Si su familia sea más grande, no ayuda la problema.
III. Sentences in which the subjunctive forms should have been used
   A. Noun clauses
     1. Volition
   (1) *Quiero que él tiene muchos intereses.
   (2) *Quiero que él puede jugar.
   (3) *El no quiere que yo trabajo.
   (4) *Mi mama no quiere que reciben...
   (5) *Quiero que mi esposo quiere hacer mucho.
   (6) *Quiero que es un hermano mayor de yo.
   (7) *Yo quiero que él será un buen jugador.
   (8) *Yo quiero que él (mi esposo) ser un americano.
   (9) *Quiero que mi esposo a tener buen sentido de humor.
   (10) *Quiero que usted me aconseja.
   (11) *Yo no quiero tú verlas.
   (12) *No quiero para él oir a mí.
   (13) *Mi padre me quiere ir a la escuela.
   (14) *¿Nos quiere ir al laboratorio usted?
   (15) *La moneda, ¿quiere dártela?
   (16) *¿Quiere usted dije mis problemas?
   (17) *Prefiero que es una profesión que...
   (18) *La escuela hace que los niños no necesitan mucho.
   (19) *Es necesario que él tiene una buena educación.
   (20) *No es necesario que la gente tienen familias grandes.
   (21) *Es muy facil que yo aprendo español.
   (22) *No es correcto que yo pienso así.

(23) *No es correcto que yo tengo miedo.
(24) *Es necesario que comprendo la realidad.
(25) *Es necesario que comprendo cuando...
(26) *Es muy necesario que yo hablo bien.
(27) *Es muy importante que él dominará la casa.

2. Doubt

(28) *Tienen miedo que es la verdad.
(29) *No estoy seguro que Tomás es el esposo perfecto.
(30) *No creo que los problemas está muy serioso.
(31) *No creo que es un problema grande.
(32) *Yo espero que yo puedo.
(33) *Yo espero que yo viajo.
(34) *Espero que trabaja por mi cuando.
(35) *Es una posibilidad que yo voy a estudiar...

B. Adverbial clauses

1. Time conjunctions

(36) *Yo no quiero casar hasta que termino la escuela.
(37) *Quiero tener un macho cuando se casa.
(38) *En el futuro cuando estoy un doctor.
(39) *Cuando recibe una diploma, seré una camarera.
(40) *Cuando vendré el próximo trimestre, tendre una pierna rota.
(41) *Para cuando saldré colegio, quiero trabajar.
(42) *Yo les visitaré cuando tendré dinero.
(43) *El tiene que cuidar los niños cuando ellos erán jóvenes.
(44) *Pienso casar cuando tener dinero.
(45) *Es necesario que comprendo cuando escribir en el futuro.
(46) *Es un buen ejemplo para yo cuando un día ser también esposo.
(47) *Pienso casar cuando termine mi educación.

2. Other

(48) *Es un jardín para la gente venir y mirar.

C. Adjectival clauses

(49) *No encontraba personas quien hablan español.
(50) *Cada persona puede estudiar que quieres.
(51) *No hagas lo que tú quieres.
(52) *Prefiero que es una profesión que él necesitaría inteligencia.

APPENDIX TWO

Sentences submitted for intelligibility judgements by native speakers. (Only those related to subjunctive are included.)

A. Sentences misunderstood by more than half of the native speakers

(1) *90% ¿Nos quiere ir al laboratorio usted?
(2) *85% La moneda, ¿me quiere dártela?
(3) *80% Pregunta y yo diga.
(4) *60% No quiero para él oír a mí.
(5) *60% No quiero tú verlas.
(6) *55% Mi padre me quiere ir a la escuela.

B. Sentences misunderstood by less than one-third of the native speakers
- (7) *30% Es necesario que comprendo cuando escribir en el futuro.
- (8) *25% ¿Qué quieres me diga?
- (9) *25% Es muy fácil que yo aprendo español.
- (10) *20% Espero que trabajé por mi cuñado.
- (11) *20% Es más importante que él dominará la casa.
- (12) *15% Cada persona puede estudiar qué quieres.

C. Sentences misunderstood by only one or two persons
- (13) *10% Cuando recibe una diploma, seré una camarera.
- (14) *10% Quiero que él tiene ganas.
- (15) *10% El anó pasado yo miro este escuela y dígales a mis padres...
- (16) *10% Pienso casar cuando terminé mi educación.
- (17) * 5% Prefiero que es una profesión buena.
- (18) * 5% Quiero que él será un buen jugador.
- (19) * 5% Si vaya a una escuela, yo pueda trabajar.

D. Sentences that no one misunderstood
- (20) *En México si no hablas correcto, ellos entiendan.
- (21) *Es muy necesario que yo hablé bien.
- (22) *Quiero que usted me aconsejé.
- (23) *Mi mamá se muera el año pasado.
- (24) *Es una posibilidad que yo voy a estudiar.
- (25) *Para cuando saldré colegio, quiero trabajar.

CHAPTER 2

The Acquisition of German Negation by Formal Language Learners[1]

Lynn Eubank
University of Texas at Austin

INTRODUCTION

Research in the acquisition of syntax and morphology by second language (L2) learners has stressed the developmental nature of interlanguage. Some researchers have claimed that there are so-called natural routes (summarized in Ellis 1985) or universal strategies and stages (Wode 1981). While most work has been conducted using English as the L2, a number of L2 studies have examined the acquisition of German, specifically the acquisition of negation. The most well known of these are the comparison of child first language (L1) and L2 development reported in Lange (1979), the analysis of child L2 development in Felix (1978), and a study of naturalistic adult L2 reported in Clahsen, Meisel, and Pienemann (1983).[2] Felix's study (which also subsumes Lange's) describes a general developmental pattern, as outlined in Table 2-1. The sequence can be summarized in terms of lexical choice and word order. Lexically, the subjects invariably began by using

TABLE 2-1 Developmental Sequence for L2 German Negation L1—English Children (Felix 1978)

Stage I: sentence → [Neg] - X - [Neg]
　　nein helfen (don't help)
　　nein spielen Katze (I don't want to play with the cat)
　　da nein (not here)

Stage II: sentence → X - [Neg] - [cop, aux] - [Neg] - Y
　　ich nein essen (I'm not eating)
　　du nicht kommt (you're not coming)
　　das ist nicht Wasser (that's not water)
　　du kannst nicht kommen (you can't come)

Stage III: sentence → X - V - Neg - Y
　　du mußt nicht das machen (you don't have to do that)
　　ich mach nicht das (I won't do that)
　　das ist gar kein Revolver (that's not a revolver)

Stage IV: sentence → X - V - NP/(object) - Neg
　　mein Vater kann das nicht (my father can't do that)
　　ich wasch die nicht (I won't wash it)

---

nein and only later added *nicht* and *kein*. (A full treatment of standard German negation is given in the Appendix.) In terms of word order (syntax), the sequence proceeds from a stage where negation is external to the utterance to a stage where negation is incorporated into the utterance.

Clahsen et al. (1983) and Clashen (1984) analyzed the speech of fifty-seven Spanish, Italian, and Portuguese guest workers and found a syntactic development for negation similar to Felix's (1978) child L2 stages. This is reported in Table 2-2. No sequences were reported for lexemic development since most learners had been in Germany long enough to have acquired all three negators.

Several observations can be made based on a comparison of these studies. The placement of a negator proceeded from sentence-external to sentence-internal position for both sets of learners. Both child and adult L2 learners also evidenced intermediate stages of variation of placement of the negator around the verb before entering the final stage of clause-final placement. In particular, both sets of learners seemed to move from a post-verbal placement to a clause-final placement as the final two stages in development (see Clahsen 1984 for more discussion). No comparisons can be made with regard to lexemic development for the reason cited previously; the guest workers already had all three negators in their speech when the Clahsen et al. (1983) study began. It can be said, however, that Clahsen et al. report a rather indiscriminate use of *kein* to negate both verbs and adjectives in adult L2 German, whereas the same was not reported in the English L1 children examined by Felix (1978).

Given that research has found certain stages of development for both child and adult learners of German L2 in a natural environment, the question raised in the present study is how foreign language learners of German (English L1) acquire

TABLE 2-2 Developmental Sequence for German Negation L2 Adults (Clahsen 1984)

Stage I: sentence → Neg - X
kein kindergarten portugiese (no Portuguese kinder)
nich hier (not here)

Stage II: sentence → X - [Neg] - V - [Neg] - Y
er nee redet mir (He doesn't talk to me)
deutschland ich nich verstehs (I don't understand German)
nich is nich agencia (This is not an agency)

Stage III: sentence → X - V - Neg - Y
ich saben nich die nummer (I don't know the number)
ich kenn nich kein kindergarten portugiese
(I don't know a Portuguese kindergarten)
ich will nich diese mann hier in zu hause
(I don't want that man to come to this house)

Stage IV: sentence → [$_{S1}$ X - Neg [$_{S2}$ Y]]
ich weiß aber jetzt nich (I don't know anymore)
hab ich danach kein geld gehabt (After that, I didn't have any money left)

negation when the only access to the language they have is in the classroom and in learner-prepared materials (largely grammar practice books). Does their interlanguage manifest stages similar to or different from the studies on German as a L2? If there are differences, are these traceable to instruction and if so, to what aspect of instruction?

SUBJECTS

All of the students who registered for beginning German at the University of Texas in September 1983 received an invitation to participate in the study. In order to encourage participation, we decided to pay subjects $3.50 per hour (for a total of $45.50 for the entire nine-month period). Of the approximately three hundred students who received invitations, fifteen signed up for the study. Of these, only six participated for the duration of the project.

The six subjects included two females (Sissy and Geraldine) and four males (Lloyd, John, Franklin, and George). They ranged between ages eighteen and twenty-two. While the two females had never learned a foreign language (FL), the four males had taken varying amounts (two to four semesters) of high school French or Spanish or both. None of the subjects had ever attempted to learn German.

INSTRUCTIONAL PROGRAM

All of the first year German classes met for fifty minutes each day, five days a week, for two semesters. The program of instruction was principally based on a grammatical sequence. The main textbook was *Modern German*, of which the first ten of eleven chapters were covered over the two semesters. The grammar points to be learned were explained in English in the book and were often contrasted with English grammar. The exercises were mostly the fill-in-the-blank variety, although there were a few "express in German" exercises as well. The classroom treatment of the grammar involved developing a conscious awareness through explanation and manipulative drill (usually from the textbook).

In addition to the main text, the students were required to buy *Deutsch 2000* and *The Lower Division German 4-Skills Program Supplement*. The first contained short episodes with strong visual support. It was used as a reader and as a cued-response generator for retelling the stories. The second text contained day-by-day assignments and lesson plans as well as a series of topicalized vocabulary lists for which the students were responsible.

The four-skills approach included a modest amount of listening and speaking. The speaking component was mostly in the context of controlled, intrasentential drills. During those times when less manipulative activities were done, students were strongly encouraged to produce complete, correct sentences. Listening practice was mainly accomplished by means of oral-context examples for vocabulary review. Outside of class, the students were free to go to the language laboratory, but there was neither a grade nor a requirement attached to laboratory attendance.[3]

METHOD

In order to elicit utterances that were as communicative as possible, we developed a structured task involving different types of picture descriptions. The pictures, eight-by-eleven-inch photos and line drawings culled from magazines and English as a second language (ESL) teaching materials, were used in at least two ways. One set consisted of individual pictures selected for straight description. A second set involved interactional picture games based on Upshur (1971). These two kinds of pictures were used throughout the nine months. At the end of the second month, however, two more kinds of pictures were added on a regular basis. The third consisted of pairs of pictures with (often extremely) small differences that were to be located and explained. The fourth set contained sequences of events, often accompanied by small clocks in the corner of the pictures. All of the pictures were, of course, selected in such a way that certain grammatical structures, including negation, would have a good chance of being elicited.

None of the tasks was obligatory. A subject could opt to turn to another picture at any time. The nonobligatory nature of the pictures was explained in English before every session. In addition, the role of the investigator was to respond to, rather then initiate, linguistic effort on the part of the subject. Thus, the results are in one way similar to those of unstructured communication: certain structures are sometimes underrepresented in the data.

In addition to the linguistic data, a large amount of historical and social-psychological information was collected from each subject. At the initial meeting, a language history was detailed, including parents' language(s), previous and present foreign language contacts, and reasons for taking German. At the beginning of each elicitation session, the subjects were questioned to find out what (if any) German input they received beyond their course work. Data were also collected from each subject using three instruments from language-related areas: an attitude-motivation assessment based on Gardner and Lambert (1972); a risk-taking assessment based on Beebe (1983); Rubin (1975), and Naiman, Fröhlich, Stern, and Todesco (1978); and the short form of the Modern Language Aptitude Test. (For more information about the first two instruments and the methods used to calculate scores from them, see Eubank in progress).

Each elicitation session was conducted with the author outside of class in a quiet room reserved for the interviews.[4] With each subject there were eleven sessions over the nine-month period. All sessions, which lasted between forty minutes and one hour, were taped and transcribed in standard orthography after the last subject's appointment. Meetings were spaced approximately two and one-half weeks apart, or after about thirteen hours of classroom instruction. Except for one instance of a three-day span, all meetings were arranged on two consecutive days.

RESULTS

For the purposes of this study, only instances of non-anaphoric negation with *nein*, *nicht*, and *kein* were drawn from the transcripts. *Nichts* (nothing), a combination of *nicht* and *etwas* (something), was excluded, although it was included in Felix (1978). Other negative combinations, such as *niemand* (nobody), *niemals* (never), and *nirgendwo* (no place), were not present in the data.

Formulaic expressions such as *Ich weiß nicht* (I don't know) and *Ich verstehe nicht* (I don't understand) are usually excluded from studies of language acquisition since they are typically learned as prefabricated routines or patterns. Instances of such learning would occur in naturalistic situations and in formal learning environments using audiolingual techniques. In this program, however, very little memorization beyond the range of individual words was done, and any meaningful input that the subjects received was sparse at best (cf. Wing, this volume). As a result, within the first two months, such utterances, which under different circumstances may have matched the surface of the standard variety, did not:

John 1:Ich kenne *nicht* (I'm not acquainted = I don't know)
Geraldine 4: Verstehe *nicht* (I don't understand)

These two examples, which include the subject's name and session number, are representative of such nonformulaic learning. Nonstandard instances such as these two were always included in the analysis; instances that match the surface of the standard variety were excluded after the second elicitation session.

Also excluded were some instances of negated utterances in dialogues between the subject and the author when unrecoverable portions of the sentence were deleted. Included, however, were negated utterances when, as the following exchange shows, subjects changed the lexemic or syntactic (but not morphological) use of negation:

John 3: der Student ist ah richtig richtig *nicht* (the student isn't right)
Interviewer: uh huh
John: *nicht* richtig

Interestingly, not all of the instances of apparent monitoring made the negated portion of the utterance more like the standard variety. In either case, both the original and the changed versions were counted.

As one would expect, the range of possible structures used with negation was restricted as compared with native speakers or with learners exposed to natural input. The following utterances are examples of the range of use:

A. Geraldine 1: *nein* hier (it's not here) (Neg X)
B. Sissy 2: sie *nicht* kaufe (she's not buying) (Neg Pred)
C. Franklin 4: sie hat *kein* Glas (she doesn't have a glass) (V Neg Obj)
D. Franklin 5: sie sind *nicht* froh (they aren't happy) (Cop Neg Comp)
E. Franklin 3: das Bild hängt *nicht* an die Wand (the picture isn't hanging on the wall) (V Neg Adv)
F. Franklin 3: er ißt *nicht* (he's not eating) (V Neg)
G. Franklin 3: ich seh Schild *nicht* (I don't see the sign) (V Obj Neg)
H. Franklin 8: hier steht das Uhr an die Wand *nicht* (here the clock isn't hanging on the wall) (V Adv Neg)
I. Franklin 3: ihr Haare ist schwarz *nicht* (her hair isn't black) (S Neg)

Tables 2-3 through 2-8 show the distribution of the different types of negation. The numbers are rounded percentages based on the number of uses for a particular structure compared with the total number of negated utterances. Those few utterances that do not conform exactly to the categories in the tables are marked with an asterisk and are explained below each table.

The first column after the number of the elicitation session includes figures of the mean length of T-unit (MLT)[5] and the total number of negated utterances (total). The following nine columns refer to the utterances that are, respectively, like examples A through I above. In the second column, no single-constituent utterances that were the result of dialogue deletions are included. Unless otherwise noted, all of these utterances contain the negator *nein*, as in A. Negators placed preverbally, B, or postverbally before objects, C, are shown in the next two columns. Those instances in the latter category are further divided into the lexeme chosen, *nicht* (n) or *kein* (k). Under C Neg Comp are copular structures in which the negator precedes the complement, as in D. The lexemic choices here are also divided between *nicht* and *kein*. Utterances like E, with the negator before the adverbial, are placed under V Neg Adv. Statements with postverbal negation after simple verbs, F, or verbs with objects, G, are placed in the next two columns. A few of those with objects also include a prepositional qualifier. These utterances are all instances in which, while speaking, the subject added the adverbial (adv) as

TABLE 2-3 John's Negation Development, with the Percentage of Each Structure As Compared with the Total Number of Negatives in Each Session

Session	MLT total	Single constit N X	INTERNAL				NEG END			
			N Pred	V N Obj	C N Comp	V N Adv	V N	V Obj N (Adv)	V Adv N	S N
1	3.1 7			n k	n k		70 nf/p	30 nf/p		c nf/p
2	3.5 10			n 10 k	n k 20		20 nf/p	10 nf/p		c 40 nf/p
3	4.7 10	10		n 30 k	n 40 k 20		10 nf/p	mf/p		c 10 nf/p
4	5.0 11			n 18 k	n 36 k	9	18 nf/p	9 nf/p 9		c nf/p
5	5.4 6			n k	n 50 k		16 nf/p	nf/p	16	c 16 nf/p
6	5.9 5			n k	n k	20	40 nf/p	20 nf/p		c 20 nf/p
7	5.9 13			n k	n 46 k 15		23 nf/p	8 nf/p 8		c nf/p
8	5.8 6			n 16 k	n 16 k 16		33 nf/p16	nf/p		c nf/p
9	6.1 3			n k	n k 33		33 nf/p	33 nf/p		c nf/p
10	5.9 9			n 11 k	n 56 k		11 nf/p	22 nf/p		c nf/p
11	5.6 2			n k	n 50 k 50		nf/p	nf/p		c nf/p

N = Negator

an afterthought. The V Neg and V Obj Neg columns also show those negators that are followed by either a nonfinite verb or by a particle (nf/p), as would be required in the standard variety. Utterances with *nicht* following an adverbial, as in H, are placed under V Adv Neg. The last column, S Neg, includes nonstandard structures in which the negator is placed at the end of the sentence. These utterances include the copular structure (c) as in example I and instances in which the negator follows either a nonfinite verb or a particle (nf/p).

There is a large amount of individual variation in the subjects' use of negation. Moreover, due to the small number of negative utterances produced within the

TABLE 2-4 Geraldine's Negation Development, with the Percentage of Each Structure As Compared with the Total Number of Negatives in each Session

Session	MLT total	Single constit N X	INTERNAL				NEG END			
			N Pred	V N Obj	C N Comp	V N Adv	V N	V Obj N (Adv)	V Adv N	S N
1	1.92	100		n k	n k		nf/p	nf/p		c nf/p
2	2.85	80*		n 20† k	n k		nf/p	nf/p		c nf/p
3	4.80‡			n k	n k		nf/p	nf/p		c nf/p
4	4.86	16		n k	n 33 k		nf/p	16 nf/p		c 33 nf/p
5	5.37			n k	n 14 k		28 nf/p	28 nf/p		c 28 nf/p
6	5.64			n k	n 25 k		25 nf/p	50 nf/p		c nf/p
7	5.35	20*		n k 20	n k		nf/p	40 nf/p		c nf/p 20
8	6.110			n k	n k		nf/p	60 nf/p		c 40 nf/p
9	6.08			n k	n 25 k		nf/p	12 nf/p		c 62 nf/p
10	5.78			n k	n 25† k		nf/p	50 nf/p	25	c nf/p
11	6.37			n k	n 71 k		nf/p	29 nf/p		c nf/p

*1 nicht   †1 nein

‡A failure of the taping equipment caused the loss of most of session three. Those few utterances that were recovered did not contain negatives.

N = Negator

first two sessions, it is somewhat difficult to determine just what the subject's interlanguage competence was at that point. Nevertheless, several trends common to all or most of the subjects can be identified.

The tables reveal a regularity in lexemic choice. During the first two sessions, Geraldine, George, and Sissy produced Neg X constructions with *nein*. Of these three subjects, George and Sissy also used *nicht* as a negator within the same session. The initial negated utterances by Franklin, John, and Lloyd were produced

TABLE 2-5 George's Negation Development, with the Percentage of Each Structure As Compared with the Total Number of Negatives in Each Session

Session	MLT total	Single constit N X	INTERNAL				NEG END			
			N Pred	V N Obj	C N Comp	V N Adv	V N	V Obj N (Adv)	V Adv N	S N
1	2.6 5	40		n k	n 20 k		40 nf/p	nf/p		c nf/p
2	3.9 8	25		n k 12	n k		12 nf/p	25* nf/p		c 25 nf/p
3	3.8 8			n k 37	n 12 k 37		12 nf/p	nf/p		c nf/p
4	4.1 14			n k 43	n 14 k 7		7 nf/p 7	14 nf/p		c nf/p 7
5	3.8 11			n 9 k 27	n 9 k 27	9	nf/p	9 nf/p	9	c nf/p
6	4.1 14			n k 21	n 36 k 14		nf/p 7	14 nf/p	7	c nf/p
7	4.1 19			n k 32	n 42 k	5	nf/p	21 nf/p		c nf/p
8	4.3 15		7	n k 13	n 27 k		13 nf/p	33 nf/p	7	c nf/p
9	4.1 11			n k	n 64 k		18 nf/p	9 nf/p		c nf/p 9
10	4.4 11			n k 36	n 27 k 18		nf/p	18 nf/p		c nf/p
11	4.4 9			n 11 k 45	n 11 k 11	11	nf/p	nf/p		c nf/p

*1 nein

N = Negator

with *nicht*. Common to all six subjects is that *kein* was not used until one or both of the other two negators were used. From these observations, one can propose a three-step progression from *nein* to *nicht* to *kein*, the first of which may be skipped by some learners.

The data also reveal three distinct types of word-order placement, and they seem to represent parts of a developmental trend. The first is the single-constituent Neg X variety which, as stated above, was found only during the first few sessions, with three of the subjects. The second type is one in which the negator is

TABLE 2-6 Sissy's Negation Development, with the Percentage of Each Structure As Compared with the Total Number of Negatives in Each Session

Session	MLT total	Single constit N X	INTERNAL				NEG END			
			N Pred	V N Obj	C N Comp	V N Adv	V N	V Obj N (Adv)	V Adv N	S N
1	4.0 3			n k	n k		33 nf/p	66 nf/p		c nf/p
2	3.8 9	11	11	n 22 k	n 33 k	11	11 nf/p	nf/p		c nf/p
3	4.5 8			n k	n k 50	12	nf/p 12	25 nf/p		c nf/p
4	4.6 11			n 27 k 45	n 18 k		nf/p	nf/p 9		c nf/p
5	5.4 8			n 12 k 25	n k	12	12 nf/p	12 nf/p 12	12	c nf/p
6	5.8 12			n k 33	n 25 k 8		nf/p 25*	8 nf/p		c nf/p
7	5.8 14			n k 50	n 14 k		14 nf/p	14 nf/p 7		c nf/p
8	6.0 8			n 12 k	n 37 k	12	nf/p 12	12 nf/p 12		c nf/p
9	6.2 10			n k	n 30 k	30	nf/p 20	10 nf/p 10		c nf/p
10	7.1 9			n k 78	n 11 k		nf/p	11 nf/p		c nf/p
11	6.5 8			n k 87	n 12 k		nf/p	nf/p		c nf/p

*1 N + nf + adv

N = Negator

placed at the end of a complete sentence. All of the subjects used this type of negation, most of them to produce constructions that did not match the standard variety:

George 2: das ist gut Kaffee *nicht* (that isn't good coffee)
Lloyd 2: der Mann hat Mund *nicht* (the man has no mouth)

(It should be noted that those subjects who used Neg X constructions began frequent use of sentence-final negation later than those who did not use Neg X constructions.) The third type of negation is sentence-internal negation. This type emerged after the first two types in those cases in which one or both of the first

TABLE 2-7 Franklin's Negation Development, with the Percentage of Each Structure As Compared with the Total Number of Negatives in Each Session

Session	MLT total	Single constit N X	INTERNAL			NEG END			
			N Pred	V N Obj	C N Comp	V N Adv	V N	V Obj N (Adv)	V Adv N	S N
1	3.0 1			n k	n k		nf/p	100 nf/p		c nf/p
2	4.1 1			n k	n k		nf/p	nf/p		c 100 nf/p
3	4.9 9			n 11 k	n 22 k	11	nf/p	44 nf/p		c 11 nf/p
4	5.2 10			n k 50	n 10 k		nf/p	10 nf/p		cf/p 30 nf/p
5	5.4 10			n k 20	n 30 k	10	20 nf/p	20 nf/p		c nf/p
6	5.7 12			n 17 k 8	n 33 k		nf/p 8	25 nf/p		c 8 nf/p
7	5.1 20			n 15* k 5	n 20 k 15		5 nf/p 5	25 nf/p 10		c nf/p
8	5.7 8			n k 12	n 12 k		nf/p 25	37 nf/p	12	c nf/p
9	5.5 8			n k 12	n 37 k	12	12 nf/p	12 nf/p 12		c nf/p
10	7.0 14			n 21 k 14	n 29 k 7	7	nf/p 7	7 nf/p 7		c nf/p
11	7.2 3			n k 33	n k		nf/p	33 nf/p 33		c nf/p

*1 N + nf + obj

N = Negator

two were used. These observations lead to a proposed sequence from Neg X to sentence-final negation to sentence-internal negation. Again, the first step may be skipped by some learners.

The percentage of subjects who seem to have skipped steps in the lexemic and word-order sequences is high. It may be, however, that the fixed schedule of the sessions did not capture the subjects' varying rates of development. If that is true, then it may also be the case that they did not skip steps at all. Rather, the steps were traversed between elicitation sessions. With a number of studies having confirmed a relationship between psychological factors and the development of nega-

TABLE 2-8 Lloyd's Negation Development, with the Percentage of Each Structure As Compared with the Total Number of Negatives in Each Session

Session	MLT total	Single constit N X	INTERNAL				NEG END			
			N Pred	V N Obj	C N Comp	V N Adv	V N	V Obj N (Adv)	V Adv N	S N
1	3.5 0*			n k	n k		nf/p	nf/p		c nf/p
2	5.9 7	14		n k	n 14 k		14 nf/p	57 nf/p		c nf/p
3	5.5 13			n k 85	n 8 k		8 nf/p	nf/p		c nf/p
4	5.2 15			n k 67	n k		27 nf/p	7 nf/p		c nf/p
5	5.7 14			n 7 k 14	n 7 k	21	7 nf/p	43 nf/p		c nf/p
6	5.8 13			n 8 k 62	n 15 k		8 nf/p	8 nf/p		c nf/p
7	6.0 20			n 5 k 25	n 35 k		5 nf/p 5*	25 nf/p		c nf/p
8	6.8 27			n k 15	n 30 k	11	nf/p 4*	22 nf/p 15	7*	c nf/p
9	6.9 5			n k 20	n 60 k		nf/p	nf/p	20*	c nf/p
10	6.8 21			n 10 k 33	n 38 k	14	nf/p	5 nf/p		c nf/p
11	6.5 10			n 10 k 60	n 20 k	10	nf/p	nf/p		c nf/p

*negation avoided   *N + nf + adv   *adv + N + nf
N = Negator

tion (Schumann 1978; Stauble 1978; Clahsen et al. 1983), this conclusion is supported by preliminary results from the attitude and motivation, risk-taking, and aptitude assessments shown in Table 2-9. Of interest here are the relatively low positions of Geraldine and George, the two subjects whose utterances exhibited all of the steps in both the lexemic and word-order sequences. That the other four subjects lacked the initial steps may be a result of their higher rankings on these assessments. That the subjects varied greatly in their rates of development is further supported by preliminary results of another study concerning the amount of input each subject voluntarily sought out above and beyond the course work (see

TABLE 2-9 Preliminary Results from Assessments of Attitude and Motivation, Risk-taking, and the MLAT (Short Form)

	Instrumental Motivation	Integrative Motivation	Attitude	Risk Taking	MLAT (Percentile)
Franklin	3.5	3	80	27	40
George	5	2.5	144	-2	25
Geraldine	3.5	1.8	17	23	60
John	5	5	90	22	85
Lloyd	3.5	4.3	76	16	80
Sissy	4	4.8	208	10	90
Maximum	+24	+24	+447	+45	99

TABLE 2-10 Proposed Developmental Sequence of German Negation L1—English Adults in a Formal Environment

Stage I: sentence → Neg - X
    nein hier (it's not here)
    nein fahren (they're not driving)

Stage II: sentence → S - Neg
    sie hat Geld nein (she doesn't have money)
    der Junge eßt nicht (the boy isn't eating)
    es ist Wanduhr nicht (there's no clock)

Stage III: sentence → X - V - [Neg] - NP(object) - [Neg]
    die ah Mann hat keine Heft (the man doesn't have a notebook)
    er sieht nicht ah den ander Mann (he doesn't see the other man)
    sie studiert und geh nicht aus (she's studying and not going out)

Eubank, in progress). Geraldine never attempted to obtain more input (probably from a lack of motivation), and George very rarely sought out additional input (perhaps because of a high-risk/low-gain perception). Assuming that these results do indicate different rates of development, one can posit that negation proceeded lexically from *nein* to *nicht* to *kein* and structurally from Neg X constructions to sentence-final negation to sentence-internal negation (see Table 2-10).

A comparison of Tables 2-1 and 2-10 shows that the word-order sequences are quite different. The Stage I utterances from Table 2-1 match the Neg X constructions of the formal learners, but the Stage II utterances do not. While the learners from the naturalistic studies (Felix 1978 and Lange 1979) internalize the negators (after copulas and auxiliaries, before main verbs), the formal learners place the negators at the end of the utterance after both objects and complements. In the following two stages, the naturalistic children place the negator first after main verbs before the rest of the predicate and then, for propositional negation, after objects. The final stage is found also in those guest workers (Clahsen et al. 1983) who did not use the Neg-X strategy. The formal learners, on the other hand, place the negator before and after objects and complements. No distinction comparable to Stages III and IV of the children could be identified. In sum, the most striking difference is the Stage II preverbal placement by the naturalistic learners as opposed to the sentence-final placement by the formal learners.

Comparing the lexemic sequences is not as easy since the two naturalistic groups were different. Results from the longitudinal guest-worker study indicate that these subjects used all three lexemic realizations of negation from the beginning. Moreover, the guest workers made particularly indiscriminate use of *kein* to negate verbs and adjectives. The L1-English children, on the other hand, showed a clear sequence progressing from *nein* to *nicht* to *kein* and a categorical use of *kein* for NPs. The formal learners' progression for lexemic choice is very similar to that of the children.

DISCUSSION

As a result of the comparison between the data related to the naturalistic learners and the data presented in this study of foreign language learners, one can see some similarities and some differences. While it may be that the similarities are the result of universal processes in all types of language learning, can the differences be attributed to instruction? Specifically, can the differences be traced to instruction having intervened in the psycholinguistic processes underlying acquisition?

It is important to note that instruction consists of at least two variables: (1) classroom and textbook input, and (2) expectations that students and teachers have about what is necessary in language learning and language performance. Thus, the role of instruction in the acquisition of negation in German must consider that (1) learners receive largely noncommunicative language data that may not vary to the degree that naturalistic input might, (2) learners are often presented with more rules than can be incorporated into their interlanguage systems in the early stages, and (3) there is a real or perceived demand placed upon learners to speak in complete and correct sentences.

The students in this program received instruction on negation at three different points in the semester (times one, two, and three). The first occurred on the fourth day of class about one week before the first elicitation session with the subjects. The other two (quite coincidentally!) co-occured with the second and third elicitation sessions.

After the introduction of *nicht* and *nein* as vocabulary items glossed as "not" and "no" at time one, *kein* was introduced and contrasted with *nicht* at time two. The textbook notes explicitly that *nicht* is placed at the end of the sentence before particles and locatives. The exercises are prefaced with instructions to place it after all objects and before all other complements. The explanation of *kein* makes no specific statement regarding its placement although all of the examples and exercises use it before objects and subject complements. Negation was the only grammatical material covered on that day.

At time three another explanation about the position of *nicht* was given. The textbook reiterates that it is positioned after objects but before any other element. In addition to the information in the text, the teachers had the option of using a three-page handout that detailed, in eight rules from a reference grammar, the use and placement of *nicht* and *kein*. On that day, negation was covered along with rules governing the ordering of the adverbial elements.

What impact did this instruction have on the lexemic sequence? It may be that the introduction of *kein* at time two caused it to be frequently used earlier than would otherwise have been the case. Lloyd, John, George, and Sissy began using it during elicitation sessions two and three, or shortly after its introduction. Franklin, on the other hand, began using *kein* only during session four, and Geraldine used this negator only one time— during session seven.

One must also remember, however, that *kein* was withheld from instruction until time two. This difference would explain why the formal learners did not use this negator from the beginning, as the guest workers did. Moreover, it would also explain why, at least for the developmental appearance of *kein*, the sequence matched that of the L1-English children. Nevertheless, there is reason to believe that the order of presentation in instruction did not alter the progression of the sequence radically. If the developmental model proposed in Table 2-10 is correct, then only Lloyd, John, George, and Sissy were developmentally ready to use internal negation (including *kein*) by time two. Franklin and Geraldine, on the other hand, were still processing negation at the Stage II level. From this point of view, it seems that introducing *kein* after *nicht* and *nein* was only partially successful.

Like the L1-English children, the formal learners also restricted the scope of *kein* to NPs. The guest workers, on the other hand, did not. The discrimination displayed by the formal learners may, of course, be a result of the formal instruction. On the other hand, the three groups also had different ages and L1s, suggesting that formal instruction also may not have been the only contributing factor.

The last question addressed above deals with the placement of the negator either before the verb or in sentence-final position. The formal instruction at time two would have placed *nicht* in sentence-final position after objects but before other elements. On the surface, this position is borne out in the data. However, four of the subjects were placing the negator in this position at the first session— before the formal instruction took place. Moreover, the position specified by the instruction continued to be only one of the several possible interlanguage placements for the subjects for some time after time two. Formal instruction, then, does not offer a satisfactory explanation of these learners' structures. In addition, lack of instruction does not account for the forms that were not found in the sequences of naturalistic learners.

The other aspect of formal instruction is the global environment. One might think that this environment would have little impact on the learner's development and the choice of lexical negators. However, for problems concerning word order it may be very important. For the learner, the impact of this environment can be summed up in two sentences: "German is composed of complete sentences," and "German is very complicated." A check of the MLT values in Tables 2-3 to 2-8 reveals that these learners were producing utterances with an average MLT length of 4 words at session two and 4.7 words at session three. The transcripts show that the majority of the utterances not only were complete sentences but also were produced, particularly during the initial sessions, with much halting labor. The result of the global environment in the classroom is, then, that the subjects were placed under a heavy cognitive strain which was carried over into the interviews.

Besides possible differences in cognitive load, another attribute distinguishing the formal and naturalistic learners is the need to communicate. Clahsen et al. (1983) suggest two explanations for the Neg-X strategy: (1) it is easy to process, and (2) it is very expressive. The key here is expressiveness. The naturalistic learners were in situations in which communication was the primary goal. The following example, drawn from the transcript excerpts in Clahsen et al. (1983, 360), illustrates the potential of the Neg-X strategy:

> Antonio S: . . . leute sagen: warum du *nicht* deutsche sprechen? (. . . people say: why don't you speak German?)

The scope of the negator *nicht* is clearly restricted to *deutsche*, and no other interpretation of the communicative intent of the utterance is possible. While the sentence-final placement of the negator by the formal learners generally produced statements that were distinct in meaning, it also produced utterances in which the intent was obscured:

> Geraldine (8): er hat zwei Schuhe und Socken *nicht* (he has two shoes but no socks)

The scope of *nicht* is ambiguous in that the message could also be interpreted as "he doesn't have two shoes and socks." This lack of clarity can be attributed to the fact that the formal learners were only engaging in semicommunicative performance. What was important to them was not getting the message across, but rather creating complete sentences.

Given that true communication was of secondary importance for the subjects in this study, an S-Neg strategy (placing the negator in sentence-final position) can be posited for the early stages of sentence production. Unlike the Neg-X strategy, the S-Neg strategy would only have to conform to Slobin's (1973) operating principle D, the syntactic strategy avoiding the interruption or rearrangement of linguistic units. Specifically, Slobin states:

> There is a tendency to preserve the structure of the sentence as a closed entity, reflected in the development from sentence-external placement of various linguistic forms to their movement within the sentence. (200)

While this tendency refers to L1 development, it seems justified from the data to extend it to L2-adult performance as well. At this early stage, the linguistic unit is the complete sentence, and the S-Neg strategy preserves its structure.

Like the Neg-X strategy, the S-Neg strategy also produces constructions that may or may not match the surface structure of the target variety. Consequently, the S-Neg strategy would also imply that the early standard-like placement of the negator in sentence-final position is not evidence for the acquisition of the underlying rule placing it in that position. Assuming that the stages in Table 2-10 are correct, the standard-like positioning of the negator would only be truly acquired at some point after the onset of internal negation.

CONCLUSIONS

It was found that the six learners in this study did pass through certain stages of lexemic and syntactic development while acquiring negation in German. When compared with naturalistic L2 learners, these FL learners deviated significantly in terms of the stages involving syntax. Instruction (such as grammar explanation and sequence of presentation) was only partially satisfactory in explaining these formal-naturalistic differences. It was suggested that these were best accounted for by the formal learner carrying the classroom demand of "speak in complete sentences" to the nonclassroom context.

While the data in this study suggest real stages of development for six different subjects, they cannot, at this point, be interpreted as representative of all formal learners. Nonetheless, they do provide a basis of comparison for future longitudinal studies as well as for studies using cross-sectional comparisons, grammaticality judgements, and other data-gathering techniques. As in research on L2 acquisition, FL learning research that looks at interlanguage will have to proceed step by step.

NOTE

1. This project was funded in part by a grant from the University of Texas Research Institute. I would like to thank Robert Bley-Vroman and Janet K. Swaffar for their helpful comments on an earlier version of this paper.
2. For the sake of brevity, discussion of the various L1 studies involving German negation have been excluded (e.g., Wode 1976, 1977; Park 1979, 1981; Clahsen 1982). In a nutshell, the results of these studies are similar to those described in the text. Stalb's (1977) discussion of the use of *nicht* by formal L2 learners has also been excluded. His cross-sectional error analysis did not attempt to establish a developmental sequence. Moreover, it was based not on learner utterances but on learner attempts to negate rather complex sentences presented to the subjects in written form.
3. The subjects in the study were instructed by four different teachers in each of the two semesters. Clearly, there were differences in the actual input that they received in class. These differences would be particularly great in terms of the number of nonmechanical exercises that the teacher did in class. On the other hand, due to the amount of control over the curriculum, it can be assumed that all students received the same grammatical instruction on the same day.

4. It should be noted that the author was not teaching German during the period of investigation. In addition, he did not visit the subjects' classes. It is believed that this lent credence to the idea that the author was truly an outside observer with no interest whatsoever in the subjects' success in or satisfaction with their German classes.
5. The T-unit is defined as an independent clause plus any subordinate clauses embedded within it, whereas the MLU is counted in morphemes. Examples follow:

John slept soundly but Mary tossed and turned.
T-units = 2, Morphemes = 11
MLT = 4, MLU = 11
While John slept, Mary studied.
T-units = 1, Morphemes = 6
MLT = 5, MLU = 6

The T-unit was used for average length of utterance rather than the MLU because the subjects tended to use only those morphological endings currently or recently taught in the classroom. The MLT result, which ignores such endings, is a much more stable figure (see Larsen-Freeman 1978).

REFERENCES

Beebe, L. M. 1983. Risk-taking and the language learner. In *Classroom Oriented Research in Second Language Acquisition,* H. W. Seliger and M. H. Long (eds.) 39-65. Rowley, MA: Newbury House.
Clahsen, H. 1982. *Spracherwerb in der Kindheit.* Tübinger Beiträge sur Linguistik A4. Tübingen: Gunter Narr.
Clahsen, H. 1984. The acquisition of German word order: a test case for cognitive approaches to L2 development. In *Second Languages: A Cross-Linguistic Perspective,* R. W. Andersen (ed.), 219-242. Rowley, MA: Newbury House.
Clahsen, H., J. M. Meisel, and M. Pienemann. 1983. *Deutsch als Zweitsprache.* Tübinger Beiträge zur Linguistik A3. Tübingen: Gunter Narr.
Ellis, R. 1985. *Understanding Second Language Acquisition.* Oxford: Oxford University Press.
Eubank, L. In progress. Aspects of the formal acquisition of German as a foreign language. Ph.D. dissertation, University of Texas at Austin.
Felix, S. W. 1978. *Linguistische Untersuchungen zum natürlichen Zweitsprachenerwerb.* Munich: Wilhelm Fink.
Gardner, R .C., and W. E. Lambert. 1972. *Attitudes and Motivation in Second-Language Learning.* Rowley, MA: Newbury House.
Lange, D. 1979. Negation in natürlichen english-deutschen zweitsprachenerwerb: eine Fallstudie. *International Review of Applied Linguistics* 17:331-348.
Larsen-Freeman, D. 1978. An ESL index of development. *TESOL Quarterly* 12(4):439-448.
Naiman, N., M. Fröhlich, H. H. Stern, and A. Todesco. 1978. *The Good Language Learner.* Research in education series 7. Toronto: Ontario Institute for Studies in Education.
Park, T. 1979. Some facts on negation: Wode's four-stage developmental theory of negation revisited. *Journal of Child Language* 6:147-151.
Park, T. 1981. *The Development of Syntax in the Child with Special Reference to German.* Innsbruck: University of Innsbruck.
Rubin, J. 1975. What the good language learner can teach us. *TESOL Quarterly* 9:41-52.
Schumann, J. 1978. Second language acquisition: the pidginization hypothesis. In *Second Language Acquisition,* E. M. Hatch (ed.), 256-271. Rowley, MA: Newbury House.

Slobin, D. I. 1973. Cognitive prerequisites for the development of grammar. In *Studies of Child Language Development*, C. A. Ferguson and D. I. Slobin (eds.), 175-208. New York: Holt, Rinehart and Winston.
Stalb, H. 1977. Gesetzmäßigkeiten beim L2 Erwerb. Untersuchungen zur Stellung von nicht. *Zielsprache Deutsch* 2:32-40.
Stalb, H. 1978. Warum kommt hier nicht *nicht* vor? *Zielsprache Deutsch* 4:30-35.
Stauble, A. 1978. The process of decreolization: a model for second language development. *Language Learning* 28(1):29-54.
Upshur, J. A. 1971. Objective evaluation of oral proficiency in the ESOL classroom. *TESOL Quarterly* 5:47-59.
Wode, H. 1976. Developmental sequence in naturalistic L2 acquisition. *Working Papers on Bilingualism* 11:1-31.
Wode, H. 1977. Four early stages in the development of L1 negation. *Journal of Child Language* 4:87-102.
Wode, H. 1981. Language-acquisitional universals: a unified view of language acquisition. In *Native and Foreign Language Acquisition*, H. Winitz (ed.), 218-234. New York: New York Academy of Sciences.

APPENDIX

The German System of Negation

In the standard variety of German, negation has both morphological and syntactic aspects. There are three common negative morphemes: *nein, nicht,* and *kein*. Only *nicht* and *kein* are used for nonanaphoric negation; *nein* corresponds exactly to the anaphoric use of the English morpheme "no."

The placement of the morpheme in the sentence determines whether the proposition as a whole, or only an individual constituent, is being negated. Complete propositions are negated by placing *nicht* after the finite verb and any objects.

Sie schlafen nicht. (They aren't sleeping.)
Sie hören die Musik nicht. (They don't hear the music.)

Other elements can occur after *nicht*. These elements include certain particles and non-finite verbs, both of which are governed by a common rule leaving them in sentence-final position. In addition, the finite verb itself is moved into final position in subordinate clauses.

Sie sehen mich nicht *an*. (They aren't looking at me.)
Sie können es nicht *lesen*. (They can't read it.)
Ich weiß, daß sie nicht *gehen*. (I know they aren't going.)

Alternatively, individual constituents may be negated by placing the appropriate morpheme (*nicht* or *kein*) before them.

Sie sind keine Studenten. (They aren't students.)
Sie fahren nicht nach Ulm. (They aren't going to Ulm.)

To a limited extent, there is a form-function relationship between the lexical realizations and the syntactic use. *Nein* is restricted in position to the same extent as its English anaphoric counterpart "no." *Kein* is also used for constituent negation of indefinite NPs. *Nicht,* on the other hand, is used for both propositional and constituent negation.

CHAPTER 3

Developmental Patterns of Past Tense Acquisition Among Foreign Language Learners of French[1]

Marsha A. Kaplan
University of Pennsylvania

INTRODUCTION

Learners of French must distinguish two kinds of past tenses used in the everyday spoken language: the *passé composé* (compound past) and the *imparfait* (imperfect). Although the French tense-aspect system is complex, only a small portion of it is formally presented to students at the beginning and intermediate levels. According to standard textbook explanations, the *passé composé* designates a completed event or change of state, and the imperfect designates a condition or habitual ongoing action in the past. Roughly speaking, the *passé composé* corresponds in English to the past or to the present perfect; the imperfect corresponds to the past, to the past progressive, and to "would/used to" plus infinitive. The crucial distinction here is not one of relative time frame but rather of aspect, marking what might be generally referred to as the discreteness of an action versus state of being, or what is also termed an event versus non-event distinction.

Teachers and textbooks devote a great deal of attention to the aspectual differences between the *passé composé* and the *imparfait*, perceived as particularly problematic for English-speaking learners of French. Articles regularly appear that suggest ways to clarify this distinction to students. The Input Hypothesis, however, tells us that conscious rules do not facilitate acquisition, especially for complex phenomena. Accordingly, certain explicitly taught grammatical features can remain resistant to acquisition, while other features outside of the teaching sequence can often be subconsciously acquired (Krashen 1982, 1985). If this is the case, then what might we expect regarding the development of the French past tenses in classroom learners of French with little or no outside exposure to the language, that is, learners with no natural input?

The purpose of this study is to observe the actual pattern of past tense forms during the early phases of acquisition in a formal setting and to determine what effect(s), if any, instruction has on these observed generalities. If explicit instruction does not seem to have any real impact on acquisitional patterns, then sources of explanation must be found elsewhere.

SUBJECTS AND METHOD

Sixteen informants interviewed for this study were randomly selected from beginning- and intermediate-level university students. Data collection took place by means of individual, semistructured interviews, each lasting approximately ten minutes. The *passé composé* and the imperfect were elicited through the use of both seeded questions and cues for descriptive and narrative monologues. Informants were asked, for example, to talk about what they did over the weekend, their first impressions of the campus, why they chose a particular course of study, and so forth. Four categories were established to document the percent of correct use of the *passé composé* and the imperfect in obligatory contexts as well as their errors of form and distribution. It should be pointed out that— phonological difficulties—that is, the fusion of /E/ and /e/, which in a large number of cases distinguishes the auxiliary from the preceding subject pronoun and the imperfect from the past participle ending—make it such that it is not always easy to differentiate the *passé composé* from the imperfect in the learner's output. While care was taken to properly identify the forms produced by the informant, some caution is recommended in interpreting the data that follow.

For the reader's convenience, the manner in which the learners' production of past tense forms was categorized is detailed in the Appendix. Briefly, performance was categorized as one of the four possibilities:

A. correct form, correct temporal-aspectual choice
B. correct form, incorrect temporal-aspectual choice
C. incorrect form, correct temporal-aspectual choice
D. incorrect form, incorrect temporal-aspectual choice

TABLE 3-1 Accuracy Scores for Past Tense Usage in Adult Classroom Learners of French

	passé composé	imperfect
First Semester	25%*	0%
Second Semester	0%	100%**
Third Semester	50%	23%
Fourth Semester	76%	35%
First year	5%	50%
Second year	64%	29%
All learners	50%	30%

*Only four obligatory contexts were produced by these learners.
**Only two obligatory contexts were produced by these learners.

RESULTS

Table 3-1 summarizes the accuracy scores in choice of the two past tenses. In the first part of the table, the rates are broken down by semester level. In the second part, they have been collapsed into the opposition first year/second year.

Table 3-2 contains a summary of error rates for form and temporal-aspectual choice broken down by year rather than by semester level.

It can be seen that these classroom learners of French exhibit greater overall accuracy rates with the *passé composé* as compared with the imperfect. In fact, the *passé composé* was attempted considerably more often than was the imperfect at each level. In terms of kinds of errors produced, it should be noted that more errors of form occur than do errors of distribution for the *passé composé*. For the imperfect, the pattern is reversed (see Table 3-2).

A further probing of the data, however, indicates that the range of verbs correctly supplied is four times greater for the *passé composé* than it is for the imperfect. It appears that certain verbs, all irregular, are "privileged" in the learners' interlanguage. Across all four levels, *aller* (to go) is the most frequently attempted verb in the *passé composé*, while *être* (to be) is the most frequently attempted verb in the imperfect. *Être* and *aller* are also the verbs with the greatest accuracy rate in overall learner production, with *avoir* (to have) close behind.

The imperfect is clearly underrepresented in these learners' output. Particularly interesting is that 82 percent of all errors of distribution for the imperfect are in fact the result of the learner's supplying a present tense form in an imperfect slot. On the other hand, relatively few present tense forms occurred in the *passé composé* slots.

It appears that generally the *passé composé* is acquired before the imperfect and that there are certain patterns of lexical choice, error types, and attempts at forms. It seem unlikely that order of presentation of the *passé composé* and the imperfect, coupled with grammar explanation and form-oriented exercises in instruction affect learner output. The beginning textbooks in use in these students'

TABLE 3-2 Error Rates in Past Tense Formation and Distribution for Adult Classroom Learners of French

	Passé composé		Imperfect	
	form	distribution	form	distribution
First year	86%	29%	40%	60%
Second year	31%	32%	56%	73%
All learners	43%	31%	54%	70%

program introduced the imperfect first, followed by the *passé composé* in the same or consecutive lessons. Yet, learners make more attempts at the *passé composé* than at the imperfect in the beginning levels. At the intermediate levels, where most of the past tenses occur in the data presented here, order of presentation is no longer relevant. To what, then, can the observed patterns in learner output be attributed?

DISCUSSION

One way in which investigators have attempted to account for the relative order of accuracy is to say that morphemes are acquired by learners according to increasing grammatical complexity. It would seem reasonable to expect that the imperfect, being morphologically less complex than the *passé composé*, would be supplied correctly more often. The imperfect is highly regular in form, and as in English, is a simple, not a compound, tense. The *passé composé*, on the other hand, is a compound tense involving two kinds of auxiliaries, a number of regular and irregular past participles, and sometimes gender-number agreement. The grammatical complexity argument might explain why they are more errors of form than of distribution for the *passé composé* at the beginning levels, but it does not explain the overall greater accuracy rate for the *passé composé*.

Some researchers (e.g., Larsen-Freeman 1976) have discussed the perceptual saliency of certain morphemes as a way of explaining relative accuracy rates. The phonological shape—that is an extra syllable or a particular sound—may lend a morpheme prominence. One study of the acquisition of English as a second language (ESL) (Zobl 1980) reports the systematic use of "did" in verb phrases to express past events. Thus, the sentence, "Peter got a shot" becomes in the learner's speech, "Peter did get a shot." One is let to speculate that "did" is functioning as an analytic past tense marker in the interlanguage of the learner of English. A similar principle may be operating for the learners of French in this study, whereby the compound form (consisting of the auxiliaries *avoir* and *être* contiguous to a participle ending in the sound /e/) marks past time. If, however, this type of compound form serves as a past tense marker in the learner's interlanguage, one might expect to see a good deal of overgeneralization of the *passé composé* in imperfect contexts. There is, in fact, a little bit of overgeneralization of the *passé composé*, although there is just as much overgeneralization of the imperfect in *passé composé* contexts. In sum, perceptual saliency is only partly useful for understanding the usage of past tense in the speech of learners of French. That perceptual saliency does not fully explain output behavior in this study is consistent with Larsen-Freeman's observations.

The accuracy score for the *passé composé* with respect to the imperfect may, on the other hand, be exaggerated. The lexical data reveal that much of the success for the *passé composé* may be attributed to learner strategies such as "chunking," that is, the use of holistic phrases and utterances, memorized without knowledge of structure, but which have a high functional value in communication (see Krashen 1981 for a review of relevant work, with discussion). In the raw data, *je suis allé* (I went) accounts for most of the instances where the irregular verb aller is supplied correctly in the *passé composé*. The question-answer format characteristic of traditional classroom interaction, which also formed part of the data collection procedure in this study, may indeed prompt the frequent occurrence of such a chunk (e.g., Q: What did you do over the holiday? A: I went to the movies; I went home; I went to Canada). This suggests that even though language may be analyzed and practiced in classroom instruction, classroom talk and the traditional value placed on formal accuracy at the expense of communication may nevertheless dispose the learner to privilege certain ready-made utterances.

Another factor that has been discussed in accuracy-order studies is frequency of occurrence in input. Larsen-Freeman (1976) claimed that the accuracy rate of morpheme production correlates highly with frequency in input. Informal observation of teacher talk at the time of this study suggests that the *passé composé* is more frequently used and elicited than is the imperfect. In order to substantiate this observation, a small sample of classroom talk was obtained and analyzed. As suspected, the teacher-talk data had an overwhelming proportion (84 percent) of *passé composé* for all past tenses used. Why would the imperfect be so ignored in classroom input? First, there is perhaps a sense among many instructors that the past tense is synonymous with the *passé composé*—that is, that there is greater functional load in this one tense than in other past tenses. Second, given the current practice by many teachers, to use and test to exhaustion a given grammatical item only to abandon its use in order to move on to another grammatical item (what Krashen has dubbed the "structure of the day" approach), one suspects that the *passé composé* might simply be easier to elicit in isolated context than is the imperfect. The topic "What did you do last night?", prompting a list of events and hence the *passé composé*, is felt to be more productive than a question such as "How did you spend your vacation as a kid?" While the latter question may be a more interesting topic, it is quickly exhausted and does not bear up as well under repeated use as an eliciting device for conversation requiring past tense.

Frequency of input, then, seems a plausible explanation for the higher accuracy rates of the *passé composé* as well as for the marked absence of the imperfect. But this absence requires a closer examination. The higher frequency of distribution errors for the imperfect with respect to the *passé composé* may have to do with the possibility that the aspectual notion of the imperfect is more subtle, less easily perceived than that of the *passé composé*. For the learner, the quality of "pastness" is not as evident for ongoing and habitual conditions as it is for discrete events or actions. An argument could also be made for semantic complexity, that is, that the imperfect form actually encodes more than one aspect (durative, iterative, imperfective, and so forth) and that this semantic complexity may diffuse or weaken for the learner the semantic value of the imperfect.

Interestingly, other studies of morpheme acquisition for child first language (L1) and adult second language (L2) learners of French also indicate a delayed understanding of the functions of the imperfect. Bronckart and Sinclair (1973) observe that French L1 children mark aspectual differences with forms found in adult language but that these forms are not necessarily the correct ones. They note that imperfective actions are almost never expressed by past tenses and that while the present is rarely substituted for the *passé composé*, it is often substituted for the imperfect. In Veronique's (1984) study of immigrant adult Arabic learners of L2 French, the oral data show higher accuracy scores for the *passé composé* compared with the imperfect. Similar results can be found in other Romance languages. Both van Naerssen (1981) and VanPatten (1981) found that the preterit in Spanish (the functional counterpart of the *passé composé*) obtains overall higher accuracy scores when compared with the imperfect.

To insist, however, on relative order of acquisition, i.e., *passé composé* before imperfect, as an indication that the aspectual meaning of the imperfect has not yet been acquired, may obscure the entire developmental process of tense-aspect acquisition. Examining morpheme acquisition in terms of a dynamic system of gradually redefined oppositions (Bickerton 1981) rather than as an ordered sequence of isolated features, we discern an aspectual opposition resembling that of the target language. In the raw data, 82 percent of all errors of distribution for the imperfect at the intermediate level are due to the informants supplying a present tense form in an imperfect context. This near-systematic use of the present in an imperfect (and not *passé composé*) context indicates that some functional distinction is being made at this level. In standard French, the *présent* versus *passé composé* would be treated as a simple *temporal present* versus *past opposition*, but to interpret the forms as such in the learner's interlanguage is to ignore an already-emerging aspectual system. This system can be schematized in this figure.

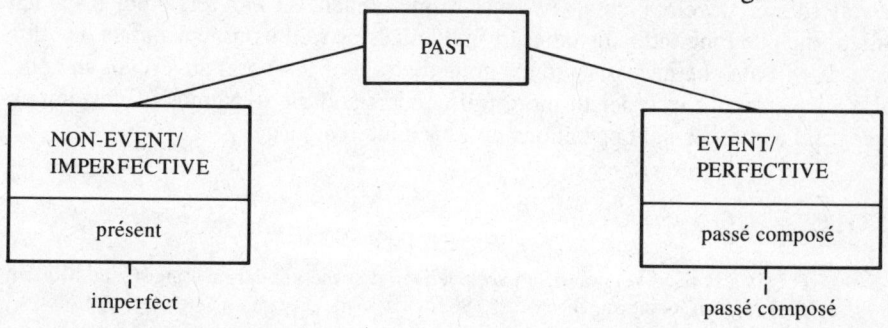

Here, the aspectual distinction may be tentatively identified as perfective (event)/imperfective (non-event). Representing the verbal forms in opposition rather than in sequence allows one to observe in the learner's interlanguage a subsystem that makes aspectual distinctions, using a reduced verbal paradigm. In other words, the aspectual distinction is partially achieved at the intermediate level, although the imperfect form does not yet consistently mark the imperfective aspect. This process of aspectual distinction, followed at a later stage by the insertion of target forms, is consistent with Bronckart and Sinclair's L1 data (cited above) as well as with Veronique's adult L2 data (also cited above). Indeed, the precedence given to aspectual organization over time-marking may be a universal feature in language acquisition. Kumpf (1984) reports a similar pattern for her ESL subject whose interlanguage developed aspectual distinction but not temporal distinction.

CONCLUSION

In this study the pattern of past tense morpheme acquisition among adult learners of French in a formal setting has been examined. While one could certainly claim that the study is limited in terms of the number of subjects studied and the quantity of data gathered, an overall pattern of early success with the *passé composé* relative to the imperfect was observed. This discrepancy would obstensibly reflect learner difficulties with the aspectual distinction between the *passé composé* and the imperfect. It was suggested, however, that by approaching the results as a holistic system rather than as an ordered sequence of isolated morphemes, the development of perfective/imperfective-event/non-event aspectual distinctions is brought to light.

Various explanations were advanced to account for the learner's success with the *passé composé* and the relative absence of the imperfect form, including grammatical and semantic complexity, phonological saliency, frequency of occurrence in input, and communicative strategies. While it is beyond the scope of this study to argue for the relative contribution of such factors (given the limitations mentioned above), it is hypothesized that perceptual saliency and semantic complexity may be operating in conjunction with frequency in input. Such arguments await further developmental evidence from French L2 and FL studies, which might include longitudinal studies of individuals as well as group studies like this one. It will also be necessary to examine the role of temporal adverbials in addition to verb types in order to more fully understand the dynamics of developing temporal and aspectual oppositions in French interlanguage.

NOTES

1. This is a revised version of a paper delivered at the annual meeting of the Modern Language Association, December 1983, New York City.

REFERENCES

Bickerton, D. 1981. *Roots of Language*. Ann Arbor: Karoma.
Bronckart, J. P., and H. Sinclair, 1973. Time, tense and aspect. *Cognition* 2:107-130.
Krashen, S. D. 1981. *Second Language Acquisition and Second Language Learning*. Oxford: Pergamon.
Krashen, S. D. 1982. *Principles and Practice in Second Language Acquisition*. Oxford: Pergamon Press.
Krashen, S. D. 1985. *The Input Hypothesis*. London: Longman.
Kumpf, L. 1984. Temporal systems and universality: a case study. In *Universals of Second Language Acquisition*, F. Eckman, L. Bell, and D. Nelson (eds.), 132-143. Rowley, MA: Newbury House.
Larsen-Freeman, D. 1976. An explanation for the morpheme accuracy order of learners of English as a second language. *Language Learning* 26:125-135.
van Naerssen, M. 1981. How similar are Spanish as a first language and Spanish as a second language? In *Second Language Acquisition Research*, S. D. Krashen, and R. Scarcella (eds.), 146-163. Rowley, MA: Newbury House.
VanPatten, B. 1981. The acquisition of *ser* and *estar* and the preterit tense in two learners of Spanish. Unpublished M.A. thesis, University of Texas at Austin.
Veronique, D. 1984. The acquisition and use of aspects of French morphosyntax by native speakers of Arabic dialects (North Africa). In *Second Languages: A Cross-Linguistic Perspective*, R. W. Anderson. (ed.), 191-213. Rowley, MA: Newbury House.
Zobl, H. 1980. Developmental and transfer errors: their common bases and (possibly) differential effects on subsequent learning. *TESOL Quarterly* 14: 469-482

APPENDIX

Categories for Learners' Use of the *Passé Composé* and the Imperfect

A. Learner supplies correct form of the tense in an obligatory context.

B. Learner produces a structurally faulty but identifiable form of the *passé composé* or the imperfect in an obligatory context. For the *passé composé*, the error invariably involves either use of the wrong auxiliary or an irregular participle made regular by analogy to that of another verb paradigm.

    Ex: *j'*ai* allé (je *suis* allé)
    *j'ai *lisé* (j'ai *lu*)

For the imperfect, the error generally involves a stem remade by analogy to that of another verb paradigm.

    Ex: *je *dormiss*ais (je *dorm*ais)

C. Learner supplies correct form of the tense in an inappropriate context.

    Ex: *J'*ai dansé* depuis deux ans. (Je *danse* depuis deux ans.)

The informant's misunderstanding of the question could result in the correct formation but inappropriate use of the past tense.

Ex: Tester: Comment allez-vous passer le weekend?
       (How are you going to spend the weekend?)
    Informant: J'ai passé le weekend à travailler.
       (I spent the weekend working.)

The informant hears *avez-vous passé* [avevupase] instead of
       allez-vous passer [alevupase].

The informant has produced a correct form of the *passé composé* in a context demanding the present/immediate future.

D. Learner supplies an item in a *passé composé* or an imperfect context that is incorrect in both form and function for the designated context. This category includes cases where the learner supplies the correct form of some tense (present, pluperfect, immediate future) other than the *passé composé* or the imperfect to express past time.

Ex: Quand j'étais petit, *j'*aimais* le sport (j'aimais)
    (When I was little, I like sports)

CHAPTER 4

Classroom Learners' Acquisition of *Ser* and *Estar:* Accounting for Developmental Patterns[1]

Bill VanPatten
University of Illinois at Urbana-Champaign

INTRODUCTION

Many foreign language (FL) teachers still believe that if they could explain a certain syntactic or morphological phenomenon in just the right way and then practice the structure sufficiently with their class, the students would somehow acquire the form. Second language (L2) acquisition research has shown us repeatedly that that is just not the case. In the instance of English as a second language (ESL), there is quite a bit of evidence that there are certain stages that learners must pass through in their acquisition of grammatical structure regardless of method, text, teacher, error correction, or even first language (L1). The most often cited of these research findings are (1) the so-called natural orders of acquisition of morphemes (summarized in Dulay, Burt, and Krashen, 1982, chapter 8), (2) the transitional stages of acquisition of negation (as in Ravem 1978 and Wode 1981, and (3) the transitional stages of acquisition of Wh-question formation and embedding (again in Ravem 1974, and also in Cazden et al. 1975). For example, it is well documen-

TABLE 4-1 The Acquisition of English L2 Negation (based on Dulay, Burt, and Krashen 1982)

I. S → [no, not] – Nucleus – [no, not]
　　No, no like it.
　　No play baseball.
　　Not raining.

II. S → Nom – Aux(neg) – [Predicate, Main verb]
　Aux(neg) → [no, not, don't]
　　I not this way.
　　Me no close the window.
　　I don't can explain.

III. S → Nom – Aux – [Predicate, Main verb]
　Aux → T – V(aux) – (Neg)
　　You're not playing it.
　　Lunch is no ready.
　　I'm not scare ghost.

S = sentence; T = tense; Nom = nominative; V = verb; Aux = auxiliary

ted that all learners of ESL tend to pass through the stages of negation outlined in Table 4-1 (based on Dulay, Burt, and Krashen 1982, 124).

While it has been documented that certain stages may be protracted in some learners as opposed to others (see Schumann 1979, for example) and that some may go so quickly through a stage as to virtually skip it, the stages outlined in Table 4-1 have found strong empirical support in L2 literature.

It seems appropriate, then, to ask ourselves just what we know of the language acquisition stages and processes in the adult learners with whom those of us in foreign languages typically deal. Just what does Spanish interlanguage development look like? What transitional stages can be ascertain? What can we say about the order of emergence of structure over time? To be sure, there are existing studies of learners of Spanish that use error analysis (see for example LoCoco 1975, Smith 1980, and Sager 1983), and there is even one study that has posited an acquisition order for certain morphemes and functors for adult classroom learners (van Naerssen 1981). But there is a dearth of research detailing the acquisition or development of any one particular syntactic or morphological feature. (For a notable exception see Plann 1979.)

This study reports on an ongoing study of the transitional stages of development in adult English-speaking classroom learners' acquisition of the Spanish copulas, *ser* and *estar*. Five stages are hypothesized, and unlike the claims made by van Naerssen (1981) and Smith (1980), Spanish copula does not appear to be a structure under even "moderate" control after one year of classroom exposure. The discussion will conclude with an examination of the factors that best account for the emergence of the copula, as observed in this study.[2]

DATA

The data for this paper are derived from three sources. The first is a year-long longitudinal study of six classroom learners of Spanish of various degrees of fluency who were involved in a much larger project concerning the effects of instruction on grammatical development in learners. The exact nature of the data collection, the learner profiles, and the data themselves are reported in VanPatten (1985a) and need not be repeated in detail here. Briefly, it can be noted that these were oral data, collected at two-week intervals over a period of nine months and, that they were derived from conversational interchange.

Another data subset comes from a grammaticality judgement task that is reported in Betts (1984). These data come from an entirely different set of learners, from another institution, and were used to verify the results of the longitudinal study in VanPatten (1985a). The grammaticality judgement task was also used to tap learners' knowledge of certain areas of copula usage that did not surface with enough frequency in the longitudinal data to be examined meaningfully at that time.[3] It should be noted that the grammaticality judgement task involved the learners' evaluation of written sentences in Spanish, using both timed and untimed judgements, and involved learners at three levels of university study: end of first year, end of second year, middle of third year (conversation courses). An outline of the grammaticality task and the results appear in the Appendix.

Finally, additional evidence comes from the author's experience in observing, for numerous hours, learner classroom behavior while supervising college-level teaching assistants. While observing the classroom activities, with the explicit intention of evaluating the teacher, the author has made many notations of learner use of *ser* and *estar* during class time interaction in which learner attention was on language use (e.g., conversational interchanges with teacher and peers, games), and not on language practice (e.g., mechanical drill). (Admittedly, this form of data collection is not always a sound methodological procedure: since one cannot obtain recorded samples, one cannot listen to the data more than once, double checking its accuracy.) However, one can derive only one additional stage of transitional competence from these notations, a stage that was not tapped either in the longitudinal study or in the grammaticality judgement task (see discussion below). It is therefore believed that this particular means of collecting information about learner verbal performance served this study well and does not constitute a real problem for the acceptability of the stages posited in this research.

Table 4-2 summarizes the results of the longitudinal study (VanPatten 1985a). As one can see, only three stages for the acquisition of *ser* and *estar* were reported in that study.

Classroom observation and the grammaticality judgement task confirmed these three preliminary stages and yielded two other significant stages. The revised sequence of development is reported in Table 4-3.

The reader's attention should be drawn to the fact that copula omission (Stage I), as reported in Table 4-3, was found during classroom observation of the first

TABLE 4–2 Developmental Stages in the Acquisition of Spanish Copulas (based on VanPatten 1985a)

I. Learners selects one copula to perform a majority of the functions of both copulas. That verb is *ser*.
   María es inteligente. (Mary is smart.)
   *María es furiosa. (Mary is angry.)
   *María es allí. (Mary is there.)

II. Consistent appearance of *estar* with locative expressions. *Ser* still overgeneralized elsewhere.
   María está allí.
   *María es furiosa.

III. Consistent appearance of *estar* with adjectives of condition.
   María está furiosa.

TABLE 4–3 Revised Development of the Spanish Copulas

I. Absence of copula in learner speech.
   *Juan alto. (John is tall.)
II. Selection of *ser* to perform most of copula functions.
   Juan es alto.
   *Juan es enfermo. (John is sick.)
   *Juan es estudiando. (John is studying.)
III. Appearance of *estar* with progressive.
   Juan está estudiando.
IV. Appearance of *estar* with locatives.
   Juan está en la clase. (John is in the classroom.)
V. Appearance of *estar* with adjectives of condition.
   Juan está enfermo.

several weeks of instruction and is not a stage that seems to last for long. Omission of the copula probably did not surface in the longitudinal study since taping of the oral conversations began during the eighth week of instruction. By that time, it is likely that the six learners in that study had already passed through that particular stage. It is also interesting to note that copula omission seems to surface more frequently in oral language than in written language (an observation the author made when comparing the classroom verbal performance with learners' diary entries). This observation may be explained by Monitor usage. It is suggested that the conditions of Monitor usage (see Krashen 1982) were met during diary writing but not during class time, and therefore learners may have inserted a copula in written language via monitoring in the earliest stages of acquisition (cf. Dvorak [this volume], who has found some structural differences between written and oral language). This may be especially true if the learners were thinking in English and writing in Spanish.

The posited stage of appearance of *estar* with progressive (Table 4-3, Stage III) was found via the grammaticality judgement task. In that task, it was found that learners recognized ungrammatical sentences most often with progressive, then locative, and finally with adjective of condition. This performance supports the stages outlined in Table 4-2.

As is evident from the data, not all functions of the copula as used in native-like speech appear in this study. For such to be investigated, a longitudinal study of many years would be needed. It is doubtful, if not impossible, that learners, after one or two years of classroom instruction, could be exposed to, let alone internalize, the variety of native-like usage of the Spanish copulas as reported in Solé and Solé (1977) and in Franco (1979). What is reported here, then are the data that have been obtained by using learners who have undergone either one year of language study, as in the longitudinal study, or one to two and a half years of study, as in the grammaticality judgement task.

DISCUSSION

The stages in the acquisition of *ser* and *estar*, like the stages of transitional competence found for ESL and English as a foreign language (EFL) learners, cannot be explained by classroom teaching approaches or sequence of instruction. That is, *ser* does not appear first in learner speech because *ser* is taught first. Indeed, for all learners who participated in this study, both copulas and their usage with common adjectives were taught on the first day of instruction and were reviewed every day for a week; they were also used regularly in classroom conversation. Furthermore, the different stages for the emergence of *estar* with its specific functions cannot be explained via teaching order since *estar* and all of its functions were presented in one chapter and were reviewed holistically at various intervals. Finally, it would be difficult indeed to link stages to instruction since teachers of Spanish do not practice copula omission with their learners.

The transitional stages observed for the Spanish copulas in adult speakers of English can, however, be accounted for by a complex interaction of at least four factors known to be involved in L2 acquisition. These factors are simplification, communicative value (see below), frequency in input, and L1 transfer. These factors have been discussed in L2 literature before, but generally independently. The following discussion will be an attempt to interrelate these factors to see how they interact during the development of learner language.

The one factor of acquisition that is immediately evident in the data is simplification. Simplification is a term with a long history in language studies. One of the earliest definitions used in L2 studies comes from Richards (1975). He claimed that simplification was an acquisition strategy whereby "the immediate objective for a language learner is to construct an optimum grammar, that is, a grammar in which the fewest number of rules do the maximum amount of work" (118). In this case, the numerous rules for the usage of *ser* and *estar* were reduced to copula omission or the overuse of *ser* or both. Research has shown that simplification is a very important factor in L2 acquisition; however, the research is also replete with debates on just what simplification is. Richard's definition does not satisfy many who are involved in the ongoing research of pidginization or language contact. Is simplification a strategy or a process; or is it merely a description of a product? (See Meisel 1983 and Traugott 1977 for appropriate discussions.) In this study, the position is taken that simplification is at least a set of processes by which learners constrain and filter input. In other words, input (language directed to the learner for communicative purposes) is simplified by the learner during intake (that moment in which incoming language is processed for meaning) because of the constraints on the human information-processing system. Learners cannot and do not attend to all linguistic items in an utterance directed to them. (See VanPatten 1985b for a more thorough discussion of how learners may process input for meaning.) The simplified system that evolves from these processing constraints forms the basis for interlanguage.

It is important to point out that copula omission is possible in the developing system in the early stages due to the influence of communicative value on simplification. Copulas tend to be meaningless functors in the propositional context of utterances. That is, they generally do not add any real information to a message contained in a sentence, and they may either be deleted in speech or unattended to in input without any particular interference in communication. Indeed, some languages do not even have surface realizations of copulas in most utterances, and many pidgins develop similar grammatical systems allowing copula omission or deletion (see Ferguson 1971 for an interesting discussion). Copula omission is also a well-documented feature of early-stage child L1 acquisition in English and of English foreigner talk. The copula is, of course, eventually acquired by child L1 learners, but that is not testimony about the evolving communicative value of copulas. Rather, it is taken as evidence that acquisition is proceeding toward adult-like norms, where grammatical "frills" are necessary in order to sound like an adult.

Any discussion of simplification in the acquisition of Spanish copula in this study necessarily leads the researcher to the question, "Why do learners select *ser* instead of *estar* as the primary copula verb in the early stages?" It is here that one finds the interaction of communicative value with frequency of occurrence in input, both intersecting with simplification. VanPatten (1984 and 1985b) has suggested that when two forms (grammatical structures and even lexical items) are of the same communicative value (i.e., the two are equally important or equally unimportant to the learner for understanding the proposition[s] contained in an utterance), frequency of occurrence in input determines which item will be acquired first. Input here is used in the manner discussed by Hatch (1983), Scarcella and Higa (1982), and Krashen (1982): meaningful, communicatively centered input directed to the learner that is appropriate for his level of comprehension and language development. To summarize, then, if form X equals form Y in terms of communicative value, then X will be acquired before Y if X is more frequent in the input (cf. Larsen-Freeman [1976], who addresses frequency of occurrence in input in absolute terms without reference to its interaction with other processes or factors).

The hypotheses of the interaction between communicative value and frequency of occurrence accounts for the earlier emergence of *ser* in the speech of the subjects involved in this study. Since both verbs belong to the syntactic category of "copula" and, in spite of instructional efforts rarely contrast in meaning for the early-stage language learner (that is, the probability is quite low that the main proposition of an utterance is not grasped by the learner if one verb is substituted for the other in the input), they can be considered of equally low communicative value. Since *ser* is more frequent in the input, it is thus picked up first and is then overgeneralized.[4] It should be noted that no reference is made here to semantic value for adult native speakers of Spanish. Semantic value for native speakers is a result of L1 acquisition and emerges over time like other aspects of the linguistic system, while communicative value for the L2 learner is a dynamic, evolving part of the interlanguage. One should keep these two concepts separate since semantic value has connotations derived from linguistic inquiry in which native use of languages is investigated, but communicative is a term that is often used with reference to language learning. The distinction is important, for what may have semantic value for adult native speakers may not have communicative value for the early-stage learner. As a last point about this matter, it should be noted that while they may be taught or explained as a grammar point, distinctions such as *es verde/está verde* rarely occur in communicatively centered input used in the classroom.

Before continuing, it might be helpful to summarize. The data on the acquisition of Spanish copula by adult speakers of English is explained via the interaction of simplification and communicative value in Stage I and the interaction of these two with frequency of occurrence in input in Stage II. Subsequent stages may be governed by frequency of occurence in input. Thus, simplification does not occur haphazardly or in individually different ways for every language learner, nor does it operate independently of other factors. Furthermore, frequency of occurrence in input does not seem to operate as an autonomous factor or as the dominant factor.

It is interesting to note that most classroom learners appear to spend a long time in Stage II, the overgeneralization of *ser*. One subject in the longitudinal study, for example, after one year of classroom exposure showed almost no development with *estar*. This subject's accuracy scores for *ser* and *estar* are presented in Figure 4-1, a longitudinal account of the copula in his conversational interchanges during one year. The reader's attention is drawn to the consistently high scores for *ser* and the consistently low scores for *estar*. While this is the profile for just one learner, the other learners in the longitudinal study exhibited similar development (see VanPatten 1985a).

The question arises as to just why most classroom learners seem to spend such a long time in the second stage, overgeneralizing *ser*. (It is important to note that

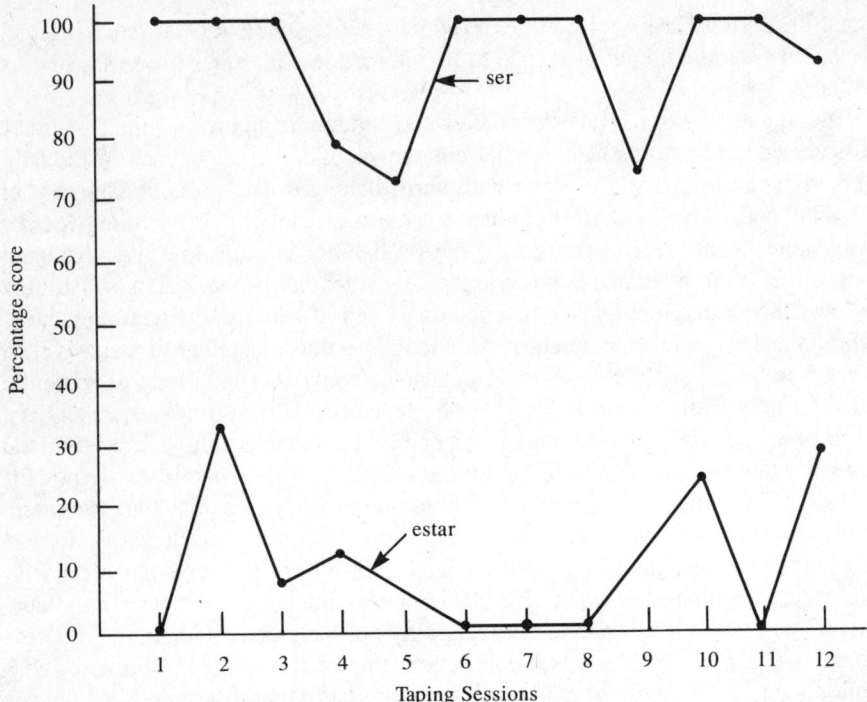

Figure 4.1 Accuracy Scores for Spanish Copula for One Learner (from VanPatten 1985a)

learners do not move crisply and clearly from one stage to another. There is some overlap. While learners are clearly in stage two we see some beginnings of the emergence of later stages.) It is here that the concept of L1 transfer apparently plays a major role.

Few researchers of L2 acquisition adhere to early accounts of L1 transfer as first put forth by Lado (1957) and Stockwell, Bowen, and Martin (1965). The automatic transfer of habits is not longer a viable explanatory model for adult language learning. Nonetheless, the concept of L1 transfer has been reinvestigated in such a way that more sophisticated hypotheses of the interaction of a given L1 and L2 acquisition do indeed help to account for certain aspects of interlanguage data. Current approaches to the role of L1 transfer allow for the natural stages and processes in L2 acquisition that are seemingly universal in scope and that limit the role of the L1 to those stages at which there is convergence between L1 structure/function and the developing interlanguage. Such is the approach of Zobl (1980 and 1982) and also of Andersen (1983).

Andersen, for example, has developed the "Transfer to Somewhere Principle," which claims,

> A grammatical form or structure will occur consistently and to a significant extent in the interlanguage as a result of transfer *if and only if* (1) natural acquisitional processes are consistent with the L1 structure or (2) there already exists within the L2 input the potential for (mis-)generalization from the input to produce the same form or structure. (192)

Andersen's principle claims that transfer operates only where there are similarities between the L1 and the developing interlanguage, not where there are differences between the L1 and L2. Furthermore, the interaction between L1 and the interlanguage cannot violate the natural processes of acquisition that are in progress (e.g., simplification, morphological restructuring). Andersen also claims that when transfer is triggered in this manner, the resultant structure in the learner's interlanguage will be more resistant to change. That is, continued development toward a native-like usage of the structure will take more time than it would if transfer were not triggered. Thus, in the acquisition of English negation by L2 learners (see Table 4-1) it has been documented that stage I is often protracted for speakers of language with L1 proverbial negation. ESL learners of Spanish L1 and Italian L2, for example, spend more time in stage I of English negation than do learners of Japanese L1, where negation is postverbal, even though eventually all learners tend to pass through the same stages (see Schumann 1979).

In terms of this study, Andersen's principle accounts neatly for our classroom learners' lingering in stage II. It can be argued that adult English-speaking learners of Spanish remain in stage II of copula acquisition for some time because of the overlap between L1 structure (one copula, "be") and that particular stage (one copula, *ser*). Progress in the acquisition of *estar* is thus hindered as compared to something like the acquisition of the possessive structure noun + *de*, where Andersen's conditions of convergence are never met during the interlanguage development of learners of Spanish. That is, as learners acquire Spanish possessive *de*, natural processes of acquisition never allow for the creation of a stage whose structure resembles English "'s." Thus, transfer is not triggered and no particular stage of the acquisition of noun + *de* is lengthened. It is true that every teacher of Spanish has encountered at some point a learner who slips and says *Juan's casa* rather than *la case de Juan*, but this is not evidence of a universal stage. These infrequent errors are generally due to reliance on the L1 for utterance initiation and can be viewed as evidence that for that particular learner, acquisition of noun + *de* has probably not even begun. Unlike the account of transfer under discussion here, these "errors" resemble what Krashen has referred to as "L1 + Monitor mode" (Krashen 1982).

In sum, four factors seem to be involved in guiding the interlanguage development of the Spanish copulas in English-speaking classroom learners of Spanish: simplification, communicative value, frequency of occurrence in input, and L1 transfer. This interaction is somewhat complex and has been summarized in schematic form in Figure 4-2.

SUMMARY AND CONCLUSIONS

It has been posited that English-speaking adult classroom learners exhibit at least five stages in the acquisition of Spanish copula and that these stages are explained

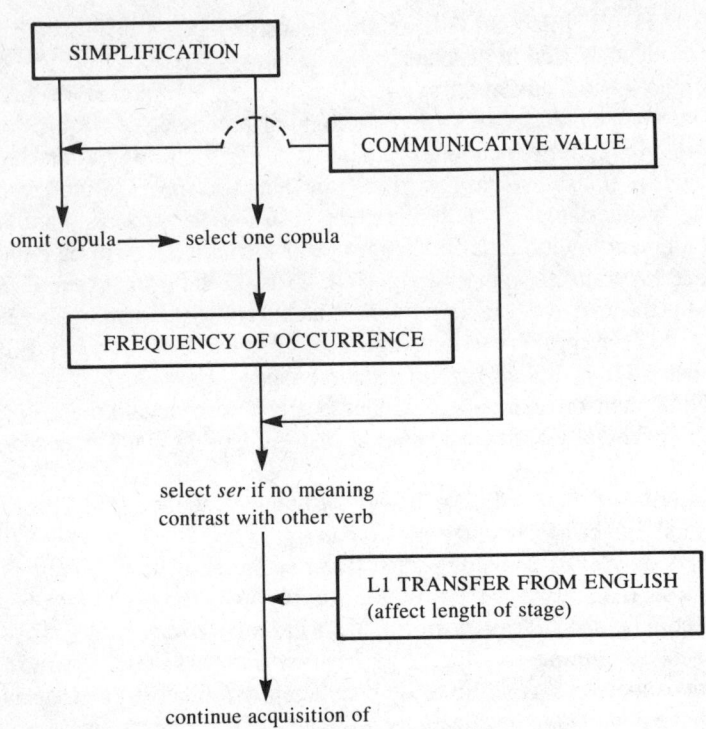

Figure 4.2 The Interaction of Four Factors in the Acquisition of *ser* and *estar*

via a complex interaction of four factors in L2 acquisition. This interaction is briefly outlined here:
1. Simplification, the primary factor, constrains input and interacts with communicative value to produce a stage of copula omission.
2. Simplification and communicative value interact with frequency of occurrence in input to select one copula to be overgeneralized: *ser*.
3. L1 transfer interacts with stage II, causing English-speaking learners to spend some time in this stage.
4. Frequency of occurrence in input eventually guides the rest of the acquisition of the functions of *estar*.

Of course, there remain questions for future research. It was suggested here that communicative value must first be considered before frequency of occurrence in input can affect language development. Is this true in the acquisition of all structure/lexicon, or is it peculiar to the explanation of copula acquisition in this study? If this is a universal, then Larsen-Freeman's (1976) study on frequency of occurrence in input as a factor in the acquisition of English morphemes would have to be reevaluated. In VanPatten (1984 and 1985b), it is suggested that communicative value (referred to in the 1984 study as "semantic clout") is just as powerful an explanatory device in the acquisition of English morphemes as is frequency of occurrence in input. Furthermore, it was suggested in this paper that frequency of occurrence in input may guide the final stages of the acquisition of *estar*, but it is conceivable that other factors not discussed here could also be at work. Patricia V. Lunn has suggested in a personal communication that cognitive grammars would predict an early emergence of correct locative usage compared to other uses of *estar*. In a different vein, Trisha R. Dvorak in a personal communication has suggested that the various functions of *estar* may appear correctly in learner speech over time because of the contrastive/non-contrastive relationship between the two copulas. That is, perhaps *estar* + progressive appears before *estar* + locative/adjective because only *estar* can occur with progressives but both *ser* and *estar* can occur with locatives and adjectives. Accordingly, the non-contrastive use of *estar* is easier to pick up. In the end, there may really be two parts to the story of the acquisition of the Spanish copulas, with two different explanations: early-stage acquisition with one set of guiding principles, and the acquisition of *estar* with another set of guiding principles. This question will be left for future discussion and research.

Another question to be answered is whether or not Andersen's (1983) account of L1 transfer can be tested by examining the acquisition of Spanish copula by speakers who have no copula in their L1. According to the hypothesis, these learners should spend more time in stage I (omission) compared to learners with English-L1 before proceeding to the stage of overgeneralization of one copula.

Finally, what does the acquisition of Spanish copula by English speakers look like in naturalistic settings? Would it parallel what we find in classroom learners? It is well known that in spite of natural-like approaches or communicative interaction, classrooms cannot provide the rich array of input data that exists in the real world; but does this necessarily mean that acquisition patterns are different? This is currently being explored by VanPatten (forthcoming) using clitic pronouns as the structure(s) in question.

This study has attempted to sort out the interaction of just four factors that have been independently discussed in previous work in L2 acquisition. Recently, there has been a move to include more data in L2 research that is not derived from learners of ESL. (See Andersen 1984 for example.) It would appear that more research on FL learners can help provide the cross-linguistic data necessary to assist in the building of a more complete account of adult language learning.

NOTES

1. The research presented here was partially supported by a grant from the U.S. Office of Education and is a revised version of a paper presented at the Second Language Research Forum, University of California at Los Angeles, February 1985. I would like to thank Trisha R. Dvorak and James F. Lee for their comments on earlier drafts of this paper, with the usual caveats regarding responsibility for content.

2. For those not familiar with the copula system in Spanish, the following is an outline of how the two copulas are generally presented in first year texts and courses (based on Knorre et al. 1985, 117):
    ser: identify people and things; express nationality; used with *de* to express origin, possession, and material make-up; to express time of day; impersonal expressions; with adjectives of inherent characteristic/quality;
    estar: to express location; to form progressive; to describe health; with adjectives of condition; in certain "fixed" expressions.
3. There is some question about the appropriateness or relative merit of grammaticality judgement tasks for L2 research. Chaudron (1983) has taken up this discussion in his rather detailed review of metalinguistic tasks. It is worth pointing out that Chaudron finds such tasks to be useful and revealing if they are not the sole means of tapping learner knowledge (and if they are well-constructed tasks). The reader is reminded that the grammaticality judgement task used in this study was conducted as additional, subsequent research to the original study of learner speech production and thus cannot be viewed as data in isolation. Regarding the construct validity of the task, the reader may review the materials presented in the Appendix and compare them to Chaudron's recommendations.
4. The author knows of no published studies dealing with the relative frequency of the two copulas in Spanish. However, in a seminar on learning Spanish given by the author at Michigan State University, graduate students conducted frequency counts of certain linguistic features of Spanish, using readings in textbooks and supplementary readings aimed at first year learners. *Ser* was overwhelmingly more frequent in this type of input than was *estar*. Students reported ratios of frequency differences from 2:1 to 4:1.

REFERENCES

Andersen, R. 1983. Transfer to somewhere. In *Language Transfer in Language Learning*, S. Gass and L. Selinker (eds.), 177-201. Rowley, MA: Newbury House.

Andersen, R. (ed.). 1984. *Second Languages: A Cross-Linguistic Perspective*. Rowley, MA: Newbury House.

Betts, E. 1984. A grammaticality judgement task with *ser* and *estar*. Unpublished term paper, Spanish 860, Department of Romance and Classical Languages, Michigan State University.

Cazden, C. B., H. Cancino, E. Rosansky, and J. Schumann. 1975. *Second Language Acquisition Sequence in Children, Adolescents, and Adults*. Final report submitted to the National Institute of Education.

Chaudron, C. 1983. Research on metalinguistic judgements: a review of theory, methods, and results. *Language Learning* 33:343-377

Dulay, H., M. Burt, and S. Krashen. 1982. *Language Two*. New York: Oxford Press.

Ferguson, C. 1971. Absence of copula and the notion of simplicity: a study of normal speech, baby talk, foreigner talk and pidgins. In *Pidginization and Creolization of Languages*, D. Hymes (ed.), 141-150. Oxford: Cambridge University Press.

Franco, F. 1979. *Ser* and *estar* in the light of modern linguistics. Ph.D. dissertation, University of Minnesota at Minneapolis.

Hatch, E. 1983. Simplified input and second language acquisition. In *Pidginization and Creolization As Language Acquisition*, R. W. Andersen (ed.), 64-86, Rowley, MA: Newbury House.

Knorre, M., T. Dorwick, T. V. Higgs, B. VanPatten, F. Ferran, and W. Lusetti. 1985. *Puntos de partida*, 2nd ed. New York: Random House.

Krashen, S. 1982. *Principles and Practice in Second Language Acquisition*. New York: Pergamon Press.

Lado, R. 1957. *Linguistics Across Cultures.* Ann Arbor: University of Michigan Press.
Larsen-Freeman, D. 1976. An explanation for the morpheme accuracy order of learners of English as a second language. *Language Learning* 26:125-135.
LoCoco, V. 1975. An analysis of Spanish and German learners' errors. *Working Papers on Bilingualism* 7:96-124.
Meisel, J. 1983. Strategies of second language acquisition: more than one kind of simplification. In *Pidginization and Creolization As Language Acquisition,* R. Andersen (ed.), 120-157. Rowley, MA: Newbury House.
Plann, S. 1979. Morphological problems in the acquisition of Spanish in an immersion classroom. In *The Acquisition of Spanish and English As First and Second Languages,* R. Andersen (ed.), 119-132. Washington, D.C.: TESOL.
Ravem, R. 1978. Two Norwegian children's acquisition of English syntax. In Evelyn M. Hatch (ed.), *Second Language Acquisition: A Book of Readings* 148-154. Rowley, MA: Newbury House.
Richards, J. 1975. Simplification: a strategy in the adult acquisition of a foreign language. *Language Learning* 25:115-126.
Sager, J. 1983. El desarrollo gramatical en la adquisicion de una segunda lengua. Unpublished Ph.D. Thesis, University of Massachusetts-Amherst.
Scarcella, R., and C. Higa. 1982. Input and age differences in second language acquisition. In *Child-Adult Differences in Second Language Acquisition,* S. Krashen, R. Scarcella, and M. Long (eds.), 175-201. Rowley, MA: Newbury House.
Schumann, J. 1979. The acquisition of English negation by speakers of Spanish: a review of the literature. In *The Acquisition of Spanish and English As First and Second Languages,* R. Andersen (ed.), 2-32. Washington, D.C.: TESOL.
Smith, K. 1980. Common errors in the compositions of students of Spanish as a foreign language. Ph.D. dissertation, University of Texas at Austin.
Solé, C. and Y. Solé. 1977. *Modern Spanish Syntax.* New York: D. C. Heath.
Stockwell, R. P., J. D. Bowen, and J. W. Martin. 1965. *The Grammatical Structures of English and Spanish.* Chicago: The University of Chicago Press.
Traugott, E. 1977. Pidginization, creolization and language change. In *Pidgin and Creole Linguistics,* A. Valdman (ed.), 70-98. Bloomington: Indiana University Press.
van Naerssen, M. 1980. How similar are Spanish as a first language and Spanish as a second language? In *Second Language Acquisition Research,* S. Krashen and R. Scarcella (eds.), 146-163. Rowley, MA: Newbury House.
van Naerssen, M. 1981. Generalizing second language hypotheses across languages: a test case in Spanish as a second language. Unpublished Ph.D. Thesis, The University of Southern California.
VanPatten, B. 1984. Processing strategies and morpheme acquisition. In F. Eckman, L. Bell, and D. Nelson (eds.), *Universals of Second Language Acquisition* 88-98. Rowley, MA: Newbury House.
VanPatten, B. 1985a. The acquisition of *ser* and *estar* in adult classroom learners: a preliminary investigation of transitional stages of competence. *Hispania* 68:399-406.
VanPatten, B. 1985b. Communicative value and information processing in second language acquisition. In *On TESOL '84: A Brave New World For TESOL,* P. Larson, E. Judd, and D. S. Messerschmitt (eds.), 89-100. Washington, D.C. : TESOL.
VanPatten, B. Forthcoming. Classroom and naturalistic learning: two case studies. In *Studies in Hispanic Phonology, Sociolinguistics, and Applied Linguistics,* T. Morgan, J. F. Lee, and B. VanPatten (eds.).
Wode, H. 1981. Language-acquisition universals: a unified view of language acquisition. In H. Winitz (ed.), *Native Language and Foreign Language Acquisition* 219-234. New York: The New York Academy of Sciences .
Zobl, H. 1980. The formal and developmental selectivity of L1 influence on L2 acquisition. *Language Learning* 30:43-57.

Zobl, H. 1982. A direction for contrastive analysis: the comparative study of developmental sequence. *TESOL Quarterly* 16:169-183.

APPENDIX

Summary of grammaticality judgement task (based on Betts 1984).

Students were administered a written grammaticality task during regular class time. A total of 70 students participated (28 first year-third quarter students, 26 second year-third quarter students, and 26 third year-second quarter students). The experimenter was cautious in pointing out that the results of the task were strictly for research purposes and could not affect student grades. The task itself consisted of 46 sentences (23 test sentences and 23 distractors). Care was taken to ensure that all of the vocabulary was familiar. In order to control for "learning" during test taking, as well as for any effects of monitoring, the sentences were randomly ordered twice to create two different tests. Students were then randomly divided into groups at each level; in one group a 15-second time limit per sentence was imposed, and in the other group no time limit was imposed, allowing students to take as much time as needed to finish the task. The following instructions were read to the students:

> You will receive a packet of three pages. Each page will have 15 to 16 sentences on it. Your task is to read each sentence carefully and then decide, based on your knowledge of Spanish, whether each sentence is grammatical or ungrammatical and circle the corresponding symbol G or U next to the sentence. [Here students were informed of the amount of time they had, depending upon group assignment, as described above.] Do the best you can. Are there any questions?

Following are the actual test sentences:
1. Ellos son cansados después del examen.
2. Los cuadernos amarillos no están aquí.
3. Mis amigos están estudiando en la biblioteca.
4. Los médicos están furiosos esta tarde.
5. Los estudiantes son cerca del río.
6. Los Ewing están en Texas.
7. Algunos profesores están irritados en clase.
8. Los padres son frustrados hoy.
9. Tus amigos no están muy tristes ahora.
10. Los directores son hablando mucho.
11. Hoy los bancos están cerrados.
12. Las niñas son allí.
13. Esas niñas están con su mamá.
14. Los pacientes en el hospital son enfermos.
15. Los amigos están el bar.
16. Tus zapatos están detrás de la puerta.
17. Los jóvenes son bailando el rock ahora.
18. Las bebidas están frías.
19. Los estudiantes están nerviosos en la clase.
20. Las profesoras están enseñando ahora.
21. Susana y Ana son en la biblioteca.
22. Los pacientes son con el médico.
23. Las muchachas son muy contentas hoy.

Student responses were scored for accurate detection of ungrammaticality, including correct and incorrect assignments of grammaticality. Since the purpose of the study was to find support for the stages suggested in VanPatten (1985a), the percentages reported in the table that follows indicate how successful the students were in judging the sentences that required *estar*, that is, progressive, locative, conditional adjective. While the scores are close, they do indicate a definite pattern of difficulty across the different levels.

	progressive	locative	adjective
1st year	78.5	74.6	69.6
2nd year	87.5	83.0	78.0
3rd year	95.8	94.0	83.0

PART TWO

Skills and Strategies

CHAPTER 5
Is Written FL Like Oral FL?

Trisha R. Dvorak
University of Michigan

INTRODUCTION

What are the relationships between written and oral language? Is written language basically a graphic version of speech, or does it have characteristics not shared by oral language? There is no doubt that the contexts for speech and writing are different in important ways (Emig 1977; Rubin 1980), but what is known about differences in the form and structure of the language used in each context? Research in first language (L1) acquisition has begun to identify a number of areas of similarity and divergence between oral and written language development.

SIMILARITIES BETWEEN ORAL AND WRITTEN FIRST LANGUAGE

The work of Hunt (1965) and others has shown that as children mature, the syntactic complexity of their speech and writing increases in similar ways. Mean length of T-unit increases (Hunt 1965, 1970; Loban 1976; O'Donnell, Griffin and Norris 1967). First developed by Hunt in 1965, the T-unit is defined as an independent clause plus any subordinate clauses embedded within it, as illustrated in the following examples.

Sentence	T-units	words/T-unit
There is a little boy.	1	5
The boy has some money / and wants to buy a toy / but he sees a blind man on the street who has no money.	3	8
The boy is sad because he has money and the blind man doesn't.	1	13

The syntactic complexity of language can be increased via coordination, subordination, or clause reduction. Through coordination one can take two simple sentences like "I have a dog/His name is Jupiter" and produce "I have a dog and his name is Jupiter." The process of subordination results in "I have a dog whose name is Jupiter" while "I have a dog named Jupiter" is the result of clause reduction. In L1 written and oral language, coordination is the first device acquired, followed by subordination and clause reduction (Gaies 1980). In L1, oral and written language react similarly to mode of discourse (Crowhurst and Piche 1979; Perron 1976; Rosen 1969; San Jose 1972): mean length of T-unit is greater for argumentation than for description, with exposition and narration falling somewhere in between. Accuracy and fluency of expression are both improved when the speaker or writer works with a topic that is familiar and of high interest (Perl 1979).

DIFFERENCES BETWEEN ORAL AND WRITTEN FIRST LANGUAGE

Speakers (Cazden 1970; Jensen 1973; Shatz and Gelman 1973) as well as writers (Crowhurst and Piche 1979; Smith and Swan 1976) adjust their language according to their audience, although this ability develops much earlier in speech than in writing. Written language is usually described as being a more "elaborative" code than oral language, and the characteristics that make it so become gradually more prominent with age and maturation: after about grade three, the mean length of T-units is longer in writing than in speech (O'Donnell, Griffin and Norris 1967), and the ratio of adjective and adverb clauses to T-units increases. Not only does the language change, but also the structure and organization of written messages begin to look less and less like those of oral messages (Bereiter 1980; Britton, et al. 1975; Kroll 1981; Stahl 1974, 1977).

SIMILARITIES BETWEEN ORAL AND WRITTEN SECOND LANGUAGE

In the foreign language (FL) and second language (L2) fields, written language has been studied relatively little, perhaps because of the common assumption that the lexical and structural characteristics of written language would essentially mirror the lexical and structural characteristics of oral language. The development of the T-unit as a measure of syntactic complexity sparked a number of studies that have indeed revealed many of the same patterns of similarity between oral and written L2 as those documented for L1. Mean T-unit length increases with language proficiency in German (Akin 1975), French (Cooper 1976; Cooper and Morain 1980), Spanish (Cooper 1981), and English as a second language (ESL) (Kameen 1979; Klassen 1976; Perkins 1980). Although the process of "syntactic maturation" occurs much more rapidly in the second language than in the first, the progression from coordination through subordination to clause reduction is essentially the same as that for L1 (Gaies 1980; Monroe 1975). As with L1, learners are both more talkative and more accurate when they are interested in and familiar with the topic of discourse (Winfeld and Barnes-Felfeli 1982).

DIFFERENCES BETWEEN ORAL AND WRITTEN SECOND LANGUAGE

Much less is known about possible differences between oral and written language, whether L2 or FL. Vann (1979) showed that the average length of T-units tends to be longer in written language than in spoken language and that written language tends to contain a higher percentage of adjective and adverb clauses than does speech. Little else has been published specifically comparing the two. Is the elaboration (e.g., the use of adjective and adverb clauses) of the FL written code related to level of language proficiency? What effect(s) does mode of discourse exert on the accuracy, complexity and elaboration of the oral and written codes? This study was designed to investigate these questions.

METHOD

SUBJECTS

Four students from each of four levels of Spanish instruction at the University of Michigan volunteered to participate in the experiment. Counting each year of high school language study as one-half and each semester of college study as one year, students in level one had studied Spanish an average of three years (e.g., two years in high school and two semesters in college), those in level two an average of 4.25 years, those in level three an average of 6 years and those in level four an average of 6.7 years, plus a period of extended residence (an academic semester or more) abroad. Each student gave a written and an oral version of a story suggested by picture sequence #28 of *Composition through Pictures* (Heaton 1966), and a written and an oral version expressing their opinion on a specific topic. Two modes of discourse— narration and argumentation— were chosen for the study, since previous L1 research had indicated that these two modes most clearly produce differences in T-unit length. In order to control for order of presentation, students within each level were randomly assigned to either speak-first or write-first conditions, argumentation-first or narration-first tasks.

MATERIALS

Four individual test booklets were prepared for each student, one for each task/code combination. Each booklet consisted of an instruction sheet stapled to a task sheet, which had enough blank space to allow students to write on it during the writing task. The picture story was chosen because it involved vocabulary that was accessible to students at all levels and because it involved not only a sequence of events but the resolution of a dilemma. It was hoped that this would provoke a longer speech sample than would a simpler picture. Keeping in mind the importance of familiarity of context on fluency, the topic for argumentation focused on the American educational system:

> Many people think that the US educational system is at a point of crisis. Do you agree? In your opinion, what are some of the problems facing American schools? Why do they exist? What kinds of solutions do you think might help to resolve them?

The instructions for oral and written versions of each task were identical, except that "talking about" and "recording" became "writing about" and "writing" in each case. (A copy of the instructions for each task is reproduced in the Appendix.)

PROCEDURE

All testing was done in the language lab at the University of Michigan, where each student could work in an individual booth in relative isolation from other students. For the oral tasks students recorded their responses from their individual booths, without feedback from or interaction with anyone else. In order to further minimize possible distractions, no more than six students were tested during a single testing session, and half of the students worked on narration and the other half on argumentation each time. Each student did the oral and written versions of the same task on the same day and returned a week later for the oral and written versions of the other task. At the beginning of each session the students were told that although they would be talking and writing about the same topic, they should not aim to duplicate in one code what they had produced in the other but to simply express their ideas as naturally as possible each time. The students were informed that their work would not be graded. Once the experimenter was sure that all of the students could properly manipulate the recording equipment, the test booklets were handed out and the students were allowed to work through the assigned version of each task at their own speed. As each student finished, she or he handed in the test booklet and was given a short "distractor activity" to perform (on one occasion a detailed description of academic background in Spanish and on another occasion detailed biographical information about the various members of their families), and when this was finished, the student was given a new test booklet with the same task and appropriate instructions. As before, the students were allowed to work through the second version of the task at their own speed.

SCORING

Following data collection, oral recordings were transcribed by the experimenter, using conventional spelling and punctuation, and written compositions were

typed, adhering to the subjects' own spelling, spacing, and punctuation. Each sample was analyzed for the following:
1. fluency: number of words (#w), number of T-units (#T),
2. complexity: words per T-unit (w/T), words per error-free T-unit (w/EFT). A number of studies (Larsen-Freeman 1978; Larsen-Freeman and Strom 1977; Vann 1978, 1979) have indicated that, given the frequency of error in L2 production, the error-free T-unit, and the ratio of error-free T-units to T-units are more valid measures of increasing syntactic ability for L2 learners than is the T-unit. The question of what constitutes an error has been answered in different ways by different researchers. This study followed Vann's (1979) procedure and accepted as "error-free" any T-unit that made sense in the given context and was free both of morphosyntactic and lexical errors. A patterned error (e.g., misclassifying a feminine noun as masculine and consistently repeating the error throughout the test) was counted as an error only at its first occurrence.
3. accuracy: ratio of error-free T-units to T-units (%EFT),
4. elaboration: ratio of adjective clauses to T-units, ratio of adverb clauses to T-units, ratio of reduced clauses to T-units, ratio of simple sentences to total sentences, and organizational structure. For the purposes of this study, reduced clauses included gerund clauses, participial clauses, and prepositional clauses, examples of which are found in Table 5-1. By organizational structure was meant the use of such devices as an introduction or a conclusion and markers such as *primero,...segundo* (first,...second), or *un problema...otro problema* (one problem... another problem).

Again following Vann's (1979) example, strings in oral data that could not be considered T-units were counted separately as mazes. Typical mazes included false starts and unintelligible strings.

TABLE 5-1 Reduced Clauses

Gerund clauses	
El niño, *mirando todos los juguetes*, no puede decidir.	The boy, *looking at all the toys*, cannot decide.
Cruzando la calle, el niño da su dinero al ciego.	*Crossing the street*, the boy gives his money to the blind man.
Participial clauses	
Asombrado por la acción del ciego, el niño se pone muy triste.	*Surprised by the blind man's action*, the boy becomes very sad.
Perdido su dinero, el niño ha aprendido una triste lección.	*His money lost*, the boy has learned a sad lesson.
Prepositional clauses	
Antes de entrar en la tienda, el niño ve que hay un ciego en la calle.	*Before entering the store*, the boy sees that there is a blind man in the street.
Al cruzar la calle, el niño da su dinero al ciego.	*Upon crossing the street*, the boy gives his money to the blind man.

METHOD OF ANALYSIS

Each measure was analyzed by a separate Analysis of Variance (ANOVA) in a 4(level) x 2(code: speak, write) x 2 (task: narration, argumentation) x 4(order: each task/each code) mixed design with repeated measures on the task and code factors. Results were tested for significance at the .05 level.

RESULTS

ORDER

Preliminary analysis of the data indicated that neither the order in which students coded each of their tasks (speaking first or writing first) nor the order of task (narration first or argumentation) had any significant impact on the syntactic variables examined. This allowed subjects to be pooled into larger groups for the remainder of the analyses.

LEVEL

The results of this study confirm those of previous researchers in a number of ways. Level of language proficiency had no effect on fluency but was significantly ($p < .05$) related to each of the indices of syntactic complexity examined in this study: in both speech and writing, mean length of T-units, ratio of error-free T-units, and mean length of error-free T-units increase as level of language proficiency increases. There were no significant interactions between level and code or level and task. The scores for each of the syntactic variables arranged by level are summarized in Table 5-2.

TABLE 5-2 Effect of Language Proficiency on Syntactic Accuracy and Complexity of FL Speech and Writing

		Level				p
		1	2	3	4	
Speech	#T	11.5	9.4	14	10.7	NS
	w/T	10.7	10.7	11.9	14.1	<.05
	#errors	15.3	14.9	14.9	5.1	NS
	%EFT	26.5	25.4	42.4	67.3	<.05
	w/EFT	5.7	5.1	9.6	13.8	<.05
Writing	#T	10.3	7.5	12.5	7.9	NS
	w/T	9.6	10.0	12.2	15.3	<.05
	#errors	9.4	11.8	14.3	5.1	<.05
	%EFT	42.3	35.6	43.3	54.9	<.05
	w/EFT	7.5	8.5	10.8	12.3	<.05

CODE

Comparison of written and oral versions of the same task revealed that students at all levels produced significantly ($p < .05$) more oral than written language on a topic, although the difference was not the twofold increase noted by Vann (1979). Students produced significantly fewer ($p < .05$) total errors when writing than when speaking, but in terms of percentage of error-free T-units, their written language was not significantly more accurate than their oral language. There was no significant difference between written and oral language in terms of syntactic complexity. The speech/writing comparisons for each of the syntactic variables are summarized in Table 5-3.

In order to examine the effect of code on elaboration in language, the tapescripts and typed versions were analyzed for the various indices mentioned earlier (i.e., fluency, complexity, and so forth). Due to the presence of a large number of zeros in the data (indicating no instances of a particular type of syntactic structure), the four levels were collapsed into two (low: 1+2 and high: 3+4) and instead of an ANOVA, Wilcoxon signed-rank-paired comparisons were used to test for differences between subjects' written and oral language on each task. These measures are summarized in Table 5-4.

Although it revealed few differences of statistical significance, comparison of the syntactic choices made for writing versus those made for speech by the two groups suggested the following patterns:

1. At both low and high levels of proficiency, the differences between speech and writing were more significant for narration than for argumentation.

2. The types of speech-to-writing adjustments made by students in the low group were different from those made by students in the high group. Lower-level students tended to use more adjective and fewer adverb clauses in writing than in speech. None of the eight lower-level students produced reduced clauses in speech, and only two of the eight produced them in writing (one clause per student!). The higher-level students tended not to vary their use of adverb clauses, but they used many fewer adjective clauses in writing than in speech and many more reduced clauses. Six of the eight students produced reduced clauses in writing; four of the eight produced them in speech.

3. Students in both low and high groups tended to use a greater proportion of simple sentences in writing than in speech, but the structure of these sentences

TABLE 5-3 Comparison of Oral and Written FL with respect to Syntactic Accuracy and Complexity

	Oral	Written	p
#T	11.39	9.52	< .05
w/T	11.85	11.79	NS
#errors	12.78	9.87	< .05
%EFT	40.37	44.13	NS
w/EFT	8.52	9.76	NS

TABLE 5-4 Elaborateness of Written versus Oral Language by Proficiency Level and Discourse Mode

	Level	1 & 2		3 & 4		All	
		S>W	W>S‡	S>W	W>S	S>W	W>S
Narration	adj. clause/T-unit	2	5*	4	2	5	8
	adv. clause/T-unit	5	1*	2	4	7	5
	red. clause/T-unit	0	1	0	4*	0	5**
	simple sentences/ total sentences	5	3	0	6*	5	9
Argumentation	adj. clause T-unit	3	3	5	2	8	5
	adv. clause/T-unit	4	3	3	3	7	6
	red. clause/T-unit	0	1	2	1	2	2
	simple sentences/ total sentences	3	5	3	3	6	8
Both tasks	adj. clause/T-unit	2	6	5	1*	7	7
	adv. clause/T-unit	5	3	3	3	8	6
	red. clause/T-unit	0	2	0	4*	0	6**
	simple sentences/ total sentences	3	5	3	3	6	8

‡S>W presents the number of students in each group whose use of the indicated measure was greater in speech than in writing. W>S presents the number of students in each group whose use of the indicated measure was greater in writing than in speech. Total N in each group was 8; since instances of "no difference" between speech and writing are not included in the totals, group Ns sometimes sum to less than 8.
*p < .05
**p < .01

was different in the two groups. The speech of lower-level students was characterized by long strings held together by the repeated use of *y* (and); when writing, these students tended to drop this coordinate conjunction and chop their ideas into a series of simple sentences. The higher-level students tended to use adjective clauses when speaking but would frequently switch to reduced clauses in writing. [A simple sentence may contain a reduced clause but not an adjective or adverb clause.]

There were few organizational differences between a student's oral and written versions of a single task. That is, the students who made frequent use of structuring devices (e.g., introduction, conclusion, markers for main and subordinate ideas) in one code, did so in the other as well, while the students who used few such devices in one code tended to use few in the other.

MODE

The results of the story versus argumentative essay comparison, presented in Table 5-5, indicate that in FL, as in L1, oral and written language are both sensitive to discourse mode. The mean T-unit length was significantly longer (p < .01) for argumentation than for narration, in both speech and writing, at each of the

TABLE 5-5 Effect of Mode of Discourse on Syntactic Complexity and Accuracy of FL Speech and Writing

		Narration	Argumentation	p
Speech	#T	12.0	10.8	NS
	w/T	9.1	14.6	<.01
	#errors	10.5	14.9	<.01
	%EFT	48.5	32.3	<.01
	w/EFT	8.0	9.1	NS
Writing	#T	10.5	8.6	NS
	w/T	10.4	13.2	<.01
	#errors	7.8	11.7	<.01
	%EFT	49.9	38.4	<.01
	w/EFT	7.9	11.7	NS

four proficiency levels. Despite students' efforts at greater fluency, argumentation proved to be considerably more demanding for them syntactically: the percent of error-free T-units was significantly lower ($p < .01$) for argumentation than for narration.

There was a significant ($p < .01$) interaction between mode of discourse and code with respect to mean T-unit length: in narration, students mean T-unit tended to be longer when they were writing than when they were speaking, but in argumentation, the reverse was true; that is, mean T-unit length was shorter in writing than in speech. There were no significant interactions between mode of discourse and level of proficiency.

DISCUSSION

This study was designed to investigate the existence of patterns of differentiation between oral and written language related to level of proficiency and mode of discourse among FL learners. As such, it produced some familiar and some unexpected results. As with L1, increasing FL proficiency is marked by increasing complexity (mean length of T-unit) and accuracy (percentage of error-free T-units) in both oral and written language. Although this study did not find the mean length of T-unit to be significantly greater for writing than for speech, one notes in the FL data a slight suggestion of the maturational shift documented by O'Donnell, Griffin, and Norris (1967) for L1: before grade three, mean length of T-unit in L1 is longer in speech than in writing; after grade three, mean length of T-unit is longer in writing. In this study, for the FL students at proficiency levels one and two, the mean length of T-unit is slightly greater for speech than for writing; for students at proficiency levels three and four, the mean length of T-unit is slightly greater for writing than for speech.

As with L1, FL written language is sensitive to mode of discourse, with argumentation producing more complex but less accurate language than narration.

Indeed, as with L1, the average difference in mean T-unit length between narration and argumentation at the same level (4.1 words) was considerably greater than that between narrations across levels (2.1 words). This researcher is unaware of any studies that explicitly examine L1 oral language across modes, but FL oral language was clearly found to be "mode-sensitive." The significance of mode of discourse suggests that researchers into oral and written FL development should take care to control for this factor in gathering and interpreting data.

As with L1, and consistent with Vann's findings (1979) for ESL students, written and oral FL are similar but not the same. When switching between speech and writing, FL learners make a variety of structural adjustments in their language. On the one hand, while the nature of these adjustments clearly does not always point toward greater elaboration (at least as presently measured), neither does it seem to have been motivated solely by a concern for increased grammaticality or formal correctness. In other words, the written tasks were not primarily "grammatically cleaned-up" versions of the oral tasks. In this context, it seems important to note that the type of adjustment appears to have been different for different levels of proficiency and also for different modes of discourse. Explanations of the source of these adjustments must remain speculative at this point. One can fairly quickly eliminate FL-composition training as a possible source: if the subjects were typical FL students, what training they might have had in FL composition would most likely have focused only on the elimination of grammatical errors. Exposure to FL reading is also an unlikely candidate: few of the students, and certainly none of those at the lower levels of proficiency, would yet have had a great amount of FL reading exposure. What about the transfer of L1 skill and training? Although there is no way of gauging the extent of the subjects' reading and writing experience in English, one may safely assume it to have been more extensive than that afforded by their FL study. It seems plausible, therefore, that at least some of the differences between oral and written language observed in this study represent L1 influence drawn from the subjects' experience with native-language written models. Additional research will be necessary to test the validity of this suggestion.

Suprisingly, it was narration rather than argumentation that produced the most changes between speech and writing at all levels of proficiency. If students clearly "switch gears" for narration, a discourse mode so closely associated with oral language that similarity between writing and telling might have been expected, why don't they do so for argumentation, where speech and writing have traditionally been assumed to diverge? One likely explanation is that the conditions for oral language in this study, in which a student talked into a microphone rather than to another person, significantly affected the nature of the oral language the students produced. While the students may have found it possible to be both conversational and author-like in narrating a picture sequence to a microphone, it may be that the lack of an interlocutor for argumentation really precluded a conversational tone. In both speech and writing, then, students might have produced basically a single register of argumentative language.

CONCLUSION

Additional research is needed to clarify the extent to which FL oral and written language are affected not only by the mode of discourse but also by the contexts for language use. Strongly suggested by this study, however, is that written FL is indeed something other than oral language on paper, even for learners whose exposure to the FL has been fairly limited. Many questions still remain. What may be the source(s) of the oral and written language differences? What is the relative contribution of L1 writing skill, L2 oral fluency, input from written models (see Krashen 1984 for a discussion of the evidence relating extensive reading to writing improvement), and formal FL writing instruction? To what extent are language learners conscious of the adjustments they make in switching from one code to the other? In this study language proficiency levels were established only on the basis of length of FL study; when proficiency is interpreted in terms of FL ability, what similarities and differences between oral and written language emerge? Is there a relationship between the degree of differentiation and the perceived quality of the written language, a relationship that is often suggested for L1?

This study looked at only a few specific aspects of the oral/written language contrast, but other aspects need to be examined as well: the information content in one code versus the other, the rhetorical structure and coherence/cohesiveness of the oral versus written texts. The development of writing skill involves mastery of a great number of subskills that progressively widen the difference between conversing and composing. The writing of the students in this study had already begun to evidence some of these differences; future research may help to explain when and how they acquire others as well.

REFERENCES

Akin, J. 1975. Enhancing the syntactic fluency of beginning foreign language learners through sentence-combining practice. Ph.D. dissertation, University of Georgia.

Bereiter, C. 1980. Development in writing. In *Cognitive Processes in Writing*. L. Gregg and E. Steinberg (eds.), 73-93. Hillsdale, NJ: Lawrence Erlbaum.

Britton, J. L., T. Burgess, N. Martin, A. MacLeod, and H. Rosen (eds.). 1975. *The Development of Writing Abilities*, 11-18. London: MacMillan.

Cazden, C. B. 1970. The neglected situation in child language research and education. In *Language and Poverty*. F. Williams (ed.), 81-101. Chicago: Markham.

Cazden, C. B., H. Cancino, E. Rosansky, and J. Schumann. 1975. *Second Language Acquisition Sequences in Children, Adolescents, and Adults*. Final report to the National Institute of Education.

Cooper, T. 1976. Measuring written syntactic patterns of second language learners of German. *Journal of Educational Research* 69(5):176-183.

Cooper, T. 1981. Sentence combining: an experiment in teaching writing. *Modern Language Journal* 65(2):158-165.

Cooper, T., and G. Morain. 1980. A study of sentence-combining techniques for developing written and oral fluency in French. *French Review* 53(3):411-423.

Crowhurst, M., and G. L. Piche. 1979. Audience and mode of discourse effects on syntactic complexity in writing at two grade levels. *Research in the Teaching of English* 13(2):101-109.
Emig, J. 1977. Writing as a mode of learning. *College Composition and Communication* 28:122-128.
Gaies, S. J. 1979. Linguistic input in first and second language learning. In *Studies in First and Second Language Acquisition*. F. Eckman and A. Hastings (eds.), 185-193. Rowley, MA: Newbury House.
Gaies, S. J. 1980. T-unit analysis in second language research: applications, problems and limitations. *TESOL Quarterly* 14(1):53-60.
Heaton, J. B. 1966. *Composition through Pictures*. Harlow, England: Longman.
Hunt, K. W. 1965. *Grammatical Structures Written at Three Grade Levels*. NCTE Research Report No. 3. Urbana, IL: NCTE.
Hunt, K.W. 1970. Do sentences in the second language grow like those in the first? *TESOL Quarterly* 4(3):195-202.
Jensen, J. M. 1973. A comparative investigation of the casual and careful oral language styles of average and superior 5th grade boys and girls. *Research in the Teaching of English* 7(3):338-350.
Kameen, P. 1979. Syntactic skill and ESL writing quality. In *On TESOL '79*, C. Yorio, K. Perkins, and J. Schacter (eds.), 343-350. Washington, D.C.: TESOL.
Klassen, B. R. 1976. Sentence-combining exercises as an aid to expediting syntactic fluency in learning English as a second language, Ph.D. dissertation, University of Minnesota.
Krashen, S. D. 1984. *Writing: Research, Theory and Application*. New York: Pergamon Press.
Kroll, B. 1981. Developmental relationships between speaking and writing. In *Exploring Speaking-Writing Relationships: Connections and Contrasts*. B. Kroll and R. Vann (eds.), 32-54. Urbana, IL: NCTE.
Larsen-Freeman, D. 1978. An ESL index of development. *TESOL Quarterly* 12(4):439-448.
Larsen-Freeman, D., and V. Strom. 1977. The construction of the second language index of development. *Language Learning* 27(1):123:134.
Loban, W. 1976. *Language Development: Kindergarten through Grade Twelve*. NCTE Research Report No. 18. Urbana, IL: NCTE.
Monroe, J. H. 1975. Measuring and enhancing syntactic fluency in French. *French Review* 48(6):1023-1081.
O'Donnell, R. C., W. J. Griffin, and R. C. Norris. 1967. *Syntax of Kindergarten and Elementary School Children: A Transformational Analysis*. Research Report No. 8. Urbana, IL: NCTE.
Perkins, K. 1980. Using objective methods of attained writing proficiency to discriminate among holistic evaluations. *TESOL Quarterly* 14(1):61-70.
Perl, S. 1979. The composing process of unskilled college writers. *Research in the Teaching of English* 13(2):317-336.
Perron, J. D. 1976. *The Impact of Mode on Written Syntactic Complexity*. Report No. 27. Athens: Georgia University Department of Language. ERIC ED 128 827.
Rosen, H. 1969. An investigation of the effects of differentiated writing assignments in the performance in English composition of a selected group of 15-16 year old pupils. Ph.D. dissertation: University of London.
Rubin, A. 1980. A theoretical taxonomy of the differences between oral and written language. In *Theoretical Issues in Reading Comprehension*. R. J. Spiro, B. C. Bruce, and W. F. Brewer (eds.), 411-438. Hillsdale, NJ: Lawrence Erlbaum.
San José, C. P. M. 1972. Grammatical structures in four modes of writing at fourth grade level. Ph.D. dissertation: Syracuse University.

Shatz, M., and R. Gelman. 1973. The development of communication skills: modifications in the speech of young children as a function of listener. *Monographs of the Society for Research in Child Development*, 38.

Smith, W. L., and B. Swan. 1976. *Adjusting Syntactic Structure to Varied Levels of Audience*. Consortium for Basic Research in English, Report No. 4. School of Education, University of Colorado at Denver.

Stahl, A. 1974. Structural analysis of children's compositions. *Research in the Teaching of English* 8(2):184-205.

Stahl, A. 1977. The structure of children's compositions: developmental and ethnic differences. *Research in the Teaching of English* 11(2):156-163.

Vann, R. J. 1978. A study of the oral and written English of adult Arabic speakers. Ph.D. dissertation, Indiana University.

Vann, R. J. 1979. Oral and written syntactic relationships in second language learning. In *On TESOL '79*, C. Yorio, K. Perkins, and J. Schachter (eds.), 322-329. Washington, D.C.: TESOL.

Winfeld, F., and P. Barnes-Felfeli. 1982. The effects of familiar and unfamiliar cultural context on foreign language composition. *Modern Language Journal* 66(4):373-378.

APPENDIX

Task instructions: Narration
The six pictures on the next page form a story. Look over the picture sequence to familiarize yourself with what the situation is, who is involved, what happens and what the possible consequences may be. Your task is not to describe the pictures, but to tell the story in Spanish as clearly as you can, so that a person who has not seen the pictures could understand exactly what happens. NOTE: Telling (Writing) the story may involve vocabulary and/or structures that you do not know. Do the best you can.

Turn the page and begin recording (writing) the story as soon as you are ready.

Task instructions: Essay
The topic on the following page presents a problem and asks for your opinion. There is no correct or incorrect answer. Look over the topic carefully and then express your opinion as clearly as you can such that a person who was not familiar with this topic could easily understand the nature of the problem you are discussing. NOTE: Talking (Writing) about this topic may involve vocabulary and/or structures that you do not know. Do the best you can.

Turn the page and begin recording (writing) your opinion when you are ready.

CHAPTER 6
Learner Self-Correction of Written Compositions: What Does It Show Us?

Diana Frantzen
Dorothy Rissel
Indiana University — Bloomington

INTRODUCTION

An integral component of the development of writing as a skill is the ability to edit one's written language for grammatical, stylistic, organizational, and other features. Of concern to most foreign language (FL) teachers is a student's ability to edit for grammatical features. The role of conscious grammar and its utility to students in writing (and speaking) is receiving increasing attention. As Krashen states, "application of conscious rules to one's output can result in a real increase in accuracy" (Krashen 1978, 25) at least for optimal users of the monitor. The questions that remain are: which rules lend themselves best to conscious rule application, and given the proper condition, how successful are students at applying these consciously?

Conscious (or learned) rules are viewed as serving as an editor or monitor that can be used under three conditions: (1) there is sufficient time to monitor, (2) performers are focused on form in addition to meaning, and (3) they know a rule to apply (Krashen 1982, 16). The purpose of the present study is to examine, to the extent possible, the language used in the compositions of fourth-semester college students of Spanish in order to discover which of a set of specified morphemes, grammatical categories, and grammar-bound semantic distinctions have been acquired. The study will also explore the degree to and manner in which these students can monitor (self-correct) their written output when their attention is drawn to errors. Finally, an item's accuracy rate will then be compared with the degree to which it is correctable to determine what relationship, if any, exists between the two.

METHOD

SUBJECTS

The subjects for this study were twenty-two students in Frantzen's fourth-semester Spanish class at Indiana University. Individual prior experience with Spanish varied since many had placed into the sequence from high school while others had followed the sequence or parts of it at the university. Due to absences on days when activities related to the project were carried out in class and other vicissitudes of the semester, complete data were collected from fourteen students. Hence, the study was based on those fourteen.

PROCEDURE

A total of three compositions were assigned at four-to-five-week intervals over the course of the semester. The instructor corrected the compositions in the following fashion to create what Krashen (1982, 106) terms a type-4 focused monitoring situation:
1. The whole word where an error occurred was circled.
2. A circle was made where a missing word should have been.

Compositions were then returned to students who were given ten minutes of class time to correct their errors and resubmit their corrected versions. Recopying was not required, and an incentive of a slightly improved grade on the composition was offered to those who corrected at least 75 percent of their circled errors. The first time this procedure was followed the instructor gave the class some hints about what to look for: for example a circled adjective might indicate a mistake in number, gender, or both; a circled verb might indicate a mistake in tense, mood, person, and so forth. Frantzen then reviewed the compositions again and collected data in the following categories:
1. The definite articles: *el, la, los, las*
2. The indefinite articles: *un, una*

3. Adjective agreement
4. Verb inflection (morphology only, not selection of tense, mood, aspect)
5. The use of the preterit and the imperfect
6. The use of *ser* and *estar*
7. The use of the indicative and the subjunctive

Some other categories were examined, but too few obligatory contexts were found to make valid inferences. A minimum of ten obligatory contexts (Krashen 1978) was held as an ideal, although individual scores on one composition did not always reach this criterion because errors of one particular type at times were not that frequent.

In each of the categories mentioned above, the following statistics were calculated:

1. Number of Obligatory Contexts for each (OC)
2. Number of Original Correct Usages in obligatory contexts (OCU)
3. Percent Original Correct Usage (%OCU)
4. Number of Errors in each category (#E)
5. Number of Corrected Errors (#CE)
6. Correction Rate (%CR)

The described procedure strikes a middle ground between integrative tests, which have been shown to reveal a natural order of language acquisition, and discrete-point tests, which tend to bring out conscious learning (Krashen 1978). There is a distinction, of course, between the present approach and a discrete-point test. In this case students were not given specific instructions about which rule or set of rules to apply (e.g., "Fill in the correct form of the verb in parentheses"). They needed not only to know the rule but also to know which rule or rules to apply in a given case.

Obviously, any "covert monitoring" (Krashen 1982) that took place before the compositions were submitted the first time cannot be explored in this fashion. However, the procedure should reveal a good deal about students' interlanguage: what they have mastered, what "slips" they are able to fix, what errors they can monitor consciously, and the limitations of their conscious rules.

RESULTS

DEFINITE ARTICLES

Whole class results (Table 6-1) showed the highest percentage of original correct usage (98%) for the masculine plural article *los*. The second highest was for the feminine plural *las* (97%), followed by a tie between the masculine and feminine singular (*el, la* - 96%). However, we should note that while errors in the masculine singular and plural are 100% correctable, those in the feminine (73% when singular and plural are considered together), are not. Moreover, while nine

TABLE 6-1 Whole Class Results—Articles

Definite Article

	COMP.#	OC	OCU	%OCU	#E	#CE	%CR
EL	C#1	96	92	96%	4	4	100%
	C#2	91	86	95%	5	5	100%
	C#3	96	95	99%	1	1	100%
	total (all 3)	283	273	96%	10	10	100%
LOS	C#1	69	68	99%	1	1	100%
	C#2	91	90	99%	1	1	100%
	C#3	22	21	95%	1	1	100%
	total (all 3)	182	179	98%	3	3	100%
LA	C#1	71	67	94%	4	4	100%
	C#2	100	94	94%	6	4	67%
	C#3	83	82	99%	1	1	100%
	total (all 3)	254	243	96%	11	9	82%
LAS	C#1	64	62	97%	2	2	100%
	C#2	56	54	96%	2	0	0%
	C#3	24	24	100%	0	—	—
	total (all 3)	144	140	97%	4	2	50%

Indefinite Article

UN	C#1	39	39	100%	0	—	—
	C#2	54	46	85%	8	8	100%
	C#3	37	36	97%	9	9	100%
	total (all 3)	130	121	93%	17	17	100%
UNA	C#1	41	34	83%	7	7	100%
	C#2	28	26	93%	2	2	100%
	C#3	30	25	83%	5	4	80%
	total (all 3)	99	85	86%	14	13	93%

students committed errors in the singular, only six committed errors in the plural. We note, however, that the %OCU for all forms of the definite article are far above the usual 90 percent mark traditionally considered to be the level of mastery.

Based on correctability, gender agreement develops later than number agreement, at least with regard to articles. Because it is the more frequent or salient masculine form that tends to be overextended, accuracy figures calculated in the traditional manner of determining the number of correct usages in obligatory contexts may be deceiving. The masculine forms were indeed used in obligatory contexts that required them, but they were also substituted for the feminine, contributing to lower accuracy in that category.

Some of the errors that students could not correct, or corrected erroneously, provide interesting information:

1. *...*la* decisiones...> **los* decisiones
   the decisions

2. *...del escuela. (no change)
   from the school
3. *...al familia. (no change)
   the family

Example 1 suggests that, at least for this student, the masculine form is salient in the plural. Although the gender agreement was correct in the first attempt, the student recurred to the masculine for the correction. Examples 2 and 3, in which both errors were committed by the same student, seem to indicate that the contractions *del* and *al* may be single lexical items for this individual, as the English contractions "can't" and "doesn't" are in early-learner systems. The student therefore could not break them into their component parts to make the necessary corrections. This pattern was not generalized. Other students made corrections such as *del sangre > de la sangre. At times, articles were successfully corrected while other intervening modifiers were not:

4. *el tercero razón > la *tercero razón
   the third reason
5. *el segundo razón > la *segundo razón
   the second reason

INDEFINITE ARTICLES

Only the singular forms of the indefinite article were counted since plurals occur very infrequently.

The results (Table 6-1) indicate that use of the masculine indefinite article has passed the 90 percent mark for acquisition (93%) while use of the feminine has not (86%). Again, we find errors in the use of the masculine to be more correctable than in the case of the feminine (100% vs. 93%). Furthermore, more students committed errors in contexts that required the feminine (8 students) than in those requiring the masculine (3 students).

ADJECTIVE AGREEMENT

This is a category (Table 6-2) in which absolutely no student's composition was entirely error free. Five individuals committed errors in masculine singular, ten in masculine plural, eleven in feminine singular and twelve in feminine plural. Only the masculine singular (98%) has passed the 90 percent mark. The remaining forms cluster around 80% (masculine and feminine plural, 81%; feminine singular, 80%). Errors in the masculine singular were not as highly correctable as they were in the case of the articles.

With regard to correctability, the order seems quite unusual. The feminine singular was accurately corrected most often — in fact with the same degree of success as the feminine definite article. Masculine plural and feminine plural adjectives fell in the midrange; and surprisingly, the most difficult item to correct was the masculine singular, the only form that passed the 90 percent mark in %OCU. Bear in mind, however, that the high %OCU (98%) meant that there were very

TABLE 6-2 Whole Class Results—Adjectives

Masculine Singular						
COMP.#	OC	OCU	%OCU	#E	#CE	%CR
C#1	77	74	96%	3	2	67%
C#2	74	74	100%	0	—	—
C#3	96	94	98%	2	1	50%
total	247	242	98%	5	3	60%
Masculine Plural						
C#1	70	51	73%	19	16	84%
C#2	72	62	86%	10	7	70%
C#3	41	36	88%	5	3	60%
total	183	149	81%	34	26	76%
Feminine Singular						
C#1	76	56	74%	20	14	70%
C#2	92	73	79%	19	18	95%
C#3	82	70	85%	12	10	83%
total	250	199	80%	51	42	82%
Feminine Plural						
C#1	110	90	82%	20	17	85%
C#2	66	53	80%	13	8	62%
C#3	16	12	75%	4	1	25%
total	192	155	81%	37	26	70%
All Adjectives Combined, by Composition						
C#1	333	271	81%	62	49	79%
C#2	304	262	86%	42	33	79%
C#3	235	212	90%	23	15	65%

few errors to be corrected, and the %CR of 60 represents 3 of 5 items. A look at some examples of items that were not corrected shows us the complexity of the contexts in which masculine agreement was missed:

6. *El momento más vergonzoso de mi vida es muy *humorosa* ...(no change)
   the most embarrassing moment of my life is very funny ....
7. *...un *buena* par de zapatos > *un *buenos* par de zapatos
   a good pair of shoes

In both cases we have nouns modified by prepositional phrases containing another noun that could be, and was, mistaken for the noun to which the adjective referred. In example 6, the adjective is also seven words away from the noun it modifies. Example 7 is slightly different because it involves an apocopated form, buen, which the student evidently does not have available.

If we take into consideration the difficulty of the few obligatory contexts for masculine singular adjectives that could not be corrected, then the %CR seems to indicate that with regard to modifiers other than the articles, plural agreement of adjectives is much more difficult to acquire than is singular agreement. Mistakes where masculine singular was used instead of feminine were generally easily corrected. There were some exceptions, particularly in cases where arbitrary grammatical agreement seems to violate rules of logic. In Spanish the masculine is the unmarked form used for mixed human groups in the plural and in the singular when sex is unknown or irrelevant. However, *persona* is grammatically feminine and causes many problems for students:

8. *La persona tiene sed, hambre, y cansado. > *La persona tiene sed, hambre y está *cansado.*
The person is thirsty, hungry and tired.

The student corrected the important *tener/estar* error but did not notice the agreement problem.

We see that in the category of adjective agreement, there is one form, the masculine singular, that appears to be the basic one. It is certainly the most accurately used in obligatory contexts, although it is subject to overextension into obligatory contexts for the other forms. We must agree with Plann (1979) that when considering mastery of a form such as this, its use in contexts where it does not belong, as well as in contexts where it is obligatory, should be considered.

One problem for students is that agreement of this type is purely grammatical; it carries no semantic meaning and therefore can be easily overlooked. Two types of erroneous corrections point to this phenomenon.

After *estar* the present participle appeared several times as a correction for adjective agreement:

9. *Mi hermano y yo estábamos *asustado* > *...estábamos asustando
My brother and I were scared > were scaring

Often, a different lexical item was substituted, and the agreement error remained:

10. *...músculos de los hombres son más *grande* > ...*más *fuerte.*
men's muscles are bigger > stronger

VERB MORPHOLOGY

Spanish has a very complex system of verb morphology with five or six (depending on dialect) inflections for person and number, and many more for tense, aspect, and mood. For purposes of this study, only the form of the verb (including correct person-number inflection) was considered in this category. Proper use of tense, mood, and aspect were examined elsewhere. Verbs were considered to consist of a stem and one suffix. Here, suffix includes what William Bull (1965) considered to be slots II (tense, aspect, mood) and III (person-number markers). As far as morphology is concerned, this group of students demonstrated mastery above the 90 percent level. The results were as follows:

	%OCU	%CR
all suffixes	94%	64%
all regular stems	98%	60%
all irregular stems	97%	44%

Errors in suffixes were so few that all tenses were combined in the final count. Individuals who made errors in suffixes made fewer in the preterit than they did in present tense affixes. Given the morphological complexity of the preterit and the potential for overgeneralization of the present tense to other contexts, this finding is surprising.

Correctability of all items scored — suffixes, regular stems, and irregular stems — was quite low. The last of these, irregular stems, totaled only 44%. This may reflect the low number of cases (sixteen overall) or the fact that irregular forms are frequently regularized and often fossilized in learner language, resulting in the students' inability to modify the previously formed rule.

Mastery of person-number inflection at this level is generally very good. Two broad categories of errors that could not be corrected were (1) items that are conceptually plural (at least to some people) while grammatically singular (*todo el mundo, la familia*) and (2) errors of person-number on the verb in subordinate clauses. In the second case, the infinitive was usually substituted, as in example 11 below.

11. *...muchos estudiantes que ir al colegio > *...*asistir*...
    many students who go to college

USE OF THE PRETERIT AND THE IMPERFECT

The use of both the preterit and the imperfect surpasses the 90 percent mark of acquisition (Table 6-3). Errors in the former seem slightly more correctable (78%) than in the latter (69%). It is interesting to note that there were more errors in which the preterit was used in contexts requiring the imperfect than vice versa.

Also interesting in this case was an examination of the errors that could and could not be corrected. Among the errors that were successfully corrected, all but four items involved a change from preterit to imperfect or from imperfect to preterit. Of the remaining four, three were changes from present to preterit, and one was from conditional to imperfect.

Among those errors that were not successfully corrected, the predominant type of required change was from present to imperfect. Some students made no attempt

TABLE 6-3 Whole Class Results—Preterit/Imperfect Usage

COMP. #	Aspect	OC	OCU	%OCU	#E	#CE	%CR
C#1	pret.	8	8	100%	0	—	—
	imperf.	7	7	100%	0	—	—
C#2	pret.	77	74	96%	3	2	67%
	imperf.	94	84	89%	10	8	80%
C#3	pret.	221	206	93%	15	12	80%
	imperf.	189	173	92%	16	10	63%
All Three Compositions Combined							
all pret.		306	288	94%	18	14	78%
all imperf.		290	264	91%	26	18	69%

to correct in these cases; others recurred to the preterit. It seems, then, that we once again have a form or concept — the preterit — that is salient and that is the one learners think of first when they are required to correct an apparently erroneous imperfect form or a present tense that should be in the past. Moreover, preterit and imperfect appear to be closely associated with each other. When attention is drawn to one as an error, the obvious conclusion is that the other is required.

USE OF SER AND ESTAR

The contrast in the accuracy of *ser* and *estar* was quite sharp (Table 6-4). *Ser* reached the acquisition level (%OCU = 95%); *estar* did not. In fact, the 73% accuracy rate for *estar* was the lowest of any of the usages examined, and its level of correctability (47%) was the third lowest. While *ser* was corrected 92% of the time, some of the errors that students could not correct proved to be very revealing:

12. *...el aire *fue* caliente > *...el aire *era* caliente
    the air was hot
13. *...yo pensé que *fue* en la sala > *...yo pensé que *era* en la sala (referring to an object)
    I thought it was in the room
14. *...que ahora ella *será* con Dios > *...que ahora ella *sería* con Dios
    that now she is with God
15. *El agua *era* frío > *El agua *tenía* frío
    the water was cold

Examples 12 and 13 illustrate a frequently occurring type of erroneous correction. There were many cases in which students substituted imperfect for preterit or vice versa, without considering that a misuse of *ser* or *estar* might be involved. In some cases there was an error of aspect as well as of *ser/estar* choice. When there were two errors, usually the preterit/imperfect choice was changed rather than *ser* or *estar*. Example 14 illustrates another instance in which a student chose to

TABLE 6-4 Whole Class Results—*Ser/Estar* Usage

COMP. #	Verb	OC	OCU	%OCU	#E	#CE	%CR
C#1	ser	130	122	94%	8	8	100%
	estar	16	14	88%	2	0	0%
C#2	ser	109	105	96%	4	3	75%
	estar	34	20	59%	14	3	21%
C#3	ser	40	39	98%	1	1	100%
	estar	51	40	78%	11	5	45%
All Three Compositions Combined							
all *ser*		279	266	95%	13	12	92%
all *estar*		101	74	73%	17	8	47%

change tense rather than *ser* or *estar*. In example 15 we see another error of lexical selection. The item chosen, *tener*, is one that frequently is used in a context where English employs "to be."

Most of the errors that could be corrected were simple substitutions of *ser* for *estar* or vice versa, with no additional changes required in tense, aspect, or mood. There were slightly fewer cases in which *estar* was used for *ser* than vice versa.

Ten students erred in the direction of substituting *ser* for *estar*. Six did the opposite. *Estar*-for-*ser* errors were more correctable (75%) than was misuse of *ser* for *estar* (33%).

USE OF INDICATIVE AND SUBJUNCTIVE

The use of the indicative, as one would expect, displays a very high level of accuracy (Table 6-5). Interestingly, seven people made errors in which the subjunctive was used where the indicative was required, but they were able to correct these readily. On the other hand, the subjunctive contexts generated were few. Five students created no obligatory contexts at all; the remaining nine created between one and five each. Also interesting, within the limited number of contexts created, individual %OCUs were either 100% or zero. There seemed to be no middle ground.

Subjunctive-for-indicative errors were highly correctable; indicative-for-subjunctive errors were not. Again, examples of unsuccessful corrections were very revealing:

16. *Es bueno que las mujeres *son*... > **están*
    It is good that women are ...
17. *Es importante que todas las personas *son*... > *Es importante que todas las personas *están*
    It is important that all people are
18. *...tienen miedo que *lastimarán*... (no change)
    they are afraid that they will hurt...

TABLE 6–5 Whole Class Results—Indicative/Subjunctive Usage

COMP. #	Mode	OC	OCU	%OCU	#E	#CE	%CR
C#1	indic.	443	433	97%	10	9	90%
	subj.	6	4	67%	2	0	0%
C#2	indic.	464	452	97%	12	11	92%
	subj.	8	5	63%	3	1	33%
C#3	indic.	473	470	99%	3	2	67%
	subj.	9	9	100%	0	—	—
All Three Compositions Combined							
all indic.		1380	1355	98%	25	22	88%
all subj.		23	18	78%	5	1	20%

In the two examples in which an attempt was made to correct (16 and 17), the wrong category was selected. These students thought they had made an error in *ser/estar* usage when they were actually confronting a misuse of mood. Example 18 draws our attention to another problem — there is no formally marked future tense in the subjunctive of modern Spanish. Present subjunctive is used to refer to future events.

ACCURACY VERSUS CORRECTABILITY

All of the grammatical items examined in the study were ranked according to %OCU (percent of original correct usage). Of the nineteen items examined, thirteen attained an accuracy level of 90 percent or better and thus can be considered to have been acquired. Six items fall below this level and are considered not to have been acquired yet. Similarly, all of the items examined were ranked according to %CR (correction rate). The two rankings are displayed in Table 6-6. Particularly low in terms of both accuracy and correctability are subjunctive use and *estar*.

DISCUSSION AND CONCLUSIONS

The purpose of this study was to examine the written output of fourth-semester college students of Spanish in order to discover which of a set of specified morphemes, grammatical items, and grammar-bound semantic distinctions had been acquired. Furthermore, the study explored the degree to which these students could monitor their written output (what we term correctability) once their attention was drawn to an error. The results of the study are discussed first in terms of an accuracy order and subsequently in terms of correctability.

ACCURACY ORDER

In order to determine an accuracy order, the data were analyzed for the percent of correct usages in obligatory contexts. As can be seen in Table 6-6, the majority of the items examined reached the 90 percent level of accuracy accepted as the criterion for acquisition. Those that did not are the feminine singular indefinite article, feminine and masculine plural adjectives, feminine singular adjectives, use of the subjunctive, and use of *estar*.

Plann (1979), in her study of the oral Spanish of children enrolled in the Culver City, CA, immersion program, was able to order definite articles from most to least accurate. The results of the present study do not allow for such an ordering since all forms of the definite article were at least 96 percent accurate. On the other hand, both Plann and the present study found that the development of the agreement of adjectives with the nouns they modify lags behind that of agreement of the definite and indefinite articles. This contrasts with van Naerssen's (1981) order for L2. For adjective agreement we can only conclude that the acquisition of

TABLE 6-6 Accuracy Versus Correctability

Accuracy Rank	%OCU	Correctability Rank	%CR
use of indicative; *los;* regular verb stems; masculine singular adjectives	98%	*los/el/un*	100%
		una	93%
las; irregular verb stems	97%	use of *ser*	92%
el/la	96%	use of indicative	88%
use of *ser*	95%	*la;* feminine singular adjectives	82%
use of preterit; verb suffixes	94%	use of preterit	78%
un	93%	masculine plural adjectives	76%
use of imperfect	91%	feminine plural adjectives	70%
una	86%	use of imperfect	69%
feminine plural adjectives; masculine plural adjectives	81%	verb suffixes	64%
		masculine singular adjectives; regular stems	60%
feminine singular adjectives	80%	*las*	50%
subjunctive use	78%	use of *estar*	47%
use of *estar*	73%	irregular stems	44%
		subjunctive use	20%

masculine singular precedes that of the other three forms (cf. Plann's study, where all four adjective inflections were ordered). This finding is comparable to Plann's in that the most accurate form in her and in our study was the masculine singular. An apparent problem for students is that agreement of this type is purely grammatical; it carries no semantic meaning. Perhaps for this reason adjective agreement is easily overlooked when students write.

Overall, verb morphology reached 90 percent mastery level. This high degree of accuracy for verb morphology is attributable to the fact that the compositions produced were self-generated material, for which students rely on acquired forms. Rissel (1981) demonstrated that learners' grammatical accuracy is greater on thematically guided free composition than on more restrictive kinds of exercises. Moreover, we caution that we made no count of the variety of lexical meanings and verb forms employed by each student. Evidence of learners using a limited number of forms from a restricted inventory of verbs can be found in numerous studies of child language acquisition. Particularly relevant to Spanish are Maez (1981) and González (1978).

Both preterit and imperfect usage reached the level of acquisition in this study. This is in contrast to Kaplan's findings (this volume) that fourth semester learners have yet to acquire the aspectual distinctions these verb forms convey. This difference could be attributable to the fact that Kaplan collected oral data and we collected written data. The writing task would in theory allow for more initial or "covert" monitoring. Moreover, with thematically guided compositions, the students have total control over the form of their output, thus raising the accuracy scores. To elicit past tenses, Kaplan used an interview format. She probed her subjects, forcing them to produce past tense contexts. Given this more restrictive format, we would expect differences in accuracy scores between the two studies.

The contrast in accuracy in the use of *ser* and *estar* was quite sharp. *Ser* reached the acquisition level, whereas *estar* was the lowest in accuracy of all of the items examined. Most of the errors that occurred were substitutions of *ser* for *estar* with only a few instances of the opposite. This appears to be an error type common to adult learners of Spanish. Both VanPatten (1985) and van Naerssen (1981), using oral data, report the same accuracy order and direction of error for *ser* and *estar*.

A great disparity exists between the accuracy of indicative use (98 percent) and subjunctive use (78 percent). As van Naerssen's (1981) summary of other studies and Blake's (1980) research on the acquisition of the subjunctive by monolingual Mexican children show, the use of the subjunctive is acquired late. The ranking of the subjunctive above *estar* in the accuracy order may in part be due to the low number of obligatory contexts generated for the subjunctive. Whereas Bull (1947) found that the subjunctive comprises some 5 percent of the verb forms used in written Spanish, the compositions examined in this study show less than 2 percent of all verb forms expressed in the subjunctive.

The accuracy order posited here may be a manifestation of the processes of simplification and overgeneralization inherent in language acquisition. In each of the categories examined, there seemed to be one form that was basic — one form that was somehow salient and overgeneralized to contexts in which other forms were obligatory. As Plann (1979, 126) reports, several factors, such as frequency of appearance, perceptual saliency, and semantic importance, contribute to this. In the present study, the basic forms were these: *ser* for copula; the masculine singular for definite articles, indefinite articles, and adjectives; preterit for past tense; and indicative for mood. Note that, to the extent that the structures examined overlap, there is essentially no disagreement between the findings of the present study and those of Plann (1979), van Naerssen (1981), and VanPatten (1985) with regard to the question of which is the basic form in each grouping. We now turn our attention to the question of correctability.

CORRECTABILITY

To characterize the way in which learners correct their output, we posit the following as a correction strategy:

Learned rules are applied in a binary fashion.
The form in which learned rules are applied reveals a problem-solving approach that could be influenced by the classroom learning situation. This binary-correction strategy, a very frequent error type, is evidenced by an overextension of the salient form (*el, un, ser*, masculine singular adjectives, preterit, and indicative) into contexts in which another member of the same grouping should be used. Errors in the use of these basic forms are more correctable than those committed

with reference to their counterparts. As Table 6-6 shows, the only exception to this is the correction rate of masculine singular adjectives, for reasons explained above, and categories such as regular and irregular verb stems that cannot be treated in this either-or fashion. For categories amenable to the binary approach, there seems to be an operating strategy that works something like this: a circled (error) form of *estar* goes to *ser*, a circled form of the imperfect goes to preterit, a circled form of the subjunctive goes to indicative, a circled article or adjective not in the masculine singular goes to the masculine singular. This strategy may be one created by the effects of the learning situation and the task at hand, or it may be an operating principle used by performers in acquisition and learning situations. Van Naerssen (1981) makes an interesting observation with regard to differences between first language (L1) and L2 acquisition of the copula in Spanish. In L1 acquisition, the copula is frequently omitted, but the *ser/estar* distinction develops comparatively early. Adults for whom Spanish is a second language tend not to omit the copula (but see VanPatten, this volume), but the *ser/estar* distinction is mastered relatively late. It appears then that there is a difference between child L1 and adult L2 strategies and orders of difficulty in this instance. What we do not know is whether they are due to cognitive development and acquisition strategies or to the effect of classroom learning approaches. We note, however, that Plann (1979) studied an immersion program in which children were acquiring Spanish as a second language. At least with regard to agreement of adjectives and articles, results in the present study are very similar to hers. One notable exception appears to be verb inflection for person and number, which was much more accurately used by the subjects in the present study than by those studied by Plann.

Tense takes precedence over other formal features when an error in verb formation is involved.
Although we posit a binary option for error correction, there are instances in which learners have multiple options. In cases where there is more than one error involved in a single verb form (see examples 12 and 13 above), tense seems to take precedence over *ser/estar* contrast, and, although our data is scant on this, it is possible that *ser/estar* contrast may take precedence over mood selection. This is an observation that merits further investigation. Is it that the rules for the use of *ser/estar* and the subjunctive are less learnable, or is there something in the FL learning situation that delays their acquisition? Van Naerssen (1981) points out that adult L2 learners acquire the distinction later than children for whom Spanish is a second language. *Ser/estar* contrasts are frequently taught early and then not reviewed or built upon. They are also normally taught in the present tense and not reinforced when other tenses are added. As our results show, students were more successful in correcting *ser/estar* errors in present tense contexts than in others, in which considerations of tense and aspect marking, topics that receive more emphasis in class, seemed to be more salient. Certainly, the use of *ser* and *estar* is more difficult to eliminate from input than is the subjunctive, which is frequently eliminated from input in learning environments. In fact, we can assume that most of the input these students received during their study of Spanish was replete with

usage of *ser* and *estar*; hence we cannot attribute the difficulty to elimination from input. Stokes, in his 1981 doctoral dissertation suggests that focusing students on specific points of grammar before they perform an integrative task has a positive effect on accuracy of performance. Perhaps in the case of *ser/estar*, so much attention has been placed on other rules that this as-yet-unacquired distinction has been ignored. On the other hand, it could be argued that the order of correctability tends to follow order of difficulty. Those items that are closer to being acquired are more amenable to correction than are those that are still presenting difficulty.

IMPLICATIONS FOR THE MONITOR

We have seen that when attention is drawn to the existence of errors, students can correct them by applying conscious rules with varying degrees of success. It is, however, difficult for them to know which rule to apply in a given case, and in instances in which more than one error exists, the contrasting item of highest accuracy is the one that tends to be corrected. When a possibility for error in more than one category exists, the usage that is employed with the highest level of accuracy is sometimes altered, even if there is no error in it. The student needs to know not only the rule for a particular usage, but also which rule to apply in a given context. The pattern of solutions that emerges from this kind of activity reveals a problem-solving strategy that may not actually serve to improve either the learners' future performance or their competence. What is most easily corrected is the use of a less salient form in an obligatory context for a more salient one. This could point to an approach to discovering the limits of the rules, and it does increase the accuracy of a usage already approaching the target. When the more salient form is used in a context appropriate to a less salient one, conscious rule application is less successful.

It would appear that conscious rule application takes on a form that is far from what those of us who give elegant linguistic explanations of these usages would like to expect. Correcting seems to involve a binary-guessing process, success in which to some extent follows order of difficulty. Those items that are closer to or have surpassed the target for acquisition are those that tend to be corrected most easily. The monitor, then, appears to take on a very simplistic form for the majority of learners, and its successful use seems to be linked to formal features used most accurately, at least when dealing with written production under the conditions prescribed in this study.

IMPLICATIONS FOR THE CLASSROOM

We have seen that ability to apply conscious rules to certain formal features tends to be associated with level of acquisition of those features and that accurate usage of these rules develops through a progressive limiting of the overextension of a basic or salient form. Undoubtedly, the learner's interlanguage system is a central element in this process, as its development readies the individual to be better able to employ the nonsalient forms in each category as the system develops. These observations lead us to make a number of recommendations regarding classroom procedure. Obviously, opportunities for acquisition should be maximized since these comprise the basis for formation of early overgeneralizations that serve as a point of departure. Formal study of rules should be brief, cyclical, and contextualized so that overextension can become progressively more limited as the learner's interlanguage approaches the target. Features such as the distinction between *ser* and *estar* should be presented in manageable chunks in conjunction with functional contexts in which *estar*, the less salient item, is used. These functions should be reintegrated and expanded upon as new tenses and moods are added. Naturally, further study is needed to determine if this type of approach is indeed more successful than traditional practice; however, it does seem that it would more closely serve to support the process our subjects followed in employing and correcting their own errors in the features currently under study.

REFERENCES

Blake, R. J. 1980. The acquisition of mood selection among Spanish-speaking children: ages 4 to 12. Ph.D. dissertation, University of Texas at Austin.

Bull, W. E. 1947. Modern Spanish verb form frequencies. *Hispania* 30(4):451-466.

Bull, W. E. 1965. *Spanish for Teachers*. New York: Ronald Press Company.

González, G. 1978. *The Acquisition of Spanish Grammar by Native Spanish-Speaking Children*. Rosellyn, V. A: National Clearinghouse for Bilingual Education.

Krashen, S. D. 1978. The monitor model for second language acquisition. In *Second Language Acquisition and Foreign Language Teaching*, R. Gringas (ed.), 1-26. Washington, D.C.: Center for Applied Linguistics.

Krashen, S. D. 1982. *Principles and Practice in Second Language Acquisition*. Oxford: Pergamon Institute of English.

Maez, L. F. 1981. Spanish as a first language: the early stages. Ph.D. dissertation, University of California at Santa Barbara.

Plann, S. 1979. Morphological problems in the acquisition of Spanish in an immersion classroom. In *The Acquisition and Use of Spanish and English As First and Second Languages*. Roger W. Anderson (ed.), 119-132. Washington, D.C.: TESOL.

Rissel, D. A. 1981. The present/past distinction in Spanish: implications for a revised syllabus. *Modern Language Journal* 65(2):181-189.

Stokes, J. D. 1981. The effects of various discrete-point focusing strategies on performance in Spanish. Ph.D. dissertation, Indiana University at Bloomington.

van Naerssen, M. 1981. Generalizing second language acquisition hypotheses across languages: a test case in Spanish as a second language. Ph.D. dissertation, University of Southern California.

VanPatten, B. 1985. The acquisition of *ser* and *estar* by adult learners of Spanish: a preliminary investigation of stages of competence. *Hispania* 68(2):399-406.

CHAPTER 7
FL Learners' Ability to Recall and Rate the Important Ideas of an Expository Text

James F. Lee
University of Illinois at Urbana-Champaign
Terry Lynn Ballman
SUNY-Binghamton

INTRODUCTION

The process of reading in a second (L2) or foreign language (FL) has often been assumed to be the same as that of reading in a first language (L1). It was once thought that a person literate in one language would somehow be able to automatically transfer this literacy to a second or foreign language. Much research has been conducted to investigate this idea. The research presented here explores the differences between L1 and FL reading by focusing on the interaction between the reader and the text. Specifically, two experiments were conducted: one investigates the ability of learners of Spanish to recall the important ideas of a passage, and the second investigates how learners of Spanish rate the importance of idea units to the overall passage.

RELEVANT LITERATURE

There are several studies that bear directly on the methods, procedures, and expected outcomes of the present study.

Johnson (1970) was the first to examine the recall of prose as a function of the structural importance of the linguistic units. His working definition of linguistic units is that they are "pause acceptability" units; that is, junctures in the passage at which pausing serves the function of catching a breath, giving emphasis to the story, or enhancing meaning. The analysis of a text into these linguistic units results, essentially, in dividing the text into clauses. One group of college students was given a text to divide into linguistic units; a second group rated the importance of these units to the overall structure of the story; and a third group was asked to read and then recall the passage. Johnson showed that the recall of prose by college-level L1 readers was a function of the structural importance of the linguistic units. That is, the more important the rating of the linguistic unit, the more likely it was to be recalled.

Johnson's study provided the impetus for other research dealing with the recall of linguistic units. Brown and Smiley (1977) expanded on his work by examining not only college-level readers but also readers from three other levels (third, fifth, and seventh grades) in order to determine if the recall of prose by different levels of L1 readers was a function of the adult readers' ratings of structural importance. They had one group of college-level readers rate the importance of linguistic units of a passage and then had four levels of readers read and recall the passage. They showed that at all levels, those linguistic units rated as most important dominated the recalls, while those linguistic units rated as least important were rarely recalled.

In a second experiment, Brown and Smiley examined the ability of the third, fifth, and seventh graders to rate the structural importance of the linguistic units by comparing their ratings of structural importance with those of the college-level readers. It was found that the fifth and seventh graders had the same ability as the college students to rate structural importance. The third graders, however, could not identify the structurally important linguistic units. Although the third graders' recalls are dominated by the structurally important linguistic units, they are unable to overtly identify those units as the important ones. Brown and Smiley concluded that the extraction of main versus supporting ideas (important versus unimportant linguistic units) is done at a subconscious level but that the ability to identify main versus supporting ideas is related to metacognitive development.

The term linguistic units as a unit of text analysis was replaced by idea units (Bransford and Johnson 1973; Carrell 1982), more recently termed information units (Roller 1985). The idea/information unit corresponds "to either individual (simple) sentences, basic semantic propositions, or phrases" (Carrell 1982, 189).

Studies that have examined different levels of FL or L2 readers have generally established developmental patterns (Cziko 1978; Carrell 1982). That is, these studies find that the advanced learners tend to outperform the intermediate and beginning learners regardless of the task.

The present research is framed by these studies. Since developmental patterns have emerged for FL and L2 readers, as well as for L1 readers, it was decided to examine four levels of learners of Spanish as a FL. In this way, the present study could examine the effect of level on the results. The same procedures of text analysis and recall scoring used in Johnson (1970) and Carrell (1982) were adopted in order to be able to make direct comparisons with L1 research (Brown and Smiley 1977).

HYPOTHESES AND QUESTIONS

Based on the previous L2 research, it was expected that a developmental pattern would emerge in terms of the overall recall of the passage. Moreover, based on the previous L1 research, it was expected that all of these readers, as adults, would show both the ability to recall and to identify the important idea units.

The specific research questions being examined are the following:
1. Does increased exposure to the grammar of a FL increase the amount of a passage an adult L2 learner can recall?
2. What effect does increased exposure to the grammar of a language have on adult L2 learners' recall of important idea units?
3. What effect does increased exposure to the grammar of a language have on the ability of adult L2 learners to rate the importance of idea units?

EXPERIMENT ONE

SUBJECTS

In experiment one, four semester levels of FL learners who were enrolled in Spanish classes at the University of Texas at Austin volunteered to participate in the study. The sample consisted of 29 learners enrolled in the first semester, 43 in the second semester, 38 in the third semester, and 19 in the fourth semester, for a total of 129 subjects. The book used in the first two semesters of Spanish was *La leñgua española* (Castells and Leonetti 1983); the book used in the third and fourth semesters was *Español: Ampliación y repaso* (Solé and Solé 1982). In the first and second semester courses, no supplementary reader was used. In the third and fourth semester classes, *Imaginación y fantasía* (Yates and Dalbor 1983) was used as a reader. Although there were instructional differences across different classes, in the first three semesters, all of the instructors followed the same syllabus, and the students were required to take departmental exams. In the fourth semester, the instructors were responsible for the syllabus and the exams, but all of them covered the same material from the same book.

MATERIALS, INSTRUMENTATION, AND PROCEDURE

An expository passage of 253 words comprised the materials. The passage, titled *El feudalismo*[1] describes feudal society and politics. It was chosen because it was felt that many of the students, independent of their FL studies, would have at least a limited knowledge of the topic.

The two researchers worked independently to divide the passage into idea units following the procedures outlined in Johnson (1970). The results of this procedure were consistent between the two authors. Each divided the passage into the same idea units, the total number being 33. A second procedure was carried out in which the authors, again working independently, ranked the importance of the idea units in terms of their overall importance to the structure of the passage. Johnson (1970) and Brown and Smiley (1977) used the ratings of importance by adult skilled readers to define importance. For the purpose of the present study, importance was defined as the central idea(s) around which the passage was organized. This working definition is similar to the concept of hierarchically based content structures (Meyer 1975). The results of this procedure yielded 8 idea units for use in experiment two. The interrater reliability for this procedure was +.88. The two authors agreed on six idea units and through discussion came to a consensus on the other two. The disagreement was over the wording of the ideas rather than the ideas themselves. The passage, divided into idea units, and the important idea units identified by the researchers are included in the Appendix.

The subjects were tested in their classrooms. Each received a three-page packet containing an agreement form, the reading passage, and a page on which to write his or her recall. The subjects were instructed to read the passage at their own rate. At the bottom of the page on which the passage was printed were the instructions to turn the page. At the top of this third page, they were directed to recall as much of the passage as they could, without looking back, and to write their recalls in English (their native language). The subjects were allowed to write their recalls in their L1's since an earlier study (Lee 1986) established that FL learners recall significantly greater amounts of a passage when they write their recalls in their native language than when they write them in the target language.

The recalls of the 129 subjects were scored by the authors for the total number of idea units recalled correctly and subsequently for the number of important idea units recalled. A percentage was calculated for each factor and a mean was determined for each level.

The data were analyzed using one-way analyses of variance (ANOVA). The factors consisted of (1) semester level by percentage of correct recall, and (2) semester level by important idea units recalled.

RESULTS

Table 7-1 presents the means for the different levels of learners. The table includes the percentage of total recall of the passage, the mean number of important idea units recalled, and the standard deviations. In terms of total recall, the first semester learners appeared to recall as much as the third semester learners (25.18% and 26.79%, respectively). The fourth semester learners recalled the most (33.17%), as was expected, but it was the second semester learners, not the first semester learners, who recalled the least (19.80%). In terms of the number of structurally important idea units recalled, the pattern that emerged was the same as that for the total recall. The performance of the first and third semester learners is comparable (1.79 and 1.71 units, respectively). The fourth semester learners recalled more than the others (2.21 units) while the second semester learners recalled the fewest (1.51 units).

These results were submitted to two one-way ANOVAs, which revealed that the semester level of the learners proved to be a significant factor affecting total recall but that it did not prove to be a significant factor in the recall of structurally important idea units. These results are summarized in Tables 7-2 and 7-3.

DISCUSSION

Experiment one was designed to address the first two research questions; that is, does increased exposure to the grammar of a language increase the amount of a passage an adult L2 reader can recall, and does increased exposure to the grammar of a language affect the recall of the structurally important idea units? The results of experiment one indicate a main effect for level in terms of total recall. The first and third semester learners, however, showed very small differences in total recall. Since the first semester learners recalled more than the second semester learners, a strict developmental pattern cannot be posited. Apparently, ex-

TABLE 7-1 Mean Percentage of Total Recall and Number of Most Important Units Recalled

Semester	N	Total (%) (SD)	Important (#) (SD)
4	19	33.17 (3.75)	2.21 (1.60)
3	38	26.79 (4.23)	1.71 (1.37)
2	43	19.80 (3.47)	1.51 (1.10)
1	29	25.18 (4.22)	1.79 (0.90)

TABLE 7-2 Results of ANOVA of Level by Total Recall

Source of variation	ss	df	ms	F
Between groups	278.15	3	92.72	6.37*
Within groups	1820.89	125	14.56	
Total	2099.04	128		

*$p < .01$

TABLE 7-3 Results of ANOVA of Level by Important Units

Source of variation	ss	df	ms	F
Between groups	7.55	3	2.52	1.96 n.s.
Within groups	161.01	125	1.29	
Total	168.56	128		

posure to the grammar of a language, although a significant factor affecting the quantity recalled, is not the only factor contributing to differences in recall. As was expected, there were no significant differences based on the semester level of the learners for the number of structurally important idea units recalled. That there were no significant differences between the levels of these FL learners is consistent with the findings of Johnson (1970) and Brown and Smiley (1977) who found no differences in the recall of the structurally important idea units of different levels of L1 readers. There are some noteworthy differences, however, between the recall of structurally important idea units by L1 and FL readers, including the fact that L1 readers' total recalls contain from 61%-75% of the structurally important units whereas the FL readers' total recalls contain only from 19%-23% of the structurally important units. While Brown and Smiley were able to conclude that the recall of a passage by four levels of L1 readers is dominated by the structurally important units, it is not possible to draw the same conclusion for FL readers. There are two possible explanations. Due to the linguistic demands of reading in a foreign language, FL readers do not extract important information at the subconscious level as L1 readers do. The second, and more plausible, explanation has to do with a reader's perception of importance. The subjects' recalls of the passage on feudalism was dominated by the information in the second paragraph, which dealt with the relationship between lord and vassal. That is probably the information that forms the readers' prior knowledge of the topic. Due to the linguistic demands of reading in a foreign language, this information was more easily comprehended and subsequently recalled. This explanation is enforced by the fact that the subjects in this study were not given specific goals to orient their reading; only after they read the passage did they learn that they were to recall the passage. Since their reading was unguided, the information they were gathering could only be schematized along the lines of their prior knowledge.

EXPERIMENT TWO

SUBJECTS

In experiment two, four semester levels of FL learners who were enrolled in Spanish classes at the University of Texas at Austin volunteered to participate in the study. The sample consisted of 16 learners enrolled in the first semester, 11 in the second semester, 13 in the third semester, and 13 in the fourth semester, for a total of 53 subjects.

MATERIALS, INSTRUMENTATION, AND PROCEDURE

The same expository text used in experiment one was used in experiment two. The passage these subjects received was divided into the idea units that previously had been identified for the scoring of the recall protocols of experiment one. The subjects were tested in their classrooms. Each received a packet containing an agreement form, the reading passage divided into idea units, and a sheet of paper on which to write the 8 most important units. The subjects were instructed to read the passage at their own rate and to then indicate which 8 idea units they considered to be the most important to the overall story. They were allowed to refer to the passage when doing so.

SCORING AND DATA ANALYSIS

The two authors scored each of the 53 protocols by matching the idea units identified by the subjects against those that had been identified by the authors. Each protocol received a score from 0-8, which represented the match between the subject-identified units and the researcher-identified units. A score of 8 would be a perfect match while a score of 1 would mean that the subject identified only one of the units that the researchers had identified as important. A mean was calculated for each level and all possible t-tests were performed to determine significant differences between the means for each level.

RESULTS

Table 7-4 presents the means for each level of the number of structurally important idea units the learners judged correctly. As noted, the differences between the means were very small and proved to be nonsignificant (see Table 7-5).

TABLE 7-4 Mean Number of Units Judged As Important

Semester	N	Number of Units
4	13	3.85
3	13	4.23
2	11	4.00
1	16	4.06

TABLE 7-5 Results of Multiple T-tests

	2	3	4
1	.137	.318	.411
2		.364	.248
3			.559

No significant differences

SUMMARY AND DISCUSSION

The research presented here attempted to determine the effect that exposure to the grammar of a FL has on (1) total quantity of a passage recalled, (2) the recall of structurally important idea units, and (3) the ability to overtly identify structurally important idea units. It was found that although exposure to the grammar as indexed by semester level has an effect on total recall, there is not a strict relationship between quantity recalled and semester level. The first semester learners recalled more than the second semester learners and as much as the third semester learners. Also, it was found that exposure to the grammar had no effect on the number of structurally important units recalled nor did it have an effect on the ability to overtly identify structurally important units.

Insofar as a recall task can measure comprehension, reading in an L2 or FL cannot be a function solely of the exposure a learner has had to the grammar of the FL. The exposure to the grammar of the FL was indexed by semester of study. The semester classification is a traditional one and does assume certain similarities among the members of each semester level. Certainly, programmatic decisions are made based on semester level. Each semester level represents a more or less unified language group because each member of a level has received a similar amount of instruction in the grammatical structures of the FL. Hosenfeld (1977) suggested that while the learners at each semester level may form a unified language group, they may *not* represent a unified skill group. The FL instruction the subjects of this study received did not include reading-skills development. The findings of the present study, that the first and third semester learners recalled about the same amount of the passage, suggest that across semester levels, these learners may not represent different skill groups. That is, the progressive accumulation of exposure to grammar, which accrues by definition in the semester-level system, may not be accompanied by a progressive development of reading skill.

In the present study there was no significant effect for semester level in terms of the recall of the important idea units or in terms of the ability to identify the important idea units. All the learners, despite differences in their exposure to Spanish, recalled, as well as identified, about the same number of important idea units. These findings are in keeping with the results of L1 research with adults and children, but they differ from that research in two important ways. L1 readers' recalls are dominated by the structurally important idea units but FL readers' recalls are not. L1 readers develop the ability to overtly identify the structurally important units of a passage at about the fifth-grade level, but this ability seems to be adversely affected when reading in a FL.

Although the learners of this study demonstrated roughly the same ability across semester level to rate the importance of the idea units of the passage, it was only at about a 50 percent rate of comparability with the researcher-identified idea units. That such a large discrepancy exists has to do with readers' perceptions of the importance of information in expository prose. Roller (1985) found that prior knowledge, as opposed to text/content structure, is a significant factor influencing adult L1 readers' rating of important information units (her term for idea unit). The present researchers' criteria for importance was text based and therefore should not be expected to coincide completely with the readers' judgments of importance. The differences lie in the perspectives that the researchers and learners used in approaching the task. This difference in perspective may also account for the finding that the learners' recalls were not dominated by important ideas. Whereas Johnson (1970) and Brown and Smiley (1977) used reader-identified units as the measure of importance, the present study used researcher-identified units. A direct comparison of the two methods of assigning importance is called for.

FL educators have recognized that L2 reading does not occur at the same level as L1 reading. For this reason, graded readers are used and reading is delayed until the third and fourth semesters. There are problems with graded readers. By reducing the level of the language of a passage, the comprehensibility of the passage is decreased. Graded readers tend to eliminate rhetorical devices, such as transition words, that relate and sequence passage content. The rationale for delaying reading until the second year stems from the activities associated with reading passages as well as from the choice of reading material. Traditionally, readings are used as stimuli for conversations or discussions. The level of a reading is based on the grammatical structures it contains. Given the limited production abilities of a first year learner, such discussions are inappropriate activities at the beginning level. Moreover, using readings as the basis of discussion skirts the issue of using readings to develop reading skills. The passage used in the present study is an intermediate-level text in terms of its linguistic (grammatical) content. The beginning learners were, however, able to make sense of the passage and to comprehend part of it. If a passage is used specifically for the development of reading skills, then the criteria by which the passage is chosen ought not to be its linguistic content (the grammatical structures) but rather its appropriateness in terms of passage content and structure, which should reflect the reading skill to be practiced. The approach to be adopted for L2 reading is that it, too, is a skill, just as speaking, listening, and writing are. These skills are developed separately through appropriate activities. Reading may need to be developed via overt training in reading strategies that focus on comprehension processes (see Hosenfeld 1977, Grellet 1981, and Groebel 1983 for specific examples.)

Comparing these FL learners with children reading in their L1 showed certain similarities, as well as differences. Only one other study we know of has made comparisons between L1 children and L2 adult readers. Carrell (1984) compared English as a second language readers' ability to use rhetorical structure (textual organization and serial presentation of information) to the ability of adult and ninth-grade L1 readers. She found that the L2 readers used rhetorical structure far less than the ninth graders did. The similarities and differences between children reading in their L1 and adults reading in an L2 or FL has never been systematically investigated, and a direct comparison of the two may provide many insights into the reading process.

NOTE

1. This passage appeared originally in Calfee, Calfee, and Peña 1979. It is used here by permission of the authors. It is given in the appendix.

REFERENCES

Bransford, J. D., and M. K. Johnson. 1972. Contextual prerequisites for understanding: some investigations of comprehension and recall. *Journal of Verbal Learning and Verbal Behaviour* 11(6):717-726.

Bransford, J. D., and M. K. Johnson. 1973. Considerations of some problems of comprehension. In *Visual Information Processing*, W. G. Chase (ed.). New York: Academic Press.

Brown, A. L., and S. S. Smiley. 1977. Rating the importance of structural units of prose passages: a problem of metacognitive development. *Child Development* 48(1):1-8.

Calfee, R. C., K. H. Calfee, and S. C. Peña. 1979. *Interactive Reading Assessment System—Spanish Edition*. Stanford: Stanford University.

Carrell, P. L. 1982. Three components of background knowledge in reading comprehension. *Language Learning* 33(2):183-207.

Carrell, P. L. 1984. The effects of rhetorical organization on ESL readers. *TESOL Quarterly* 18(3):441-470.

Castells, M. O., and Leonetti, H. E. 1983. *La lengua española*. New York: Charles Scribner's Sons.

Clarke, M. A. 1979. Reading in Spanish and English: evidence from adult ESL students. *Language Learning* 29(1):121-150.

Cziko, G. A. 1978. Differences in first- and second-language reading: the use of syntactic, semantic, and discourse constraints. *Canadian Modern Language Review* 34(3):473-489.

Grellet, F. 1981. *Developing Reading Skills*. Cambridge: Cambridge University Press.

Groebel, L. 1983. A comparison of students' reading comprehension in the target language. *English Language Teaching Journal* 35(1):54-59.

Hosenfeld, C. 1977. A preliminary investigation of the reading strategies of successful and nonsuccessful second language learners. *System* 5(2):110-123.

Johnson, R. E. 1970. Recall of prose as a function of the structural importance of the linguistic units. *Journal of Verbal Learning and Verbal Behaviour* 9(1):12-20.

Lee, J. F. 1986. On the use of the recall task to measure L2 reading comprehension. *Studies in Second Language Acquisition* 8:201-211.

Meyer, B. J. F. 1975. *The Organization of Prose and Its Effects on Memory*. Amsterdam: North Holland Publishing Co.

Roller, C. M. 1985. The effects of reader- and text-based factors on writers' and readers' perceptions of the importance of information in expository prose. *Reading Research Quarterly* 20(4):437-457.

Solé, C. A., and Y. R. Solé. 1982. *Español: Ampliación y repaso.* New York: Charles Scribner's Sons.

Yates, D. A., and J. B. Dalbor. 1983. *Imaginación y fantasía.* 4th ed. New York: Holt, Rinehart & Winston.

APPENDIX

Text Used in the Study, Divided into Idea Units

El Feudalismo

Entre los años de 900 y 100,/ Europa Occidental estaba en gran desorden./ El imperio de Carlomagno,/ que había logrado unir esa parte del mundo,/ se estaba dividiendo en pequeños estados./ La paz y la seguridad estaban por desaparecer a medida que caían los gobiernos./ El feudalismo, un nuevo sistema político, surgió durante esta misma época./ Y por los siguientes 400 años,/ este sistema llenó un gran vacío en el mantenimiento del orden social./

El feudalismo estaba basado en un acuerdo de honor entre dos hombres./ Uno, llamado señor o don,/ controlaba mucho terreno./ El otro, llamado vasallo,/ se comprometía a servir y proteger al señor/ para que éste le permitiera usar parte de su terreno./ Mientras estaba en vigor el acuerdo,/ el vasallo podía usar la propiedad,/ inclusive los edificios y los peones,/ para hacerse más rico./ A cambio de estos derechos/ le daba parte de sus ingresos al señor/ y lo servía con lealtad en tiempo de guerra./

Con el tiempo estas relaciones feudales unieron a grandes números de personas/ así como grandes cantidades de terreno./ Los señores entablaron relaciones feudales con otros señores más poderosos/ convirtiéndose ellos mismos en vasallos./ Los estados pequeños así se fueron uniendo a veces a consecuencia de las guerras/ pero con más frecuencia por acuerdo entre los hombres./ En el proceso se fueron estableciendo sistemas de ley y justicia más perdurables./ Para el año 1200,/ cuando el feudalismo alcanzó su cima,/ Europa Occidental empezó a restablecerse del caos/ que había existido hacía 200 años./

Resercher-Identified Important Idea Units
- Europa Occidental estaba en gran desorden
- el feudalismo, un nuevo sistema político
- este sistema llenó un gran vacío en el mantenimiento del orden social
- el feudalismo estaba basado en un acuerdo de honor entre dos hombres
- se comprometía a servir y proteger al señor
- con el tiempo estas relaciones feudales unieron a grandes números de personas
- así como grandes cantidades de terreno
- en el proceso se fueron estableciendo sistemas de ley y justicia más perdurables

CHAPTER 8
Learner Comprehension of Oral and Written Sentences in German and Spanish: The Importance of Word Order

Veronica LoCoco
Santa Clara University

INTRODUCTION

Second language (L2) research has dealt primarily with speech production, but in recent years investigators have attempted to discover the strategies used by L2 learners when they are decoding a message. Message decoding occurs at least at two levels: discourse and sentence. The importance of examining the sentence-level processing strategies of foreign language (FL) learners stems from the input that characterizes classroom interaction. Teachers tend to provide only a few sentences, or more often a single question, for a learner. Beginning-level exams are generally devoid of text-type discourse, as are the majority of textbook exercises. How does the learner interpret sentences that do not form part of ongoing discourse?

Psycholinguistic research into the processing strategies of children acquiring their first language (FL) firmly established word order as a major factor in sentential processing. Bever (1970) found a stage of L1 development in which children interpreted noun-verb-noun (NVN) sequences mostly as agent-action-object. Slobin (1973) proposed the following operating principle for L1 acquisition: pay attention to the order of words and morphemes. He further stated that sentences deviating from standard word order (agent-action-object) would be interpreted at early stages of development as if they were examples of standard word order. Slobin and Bever (1982) went on to propose that children younger than four have already formed a canonical sentence schema that plays a central role in the process of sentence interpretation.

Tarone (1974) has suggested the existence of a preliminary stage of L2 speech perception in which decoding is based on feature analysis and hypothesis formation. Learners will pay attention to some feature that, through their experience with the language, they have come to regard as an important cue to finding meaning. Several researchers have reported that word order plays a role in L2 aural comprehension regardless of the L2 being acquired and regardless of L1 background (Nam 1975; Morsbach 1981; Xiao-Chun 1981; Fathman and LoCoco 1982; Stevens 1984; VanPatten 1984). The role of word order in the comprehension of L2 written sentences has yet to be explored. One might expect the same comprehension strategies to surface, but since learners can also "see" the language when they are reading, they might make use of cues that they miss during aural comprehension. The present study compares the comprehension of aural and written sentences by learners of German and Spanish. Such a comparison would not only give a cue to the strategies used (be they similar to or different from those documented in other studies) but would also point to grammar that has been taught but not yet acquired for use in aural comprehension.

SUBJECTS

The subjects used in this study were 151 adult FL learners at a university in California. Of the 151, 73 were students of Spanish and 78 were students of German. They were enrolled in first year language study, which followed an eclectic approach to classroom instruction, and all of the students were L1 speakers of English.

METHOD AND PROCEDURE

For the aural comprehension task, subjects were provided with a series of pictures depicting activities being performed (see Table 8-1). They were read sentences in the FL characterized by various word orders. The sentences were read twice at natural speed and with normal intonation by an adult native speaker of the language. No specific part of any utterance was emphasized. For every sentence there was a corresponding drawing. Subjects were instructed in English to write on an answer sheet the letter of the drawing that corresponded to the sentence heard. In this way, the subjects did not engage in either L1 or FL production. The subjects were also given a sheet with drawings of the agents and objects involved in the various activities outlined in Table 8-1. For each sentence the subjects heard, they were asked to mark with an X the person or thing that was performing the action.

A similar method was used for the written comprehension task. However, in addition to hearing the sentences, the learners simultaneously saw the utterances. It is important to note that the sentences used in the two tasks were not the same but were syntactically and semantically parallel.

TABLE 8-1 Descriptions of Drawings

Category I
Oral:
 a boy pushing a truck
 a truck pushing a boy
 a truck pushing a car
 a car pushing a truck

Oral and Written:
 a whale pulling a boat
 a boat pulling a whale
 a boat pulling an innertube
 a man in an innertube pulling a boat

Category II
Oral:
 a girl bringing beer to a boy
 a boy bringing beer to a girl
 two men bringing beer to a girl
 a girl bringing beer to two men

Oral and Written:
 a girl giving flowers to a boy
 a boy giving flowers to a girl
 two boys giving flowers to a girl
 a girl giving flowers to two boys

Category III
Oral:
 a woman pushing a child on a sled towards a man
 a man pushing a child on a sled towards a woman
 a child pushing a woman on a sled towards a man
 a child pushing a man on a sled towards a woman

Oral and Written:
 a man taking (pulling) a boy towards an older woman
 an older woman taking a boy towards a man
 a boy taking an older woman towards a man
 a boy taking a man towards an older woman

For each category (see below) both tasks were administered during one classroom period. Half of the subjects were given the aural task first; the other half received the aural-written task first.

In English, the word order of the utterance "The boy sees the girl" cannot be altered without affecting the meaning (e.g., "The girl sees the boy", "The boy the girl sees"). If the order is altered and the meaning is somehow preserved, linguistic or grammatical complexity is added (e.g., "The girl is seen by the boy" or "The girl, the boy sees"). (A comprehension task would examine the effect of both word order and grammatical structure.) However, in Spanish and German, due to overt object marking, the word order of such simple sentences can be reversed without altering the meaning. Spanish uses the object marker *a* whenever it is semantically possible for the object to perform the action.[1] German uses an inflection of the article and sometimes also of the noun (when the object is of masculine gender). The sentences used in this study were all of the type mentioned above: simple declaratives. No sentences were included in which semantic constraints would clearly limit possible interpretations (e.g., "The boy eats the cake", "The cake eats the boy").

Sentences were grouped according to different categories. In Category I, the grammatical items involved were subject, direct object, verb inflected for third person singular, and present tense. In German, two genders (masculine and neuter) were used, along with inflection of the masculine article and one noun (accusative case). In Spanish, the sentences in this category included one gender (masculine) and the direct object marker *a*, which combines with the article *el* to form *al*. These sentences are all listed in Table 8-2; the grammatical subject is italicized.

In Category II, the sentences were grammatically and semantically more complex than were those in Category I, for they included subject, direct object, and indirect object. The verb form was either third person singular or plural, but always present tense. In German, dative inflection (both singular and plural) of articles and some nouns was included. In Spanish, the preposition for indirect objects, *a*, appeared, along with third person indirect object pronouns (singular and plural). Another semantic cue was also introduced: an inanimate object that could not perform the action contained in the sentence. Again, both typical word order and permutations were used as test sentences, as shown in Tables 8-3 and 8-4.

The last group of sentences in Category III included subject, object, and objects of prepositions in each utterance. All of the subjects and objects in these sentences had the features [+animate] and [+human]; thus, any noun could be interpreted as the agent of the action. The verbs were again third person singular, present tense. The German sentences included two genders, feminine and masculine. Only masculine articles were inflected for accusative case, while both masculine and feminine articles were inflected for dative case. These latter were combined with the preposition *zu* to form either *zur* or *zum*. The Spanish sentences included two genders, feminine and masculine, and the object marker *a* by itself or combined with the article *el*. These sentences appear in Tables 8-5 (Spanish) and 8-6 (German).

TABLE 8-2 Comprehension of Category I Sentences

Spanish—26 Subjects

Oral Sentences:	Errors	%	Interpreted as Subject
El *muchacho* empuja al camión.	0	0	N1
Al camión empuja el *coche*.	13	50	N1
El *camión* empuja al muchacho.	0	0	N1
Al muchacho empuja el *camión*.	11	42	N1
El *coche* empuja al camión.	0	0	N1
El *camión* empuja al coche.	0	0	N1
Al camión empuja el *muchaco*.	15	57	N1
Al coche empuja el *camión*.	17	65	N1

Oral and Written Sentences:	Errors	%	Interpreted as Subject
La *ballena* jala al bote.	0	0	N1
Al bote jala la *cámara*.	10	38	N1
El *bote* jala a la ballena.	0	0	N1
A la ballena jala el *bote*.	8	31	N1
La *cámara* jala al bote.	0	0	N1
El *bote* jala a la cámara.	0	0	N1
Al bote jala la *ballena*.	11	42	N1
A la cámara jala el *bote*.	7	27	N1

German—25 Subjects

Oral Sentences:	Errors	%	Interpreted as Subject
Der *Junge* schiebt den Lastwagen.	0	0	N1
Den Lastwagen schiebt das *Auto*.	19	75	N1
Der *Lastwagen* schiebt den Jungen.	0	0	N1
Den Jungen schiebt den *Lastwagen*.	17	68	N1
Das *Auto* schiebt der Lastwagen.	0	0	N1
Der *Lastwagen* schiebt das Auto.	0	0	N1
Den Lastwagen schiebt der *Junge*.	19	76	N1

Oral and Written Sentences:	Errors	%	Interpreted as Subject
Der *Wahlfisch* zieht das Boot.	0	0	N1
Den Luftschlauch zieht das *Boot*.	7	28	N1
Das *Boot* zieht den Wahlfisch.	0	0	N1
Der *Luftschlauch* zieht das Boot.	0	0	N1
Den Wahlsfisch zieht das Boot.	5	20	N1
Das *Boot* zieht den Luftschlauch.	0	0	N1
Das Boot zieht der *Wahlfisch*.	2	8	N1

RESULTS

Responses were classified as correct or incorrect. For each sentence, responses for whole-sentence interpretation were matched against responses for subject-agent interpretation.

Sentences for both target languages and the number of errors that occurred are presented in Tables 8-2 through Table 8-6.

In the aural comprehension of sentences in Category I, errors consisted of interpreting the first noun as the agent. In the comprehension of sentences in

TABLE 8-3 Comprehension of Category II Sentences

Spanish—25 Subjects

Oral Sentences:	Errors	%	Interpreted as Subject
El *muchacho* le trae la cerveza a la muchacha.	0	0	N1
A los hombres les trae la *muchacha* la cerveza.	13	52	N1
La cerveza le traen los *hombres* a la muchacha.	0	0	N1
Al muchacho le trae la cerveza la *muchacha*.	14	56	N1
La *muchacha* le trae la cerveza al muchacho.	0	0	N1
La cerveza le trae el *muchacho* a la muchacha.	0	0	N2
Los *hombres* le traen a la muchacha la cerveza.	0	0	N1
A la muchacha le trae la cerveza el *muchacho*.	18	72	N1

Oral and Written Sentences:	Errors	%	Interpreted as Subject
El *muchacho* le da las flores a la niña.	0	0	N1
A los muchachos les da la *niña* las flores.	8	32	N1
Las flores le dan los *muchachos* a la niña.	0	0	N2
Al muchacho le da las flores la *niña*.	10	40	N1
La *niña* le da las flores al muchacho.	0	0	N1
Las flores le da el *muchacho* a la niña.	0	0	N2
Los *muchachos* le dan a la niña las flores.	0	0	N1
A la niña le da las flores el *muchacho*.	9	36	N1

TABLE 8-4 Comprehension of Category II Sentences

German—27 Subjects

Oral Sentences:	Errors	%	Interpreted as Subject
Der *Junge* bringt dem Mädchen das Bier.	0	0	N1
Das Bier bringt den Männern das *Mädchen*.	11	41	N2
Das Bier bringt der *Junge* dem Mädchen.	0	0	N2
Das *Mädchen* bringt dem Junge das Bier.	0	0	N1
Die *Männer* bringen dem Mädchen das Bier.	0	0	N1
Den Männern bringt das *Mädchen* das Bier.	12	44	N1
Das Bier bringen die *Männer* dem Mädchen.	1	4	N3
Dem Jungen bringt das *Mädchen* das Bier.	11	41	N1

Oral and Written Sentences:	Errors	%	Interpreted as Subject
Der *Junge* gibt dem Mädchen die Blumen.	0	0	N1
Den Jungen gibt das *Mädchen* die Blumen.	3	11	N1
Die Blumen geben die *Jungen* dem Mädchen.	0	0	N2
Dem Jungen gibt die Blumen das *Mädchen*.	2	7	N1
Das *Mädchen* gibt die Blumen dem Jugen.	0	0	N1
Die Blumen gibt der *Junge* dem Mädchen.	0	0	N2
Die *Jungen* geben dem Mädchen die blumen.	0	0	N1
Dem Mädchen gibt die Blumen der *Junge*.	1	4	N1

Category II, both learner groups made use of the semantic cue for interpretation. The *beer* was never interpreted as being the agent of the action, not even when it appeared as the first noun in the sentence. For Categories I and II, then, the learners apparently used a strategy that could be characterized by the following:

TABLE 8-5 Comprehension of Category III Sentences

Spanish—27 Subjects

Oral Sentences:	Errors	%	Interpreted as Subject
La *madre* empuja al niño hacia el padre.	0	0	N1
El *padre* empuja al niño hacia la madre.	0	0	N1
Hacia la madre empuja el *niño* al padre.	12	44	8N1,4N3,4N2
El *niño* empuja a la madre hacia el padre.	0	0	N1
Hacia el padre empuja al niño la *madre*.	17	63	7N1,10N2
Hacia la madre empuja el *padre* al niño.	14	52	2N1,12N3
El *niño* empuja al padre hacia la madre.	0	0	N1
Hacia el padre empuja a la madre el *niño*.	17	63	3N1,14N2

Oral and Written Sentences:	Errors	%	Interpreted as Subject
El *señor* lleva al niño hacia la abuela.	0	0	N1
La *abuela* lleva al niño hacia el señor.	0	0	N1
Hacia el señor lleva el *niño* a la abuela.	0	0	N2
El *niño* lleva a la abuela hacia el señor.	0	0	N1
Hacia la abuela lleva al niño el *señor*.	8	30	N2
Hacia el señor lleva la *abuela* al niño.	0	0	N2
El *niño* lleva a la abuela hacia el señor.	0	0	N1
Hacia la abuela lleva al señor el *niño*.	7	26	N2

TABLE 8-6 Comprehension of Category III Sentences

German—26 Subjects

Oral Sentences:	Errors	%	Interpreted as Subject
Die *Mutter* schiebt den Jungen zum Vater.	0	0	N1
Der *Vater* schiebt den Jungen zur Mutter.	0	0	N1
Zur Mutter schiebt der *Junge* den Vater.	17	65	15N1,2N3
Der *Junge* schiebt die Mutter zum Vater.	0	0	N1
Zum Vater schiebt den Jungen die *Mutter*.	18	69	15N1,1N3
Zur Mutter schiebt der *Vater* den Jungen.	12	46	11N1,1N3
Das *Kind* schiebt den Vater zur Mutter.	1	4	N3

Oral and Written Sentences:	Errors	%	Interpreted as Subject
Der *Mann* bringt den Jungen zur Grossmutter.	0	0	N1
Die *Grossmutter* bringt den Jungen zum Mann.	0	0	N1
Zum Mann bringt der *Junge* die Grossmutter.	0	0	N2
Der Junge bringt die *Grossmutter* zum Mann.	0	0	N2
Zur Grossmutter bringt den Jungen der *Mann*.	2	8	N2
Zum Mann bringt die *Grossmutter* den Jungen.	0	0	N2
Der *Junge* bringt die Grossmutter zum Mann.	0	0	N1
Zur Grossmutter bringt den Mann der *Junge*.	3	11	N2

interpret the first [+animate] noun in a sentence as the agent of the action. This strategy accounts not only for the correct interpretation of sentences of the word order direct object-verb-subject-indirect object and for sentences of the pattern subject-verb-indirect object-direct object, but it also accounts for the misinterpretation of sentences that follow the order indirect object-verb-subject-direct object.

In Category III, most learners that made errors in Spanish did so by either interpreting the first noun as the agent or by interpreting the noun marked by accusative *a* as an object of a preposition.

When responding to written-aural stimuli, learners seemingly relied on the same strategy that they used in aural comprehension for Category I sentences. Errors occurred when the agent appeared as the second noun in the sentence and was interpreted as the object of the action. In Spanish, the fact that *a* is not contracted with the feminine article appears to have aided correct interpretation. When compared with aural comprehension by itself, average error reduction in comprehending written sentences was 19 percent in Spanish. In German, error reduction with written stimuli was more impressive: 54 percent.

With regard to sentences in Category II, learners again relied on the strategy they used in the aural-only task. However, the learners of Spanish did focus more on the object marker, especially when that marker was not contracted with an article. For those sentences that lend themselves to misinterpretation, error reduction in both languages was greater than in Category I. For Category III, learners of Spanish that made errors seemed to continue relying on word order as the preferred cue during comprehension of written-aural sentences. In German, although errors were almost absent, those that were made appeared to have been influenced by word order. Once the object of the preposition was determined, the first of the remaining nouns was interpreted as the agent.

DISCUSSION AND CONCLUSIONS

The results of this study indicate that word order is an important cue used in comprehension. In both target languages and in all three tasks, sentences of the order subject-verb-direct object were almost never misinterpreted. When a semantic cue is available, such as an inanimate object incapable of performing the action, learners will make use of it, but the aid it provides is limited. In this study, the semantic cue helped eliminate the direct object in Category II from misinterpretation as agent. The word order of the remaining elements was still used as a cue.

If the proportion of learners who made errors on a given task is taken as an indicator of complexity or of difficulty in comprehension, sentences that provide a semantic cue (Category II) seem to be the least complex or difficult. The sentences of Category I, which are linguistically the least complex of the three categories, turn out to be the most complex perceptually.

In aural comprehension, it appears that learners of both languages had less difficulty identifying objects of prepositions marked by phonetically distinct prepositions (i.e., *hacia* and *zu*) than when they were identifying unmarked subjects, object nouns inflected for case, or object nouns marked by contracted forms that are phonetically similar to unmarked articles (i.e., *al/el* and *den/dem*). Even so, a considerable number of learners did not listen for the prepositions, relying on word order instead. Since the learners were adults who use and rely on written language as well as on oral, it was expected that the addition of written stimuli would aid correct interpretation. The results confirmed this expectation. However, when written stimuli were added, the greatest gains in correct interpretation were made by the learners of German. This points to differences in learning strategies that depend in part on the structure of the language being learned and in part on the relationship between the L1 and the FL/L2 that the learner has established.

In the case of German as a FL, although the learners' L1 does not have article case endings, learners seem to be aware of their importance for correct interpretation. It appears that it is the difference between the L1 and the FL article endings that aided learners in correctly interpreting sentences of differing word orders. Word order is also subject to more variation in German than in English, which possibly leads learners not to rely on word order alone for sentence interpretation.

Spanish articles are not inflected for case. In this respect, L1 and FL are more similar than when the FL is German. Learners of Spanish did not focus on the overt form of the article as learners of German did. The Spanish object marker *a*, when contracted with the masculine article, was frequently ignored. The highest percentage of errors occurred in sentences that had this contraction.

Spanish learners relied primarily on word order, even when a noticeable preposition such as *hacia* was present. Since Spanish word order is similar to English word order, this possibly contributes to an increased tendency to rely on it.

Even though these learners appear to have used comprehension strategies similar to those proposed for L1 acquisition, the fact that they were adult learners capable of reading and writing introduces an issue that is absent in L1 acquisition: the role that written language might play in sentence interpretation and the place its correct interpretation occupies in a four-skill language learning hierarchy.

It is Smith's (1973) belief that in language production, writing and speech occupy equivalent levels and are not hierarchically related. However, in the case of comprehension, this study indicates that although the deep structures of written and spoken language may be the same, these structures are more easily comprehended through written language.

The tasks were taken by the same learners within each category of sentences. One may assume, then, that the reduction in errors from aural only to written-aural, is in part due to the different stages at which learners find themselves. Learners who made errors in aural-only interpretation but did not do so in written-aural interpretation may have learned the grammatical rules necessary for correctly interpreting the sentences in this study; yet, these rules have not been acquired to the point that they are easily accessible and can be applied in all instances of language use.

Not only does there seem to be a sequence in the acquisition of the two language skills that were tested here (i.e., reading first, listening second), but also there seems to be a progression in comprehension strategies. Winitz (1981) explains that depending on the structure of the FL or L2, fundamental cognitive strategies that learners use to construct underlying grammatical competence may be abandoned in favor of other strategies. In the present study, the use of word order as the primary comprehension cue was followed by the additional use of other overt cues (prepositions and inflections). Reliance on word order was abandoned sooner with German than with Spanish, indicating that the structure of the FL or L2 influences comprehension strategies.

NOTES

1. A common misconception, even among native speakers of Spanish, is that the preposition *a* is used only to mark human or personified objects; hence it is called the "personal *a*." This marking of direct objects, however, is not limited to persons or personified objects: *Conozco bien a Madrid* (I know Madrid well); *El tigre atacó al león* (The tiger attacked the lion). The Real Academia Española (1983, 374) points out that *a* may be used at any time to disambiguate subjects and objects. They give as examples: *Acompaña al examen de las obras la noticia de muchos de sus autores* and *Todos le temen como al fuego*. Nonetheless, due to idiosyncratic normative usage of the "personal *a*," it would not be difficult to find some native speakers of Spanish who might object to the Category I experimental sentences. In any event, the acceptability or unacceptability of a sentence by native speakers is irrelevant to the research question here: How do learners interpret sentences of different word order? It should be noted that in both L1 and L2 studies with children, researchers purposefully use unacceptable sentences and word strings to get at syntactic and semantic processing strategies (e.g., Steven's 1984 study in which L2 learners of French were presented with utterances such as *ouvrir boîte garçon* [open box boy] and *cheval partir vache* [horse leave cow]).

REFERENCES

Bever, T. G. 1970. The cognitive basis for linguistic structures. In *Cognition and Development of Language*, J. Hayes (ed.), 279-352. New York: John Wiley and Sons.

Fathman, A., and V. LoCoco. 1982. Word order contrasts in three target languages. Paper presented at the Los Angeles Second Language Research Forum.

Nam, E. 1975. Child and adult perceptual strategies in second language acquisition. Paper presented at the annual TESOL Convention, Los Angeles.

Morsbach, G. 1981. Cross-cultural comparison of second language learning: the development of comprehension of English structures by Japanese and German children. *TESOL Quarterly* 15(2):183-188.

Real Academia Española. 1983. *Esbozo de una nueva gramática de la lengua española*. Madrid: Espasa-Calpe.

Slobin, D. I., 1973. Cognitive prerequisites for the development of grammar. In *Studies in Child Language Development*, C. A. Ferguson and D. I. Slobin (eds.), 175-208. New York: Holt, Rinehart & Winston.

Slobin, D. I. and T. G. Bever. 1982. Children's use of canonical sentence schemas: a cross-linguistic study of word order and inflections. *Cognition* 12:229-265.

Smith, F. 1973. Decoding: the great fallacy. In *Psycholinguistics in Reading*, F. Smith (ed.), 70-83. New York: Holt, Rinehart & Winston.

Stevens, F. 1984. *Strategies for Second-Language Acquisition*. Montreal: Eden Press.

Tarone, E. 1974. Speech perception in second language acquisition: a suggested model. *Language Learning* 24:223-232.

VanPatten, B. 1984. Learners' comprehension of clitic pronouns: more evidence for a word order strategy. *Hispanic Linguistics* 1(1):88-98.

Winitz, H. (ed.). 1981. *The Comprehension Approach to Foreign Language Teaching.* Rowley, MA: Newbury House.

Xiao-Chun, M. 1981. Word order and semantic strategies in Chinese sentence comprehension. *International Journal of Psycholinguistics* 8-3(23):109-122.

PART THREE
Factors Affecting FL Development

CHAPTER 9
Differentiated Cognitive Style and Oral Performance

Susan Cameron Bacon
University of Cincinnati

INTRODUCTION

Differentiated cognitive style (field dependence/independence) has been found to influence the manner by which a person seeks and processes information. Field independence (FI) is generally defined as a greater degree of differentiation of self from the environment such that there is greater self-reliance for processing information. Field dependence (FD) is generally defined as a lesser degree of differentiation, resulting in an increased reliance on others for processing information. As with any psychological construct, that of FD/FI is considered to be a continuum; in a normally distributed population, one would expect a clustering of individuals around the mean and fewer at the extremes (see Witkin and Goodenough 1979 for a review).

Several studies support the hypothesis that in second language (L2) learning (including foreign language [FL] learning), the FI individual has an advantage (d'Anglejan and Renaud 1985; McLaughlin 1980; Naiman, Fröhlich, Stern, and Todesco 1978; Parry 1984; Tucker, Hamayan, and Genesee 1976). Although the FI subject can better disambiguate both oral and written speech signals, the FD subject is suspected to have a social advantage in resolving ambiguity. Despite the acknowledgement by those involved in psychological research that an individual's degree of FD/FI is stable, some writers (Brown 1973; 1980) suggest that successful L2 students are both FI and FD.

In the traditional L2 testing situation, i.e., one that does not require the learner to speak, the FI individual is rewarded for his/her ability to hear or see how the language "puzzle" fits together. The social advantage of the FD individual, such as increased awareness of eye contact and other kinesics, for example, is notably absent from paper and pencil tests. The social awareness factor is, however, especially important in face-to-face communication. Whereas an extremely FI individual may not have to rely on another person to aid in comprehension of the L2 message or to confirm that the message has been received, the FD individual may not only use social cues to disambiguate the message received, but also may employ social strategies to enhance the message that is sent. Additional research, therefore, into the effect of body posture, eye contact, and facial expression on successful L2 communication, especially with native speakers of the target language, is essential (Pennycook 1985).

The combination of social strategies with dis-embedding abilities have led some writers to assert that successful L2 learners must be both FD and FI (Brown 1973; 1980). Psychological research, however, has consistently shown that a person's degree of FD/FI has stabilized by the time of adolescence.

A perusal of the studies that deal with differentiated cognitive style reveals, almost without exception, that the criterion for success in an L2 was based on receptive linguistic skills. When oral measures were taken, they may not have reflected a true capacity for creative speech. The oral measure reported in the Naiman et al. (1978) study consisted of a student's ability to repeat sentences rather than to produce original discourse. The oral measure reported by Hansen and Stansfield (1981) was based on the oral grade students received from their instructor, a measure that may have been biased by other confounding variables such as the teacher's opinion of the student. No study has reported on the role of differentiated cognitive style and oral communicative and linguistic proficiency as measured by a rating scale and independent raters.

Many studies outside of FL research have investigated the interaction between differentiated cognitive style and manner of testing (e.g., Witkin 1978; Freedman, O'Hanlon, Oltman, and Witkin 1972; Ruble and Nakamura 1972). These have supported the hypothesis that FD individuals are not necessarily deficient intellectually or verbally, but that they do react differently in oral-testing situations. They are more comfortable and respond more fully when the situation has been structured for them; they take advantage of social cues more than do FI subjects (Witkin 1978; Ruble and Nakamura 1972). In oral communication, therefore, the social strategies that FD individuals have developed may override the dis-embedding strengths of their FI counterparts.

How the interview treatment may interact with cognitive style has been of considerable interest in psychological studies (where L1 is the language of interaction). Freedman et al. (1972) justified their research on the interaction between field dependence and treatment by "warm" and "cold" interviewers by the fact that there are indeed "warm" and "cold" doctors. Their hypothesis that the reactions and performance of subjects would be influenced by the interaction between their cognitive style and the manner by which they were interviewed was supported. deGroot (1968) found that all subjects spoke more under "warm" rather than "cold" interview treatment, but that the increase in verbal output by FD subjects was significantly greater than that of FI subjects under the "warm" treatment conditions. In Gates (1971), subjects were asked to talk about a subject of interest to them, under a condition in which the interviewer kept silent throughout, or under a condition in which the interviewer supplied appropriate verbal or nonverbal feedback (e.g., "umm hmm," "yeah"). Although the output for the FD individuals was much lower under the nonsupportive conditions, the output of the FI individuals was not significantly affected by either treatment. These studies have led Witkin and Goodenough (1977, 663) to conclude that FI subjects "may be impervious to information from others that could actually help them."

Although some writers claim field independence to be the desirable trait in L2 performance (e.g., Birckbichler and Omaggio 1978; Reiss 1981), Ruble and Nakamura (1972) caution that

...field-dependent Ss [subjects] may be more effective in tasks or situations that involve relevant social cues. Thus it is perhaps inappropriate to refer to one cognitive style as more desirable than the other. Which style is more effective may vary with situational factors. (479)

Because oral proficiency in an L2 involves social interaction, the role of FD in performance may have implications that have not been considered previously. Given that interview testing has become an important means of assessing L2 ability, the present experiment sought to discover whether or not FI/FD interacts with the type of verbal and nonverbal behavior displayed by the interviewer - (supportive/nonsupportive) such that the quantity or quality, or both, of language produced by the L2 learner is affected.

SUBJECTS

The population consisted of students who were enrolled in Spanish 102, fall and winter quarters, 1984-85, Spanish 103, winter quarter, 1985, at Ohio State University, and in Spanish 102, spring semester at the College of Wooster.

The programs at each institution represent the second course of a sequence that uses the text *En Contacto* (Valencia and Merlonghi 1980) and its ancillary materials. The two groups were selected in order to provide an adequate number of subjects which would allow for regression analysis. The subjects were tested afer having completed between 90 and 100 hours of formal classroom instruction at the university level. Both programs of instruction include interviews by the regular classroom instructor. A pilot study confirmed the suitabilityof the instruments and procedures used.

The subjects were assigned an identification number in order to ensure anonymity and to assure them that their grade in Spanish would not be affected by their prescence in (or absence from) the study. It was hoped that the students who showed willingness to participate would represent the population of students who were most interested in learning how to speak Spanish.[1]

The students participating in the study were randomly assigned to each treatment group until there were 95 subjects (45 males, 50 females) in the supportive group and 92 subjects (45 males, 47 females) in the nonsupportive group (the difference in number being attributable to the failure of some of the subjects to complete all of the aspects of the interview). In order to protect against experimenter bias, the researcher did not have access to the scores for FD/FI until after the interview had been completed.

METHOD

The construct of cognitive differentiation was measured by the Hidden Figures Test (HFT) (French, Ekstrom and Price 1963). This test was also used by Jackson, Messick and Myers (1964) in their research on the FD/FI construct and was found to have both validity and reliability. The test, with a multiple-choice format, requires the subjects to recognize simple geometrical figures within a complex figure. The score is based on the number of correct responses minus a fraction (one-fourth) of the number guessed incorrectly. There are two ten-minute sections, each with 16 figures to dis-embed. High scores are associated with field independence; low scores are indicative of field dependence. Internal reliability was established through application of the Kuder-Richardson formula, KR-21, to a random sample representing 20 percent of the subjects tested. This procedure resulted in a satisfactory coefficient of .850.

For the interview, the subjects were provided with a randomly ordered collection of questions or topics that were based on the vocabulary and structures covered in their respective courses. Half of the topics were structured (providing guidance toward possible response), and half were unstructured (providing no guidance toward response).[2]

In order to better identify a speaking proficiency that was effectively isolated from listening skill, each question was written in English and printed on a four-by-six-inch note card. The use of the note cards served to standardize the topics as well as to enable easy randomization of order with each interview. The researcher had no control over the order in which the topics appeared to the student.

Although it is recognized that creating topics of equal linguistic difficulty is not possible, efforts were made to address pairs of similar topics in structured and unstructured ways. Reflexive verbs, for example, would be used in two topics. In two other topics subjects had the opportunity to contrast the preterit with the imperfect. (See the Appendix for examples.)

When the students appeared for their interviews, the interviewer explained that she was interested in what they could do as opposed to what they could not do. Thus, the students were allowed to speak about anything they liked, even though topics were provided. This procedure encouraged maximal communicative performance on the part of the subjects. When the subjects were finished with a card (topic), they put it aside and proceeded with another. Each interview was timed for exactly ten minutes.

The subjects were randomly assigned to two treatment groups:

1. Supportive Treatment consisted of the interviewer responding to utterances from the student with the following: *sí, comprendo, verdad*. These phrases were accompanied by affirmative head nodding. The purpose of this feedback was to indicate that the interviewer was interested in what the subject was saying.

2. Nonsupportive Treatment consisted of the interviewer providing no verbal interaction or head nodding whatsoever. The interviewer did not give any particular indication that she was interested in the subject's responses.

These treatments were based on those cited above, particularly Gates (1971), de Groot (1968), and Freedman et al. (1972). In neither treatment condition did the interviewer correct the subjects, supply them with responses, or take notes on what was said.[3]

A post interview questionnaire served to ascertain whether or not there was an interaction between the manner of interview and the cognitive style of the subject such that attitude was significantly different under the two treatment conditions.[4]

DATA ANALYSIS

The quantity of Spanish produced, as measured by the actual number of words uttered during the ten-minute interview, was assessed. Fillers that are considered English were not counted (e.g., "umm"). Those that are considered Spanish were counted (e.g., *este*). When a subject pronounced a non-Spanish word by using Spanish phonology, it was accepted only if that word had no reasonable translation into Spanish. Place names, for example, would be accepted as Spanish words if they were said with Spanish pronunciation. A 5 percent random sample of the tapes was re-counted to determine the reliability of the count. It was determined that the variability between the first and the second count was within 3 percent, which was considered a reasonable range of error. A subcomponent of the quantity of language was determined to be the development of topic. This was calculated by the mean number of words employed in response to each topic.

The quality of the Spanish produced, as measured by a separate rating of "overall communicative effectiveness," was analyzed. This measurement, "overall communicative effectiveness," was selected from consideration of the research done by Yorozuya and Oller (1980). Based on their report on the "halo effect" produced by using a rating scale with several separate categories (e.g., vocabulary, syntax, phonology, and so forth), the rating of "overall communicative effectiveness" is considered a valid measure of the quality of speech produced. The rating is based on a scale from one to five. Two graduate students in Foreign-Language Education at Ohio State University were trained to serve as raters. The variability in the rating of individual questions did not seem to seriously affect the global rating for the entire tape. It was determined, consequently, that the global score for the tape was a better indication of interrater reliability than was the score for individual questions. In no instance, however, did the raters differ more than one point on any question, nor did the global rating for the tape differ more than .500. Interrater reliability was established at .845 based on a random sample of 20 percent of the tapes.

Attitude toward speaking Spanish after the interview was assessed by agreement with the statement, "Being able to speak a second language is important to me." Agreement with this statement yielded a four or five; disagreement, a one or two; "no opinion" was scored as a three.

In order to test for the effects of treatment and the relationship of cognitive differentiation to the dependent variables under the two treatments, the analysis recommended for Aptitude Treatment Interaction (ATI) research was used (Cronbach and Snow 1977). This analysis is similar to that of analysis of covariance. With analysis of covariance, however, the use of the continuous variable is for control and is thereby designed to reduce the error term (Pedhazer 1982). In the ATI design, in contrast, the continuous variable, or variables, is used to predict the different outcomes under separate treatments. Both analyses use regression analysis of continuous variables examined in relationship to at least one categorical variable with two or more levels.[5]

RESULTS

The results of the analysis of the quantity of words produced in Spanish are reported in Table 9-1. The total variance (r) for which the proposed model accounts is only .019 ($p < .31$), which immediately casts doubt upon its appropriateness for the data at hand. The regression coefficients indicate that there is no significant interaction between FD/FI (HFT) and the treatment variables (supportive/nonsupportive) for the quantity of Spanish produced ($F = .98, p < .32$). The difference between the common regression coefficient and those reported for the treatment levels is different from zero, but not at a significant level ($p < .11$ and $p < .74$). Although the main effect of cognitive style (HFT $p < .16$) is nonsignificant, as the HFT score increases (more FI); subjects produce a greater quantity of words under the supportive treatment. The nonsupportive treatment tended to create an equalizing effect, such that the degree of FI was less of a factor in determining output for this group. The LS means statistic further suggests that treatment, by itself, does not significantly affect the quantity of language produced.

The results of the analysis for development of topic are reported in Table 9-2.

TABLE 9-1 Statistics Associated with the Dependent Variable Quantity: Total Words Produced

Source	DF	F Value	PR>F	R-Square	Mean all subjects	STD DEV
Model	3	1.20	0.310	0.019342	268.83	120.31

Source	DF	Type III SS	F	PR>F		
HFT★TRTMNT	1	14163.26	.98	.32		
TRTMNT	1	524.56	.04	.85		
HFT	1	29177.94	2.02	.16		

Parameter	Estimate	T for HO: Parameter=0	PR>T	Standard Error of Estimate		
Intercept	254.8000	12.63	.0001	20.169		
HFT★TRMNT						
1	3.3114	1.59	.11	2.082		
2	.5919	0.33	.74	1.788		
Treatment 1	-5.633	-0.19	.85	29.543		

Least Squares Means Treatment	LSMEAN	STD ERR LSMEAN	PROB> |T| HO:LSMEAN=0	PROB> |T| HO:LSM1=LSM2
1	277.89	12.33	.0001	.31
2	259.93	12.53	.0001	

TABLE 9-2 Statistics Associated with the Dependent Variable Quantity: Mean Words per Topic

Source	DF	F Value	PR>F	R-Square	Mean all subjects	STD DEV
Model	3	0.92	0.44	0.014811	48.81	34.31

Source	DF	Type III SS	F	PR>F		
HFT★TRTMNT	1	4.48	0.00	.95		
TRTMNT	1	659.59	.56	.46		
HFT	1	1634.67	1.39	.24		

Parameter	Estimate	T for HO: Parameter=0	PR>T	Standard Error of Estimate		
Intercept	41.6000	7.21	.0001	5.765		
HFT★TRMNT						
1	0.4377	0.74	.46	0.595		
2	.4861	0.95	.34	0.511		
Treatment 1	6.3119	0.75	.46	8.445		

Least Squares Means Treatment	LSMEAN	STD ERR LSMEAN	PROB> |T| HO:LSMEAN=0	PROB> |T| HO:LSM1=LSM2
1	51.70	3.52	.0001	.24
2	45.81	3.58	.001	

The total variance accounted for by this model is also small ($r = .014$). None of the independent variables, or the interactions between them, has a statistically significant effect upon the subjects' development of topic in Spanish. It is evident that topic development (as rated from audio tapes) is not influenced by cognitive style or by an interviewer's social behavior.

The results of the analysis of quality of speech produced are reported in Table 9-3. As with the previous analyses, the amount of variance accounted for is very small ($r = .018$). The interaction between treatment and FD/FDI is nor significant ($p < .81$). The HFT score, however, has more influence on the rating than it did in measuring quantity of Spanish produced ($p < .07$) though still not at a significant level. For quality of speech produced, the treatment variable was of little importance to the outcome. Although the LS mean of the supportive group is higher than that of the nonsupportive, it is clearly not at a significant level ($p < .65$).

The relevant statistics for attitude toward learning to speak Spanish are reported in Table 9-4. Although the variance accounted for by the model is low ($r = .037$), the regression coefficients indicate a small, but significant interaction between FD/FI and treatment for the variable attitude ($F = 2.23, p < .14$). (See Figure 9-1 for a graphic representation of this significant interaction.) This is considered significant in the context of ATI research (Pedhazer 1982). The difference between the common regression coefficient and that of the supportive group suggests that in this group field-dependent subjects were more inclined to respond favorably to the statement "Being able to speak a second language is important to me." In the nonsupportive group, the regression coefficient suggests that the treatment did not have a detrimental effect on the attitude of subjects who were field independent. As the HFT score increases (more FI), the favorable response to

TABLE 9-3 Statistics Associated with the Dependent Variable Quality

Source	DF	F Value	PR>F	R-Square	Mean all subjects	STD DEV
Model	3	1.14	0.34	0.018274	2.73	.54

Source	DF	Type III SS	F	PR>F		
HFT★TRTMNT	1	0.01779	0.06	.81		
TRTMNT	1	0.00141	0.00	.95		
HFT	1	0.94312	3.24	.07		

Parameter	Estimate	T for HO: Parameter=0	PR>T	Standard Error of Estimate		
Intercept	2.6288	29.02	.0001	0.091		
HFT★TRMNT						
1	0.0126	1.35	.18	0.009		
2	0.0095	1.19	.23	0.008		
Treatment 1	0.00920	0.07	.94	0.133		

Least Squares Means Treatment	LSMEAN	STD ERR LSMEAN	PROB> |T| HO:LSMEAN=0	PROB> |T| HO:LSM1=LSM2		
1	2.747	0.055	.0001	.65		
2	2.712	0.056	.0001			

TABLE 9-4 Statistics Associated with the Dependent Variable Attitude—"Being able to speak a second language is important to me"

Source Model	DF 3	F Value 2.36	PR > F 0.07	R-Square 0.037304	Mean all subjects 3.78	STD DEV 1.1
Source	DF	Type III SS	F	PR > F		
HFT★TRTMNT	1	2.53074	2.23	.137		
TRTMNT	1	7.01963	6.18	.014		
HFT	1	0.41448	.36	.547		

Parameter	Estimate	T for HO: Parameter = 0	PR > T	Standard Error of Estimate
Intercept	2.7833	19.63	.0001	0.179
HFT★TRMNT				
1	−0.0255	−1.38	.17	0.018
2	0.0108	0.68	.50	0.016
Treatment 1	0.6516	2.49	.01	0.262

Least Squares Means Treatment	LSMEAN	STD ERR LSMEAN	PROB > |T| HO:LSMEAN = 0	PROB > |T| HO:LSM1 = LSM2
1	3.95	0.109	.0001	.0324
2	3.61	0.111	.0001	

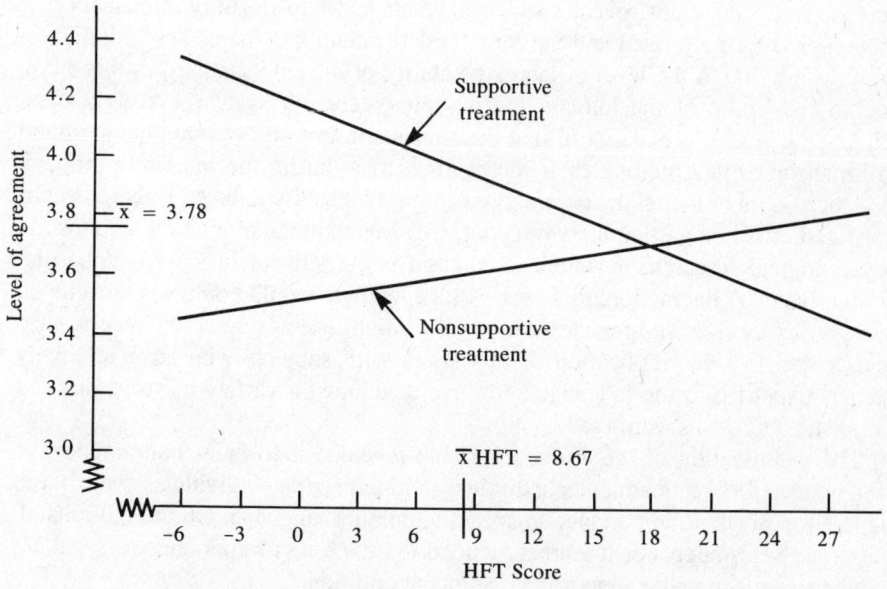

Figure 9.1 "Being able to speak a second language is important to me"

the attitude statement decreases under the supportive treatment. Moreover, very field-independent subjects were apparently unaffected by the nonsupportive treatment. Even under the nonsupportive treatment, however, field-dependent subjects maintained a fairly positive response to the attitude statement. The high LS mean for both groups ($x = 3.78$) suggests that both groups were comprised of individuals (all volunteers) who were interested in learning to speak a FL regardless of the treatment conditions.

In order to further examine the relationship between attitude and performance during the interview, correlations were calculated. Favorable response to this statement (i.e., positive attitude toward learning to speak an L2) correlated significantly with both quantity and quality of Spanish produced $r = .18, p < .01$ and $r = .20, p < .006$, respectively).

SUMMARY AND CONCLUSIONS

Previous psychological research into the cognitive-differentiation construct has focused on the field-dependent individual's reliance on social interaction with other persons to resolve ambiguity. While one might expect that field-dependent FL learners would make use of supportive treatment from an interviewer to facilitate communication, the present study did not confirm this. Moreover, though previous research on L2 learning has suggested that field-independent learners should have an overall advantage in the process of language learning, the present study does not reveal such an advantage when quantity and quality of speech produced are rated and measured independently. Perhaps these conflicting findings are due to the level of language ability of the subjects used in this study and to the limits of the human information processing system. As early-stage language learners, it is doubtful that the subjects in this study were able to attend to much more than getting their messages across during the interview process. Reliance on any other skills or strategies might be heavily reduced if there is concentrated effort on getting the words out, creating a situation quite unlike those in psychological research, in which interaction is carried out in the L1. Also dissimilar from L1 interaction, these early-stage learners would not have a developed system of L2 codes and registers which they might use as part of the face-to-face interaction. Clearly, replication of this study with subjects who have relatively greater expertise in the language and have developed a variety of strategies and linguistic abilities is warranted.

The examination of the attitude variable revealed that under both supportive and nonsupportive treatment conditions, field-dependent individuals were more inclined to attribute importance to speaking another language. On the other hand, the more field-independent learners tended to attach less importance to speaking another language under supportive treatment condition.

The findings of this study suggest several other avenues for further research. First, a comparison of the rating that would have been assigned by the interviewer (who benefitted from the social-interaction strategies of the subjects) with that of the independent raters (who only listened to audio tapes) would reveal whether or not any nonverbal strategies used by the students would significantly affect the rating. Second, an analysis of the relationship between nonverbal strategies and cognitive differentiation would also be revealing. It is possible that field-dependent individuals compensate for having less linguistic ability by employing strategies that field-independent individuals have not developed. Although nonverbal communication strategies are recognized as important in effective communication, they are not considered in oral-proficiency testing procedures that have been proposed (e.g., The ACTFL Proficiency Guidelines). It is precisely these face-to-face strategies that may prove to enhance the communicative proficiency of the FD individual.

NOTES

1. Although many students agreed to participate in all stages of the research, there was a high rate of attrition from the first test to the final interview, which made it necessary to pretest the large number of classes. In order to establish a sample of 187 subjects who completed all aspects of the study, 261 students were pretested. Following the admonition of Cronbach and Snow (1977) with regard to the ideal size of the sample to be tested, the 187 subjects represented what was considered a minimum number for ATI research:
   The ATI study must be much larger than a study where main effects of single correlations are at issue: The ATI effect is a difference of regression slopes. The sampling error of a difference of correlations is 1.4 times the sampling error of each correlation, and differences of slope are similarly hard to pin down. (46)

2. These topics were validated as either structured or unstructured by 16 seniors and graduate students in the Foreign-Language Methods course at Ohio State University, fall quarter, 1984. In order to allow a question to be used, at least 80 percent of those evaluating the topics agreed about their structure or lack of structure. Interviews with instructors in both programs confirmed the appropriateness of the two types of questions and the length of the interview (ten minutes). The level of difficulty of the vocabulary and structures that were required in order to respond to the topics was validated by one of the authors of the text (P. Valencia) and by an instructor in the Spanish program at Ohio State University. They agreed, with minor changes in vocabulary, that the topics were suitable for students at that level of instruction. Because there was no predetermined number, order, or type of question that the subjects were required to address, the internal reliability of the test was not measured.

3. The level of treatment was validated by the evaluation of the videotapes that were made during the pilot study. These tapes were viewed by nine graduate students in Foreign-Language Education at Ohio State University, fall quarter, 1984. On the basis of their evaluation, the interview treatments were judged to be either supportive or nonsupportive.

4. Rushton, Brainard, and Pressley (1983) point out that multiple measures of interrelated variables are important in cognitive-style research; thus, the validity of the assessment of cognitive differentiation will be strengthened by the use of a questionnaire in which the subject may react to the method of treatment.

5. The critical factor with the ATI design that makes it preferable to a factorial design is that each point along the continuous variable is compared with the outcome. By not forcing the continuous variable into high and low blocks or categories, the researcher avoids addressing the problem posed by the tendency of scores to cluster around their mean. The median-split, then, is not deemed appropriate to a design that attempts to relate a continuous variable to the prediction of outcome under different treatment conditions. Cronbach and Snow (1977) also advise against using a three-level design because this not only disregards within-block differences, but also ignores the order of the levels.

All analyses were performed by using the General Linear Models subprogram of the SAS package on the IBM 3081 computer at Ohio State University. The procedure specifies both Type 1 and Type III statistics. The latter are reported here because they reflect the contribution of each variable as it is added last to the equation, thereby eliminating any correlation between that variable and other variables in the equation. The least squares (LS) are reported here instead of the actual means of the two groups because the former statistic allows for different sample size, as well as for the other covariables in the equation.

REFERENCES

ACTFL Proficiency Guidelines. 1982. Hastings on Hudson, NY: ACTFL.
Birckbichler, D., and A. Omaggio. 1978. Diagnosing and responding to individual learner needs. *Modern Language Journal* 62:336-345.
Brown, H. D. 1973. Affective variables in second language acquisition. *Language Learning* 23:223-244.
Brown, H. D. 1980. *Principles of Language Learning and Teaching*. Englewood Cliffs, NJ: Prentice Hall, Inc.
Cronbach, L., and R. Snow. 1977. *Aptitudes and Instructional Methods*. New York: Irvington Publishers, Inc.
d'Anglejan, A., and C. Renaud. 1985. Learner characteristics and second language acquisition: a multivariate study of adult immigrants and some thoughts on methodology. *Language Learning* 35:1-19.
de Groot, J. C. 1968. Emotional climate of an experimental situation, interaction patterns, and field style of subject. Ph.D. dissertation, University of Cincinnati. Dissertation Abstracts International 30:843B-844B.
Freedman, N., J. O'Hanlon, P. Oltman, and H. A. Witkin. 1972. The imprint of psychological differentiation on kinetic behavior in varying communicative contexts. *Journal of Abnormal Psychology* 79:239-258.
French, J. W., R. B. Ekstrom, and L. A. Price. 1963. *Manual for Kit of Reference Tests for Cognitive Factors*. Princeton: Educational Testing Service.
Gates, D. W. 1971. Verbal conditioning, transferal of operant level "speech style" as functions of cognitive style. Ph.D. dissertation, City University of New York. Dissertation Abstracts International 32:3634B.
Hansen, J., and C. Stansfield. 1981. The relationship of field dependence-independence cognitive styles to foreign language achievement. *Language Learning* 31:349-367.
Jackson, D. N., S. Messick, and C. T. Myers. 1964. Evaluation of group and individual forms of the embedded figures measures of field independence. *Educational and Psychological Measurement* 24:177-192.
McLaughlin, B. 1980. Theory and research in second language learning: an emerging paradigm. *Language Learning* 30:331-350.
Naiman, N., M. Fröhlich, H. H. Stern, and A. Todesco. 1978. *The Good Language Learner*. Toronto: Ontario Institute for Studies in Education.
Parry, T. 1984. The relationship of selected dimensions of learner cognitive style, aptitude, and general intelligence factors to selected foreign language proficiency tasks of second-year students of Spanish at the secondary level. Ph.D. dissertation, Ohio State University, 1983.
Pedhazer, E. J. 1982. *Multiple Regression in Behavioral Research*. NY: Holt, Rinehart, and Winston.
Pennycook, Alstair. 1985. Actions speak louder than words: paralanguage, communication, and education. In *TESOL Quarterly* 19:259-282.
Reiss, M. 1981. Helping the unsuccessful language learner. *Modern Language Journal* 65:121-128.

Ruble, D. N., and C. Y. Nakamura. 1972. Task orientation versus social orientation in young children and their attention to relevant social cues. *Child Development* 43:471-480.

Rushton, J. P., C. J. Brainard, and M. Pressley. 1983. Behavioral development and construct validity: the principle of aggregation. *Psychological Bulletin* 94:18-38.

Tucker, G. R., E. Hamayan, and F. Genesee. 1976. Affective, cognitive and social factors in second language acquisition. *Canadian Modern Language Review* 32:214-226.

Valencia, P., and F. Merlonghi. 1980. *En contacto*. Boston: Houghton Mifflin Company.

Witkin, H.A. 1978. Cognitive styles in personal and cultural adaptation. *Heinz Werner Lecture Series Volume III*. Worcester, MA: Clark University Press.

Witkin, H.A. and D.R. Goodenough. 1977. Field dependence and interpersonal behavior. *Psychological Bulletin* 34:661-689.

Yorozuya, R., and J. Oller. 1980. Oral proficiency scales: construct validity and the halo effect. *Language Learning* 30:135-153.

APPENDIX

Sample of structured-question cards:
2
When you were young, how did you spend your summer vacations?
Sleeping?
Swimming?
Playing with friends?
Attending summer school?
Reading?

5
What time did you go to bed last night?
Did you fall asleep immediately?
How long did you sleep?
Did you dream?
When did you wake up?
Were you tired this morning?

Sample of unstructured-question cards:
21
You were on your way to class one morning when you remembered something important. Tell me about it.

15
Tell me what you do in the morning before class.

CHAPTER 10
Linguistic and Communicative Competence: Reassessing Foreign Language Aptitude[1]

Elaine K. Horwitz
University of Texas at Austin

INTRODUCTION

In recent years the development of communicative competence has increasingly been cited as the goal of foreign language (FL) instruction. Second language (L2) communicative competence involves the production of novel utterances that are appropriate to the demands of the communicative situation and that flexibly adapt to changing listener requirements. The abilities that facilitate the development of communicative competence may be different from those that have been found to relate to the development of linguistic competence.

In order to determine the abilities that are necessary for L2 communicative competence, it is first necessary to describe what a learner must be able to do "to function in a truly communicative setting, that is, in a spontaneous interchange involving one or more persons" (Savignon 1978, T-15).

Researchers in first language (L1) acquisition have found the concept of perspective-taking useful in the description of the development of L1 communicative competence. Flavell and his colleagues (Flavell et al. 1968) and Glucksberg and his colleagues (Glucksberg, Krauss, and Higgins 1975) have found that the ability to adapt one's communications to varying listener requirements emerges at a later age and develops at a more gradual pace than does linguistic competence. Other researchers (Feffer and Schotliff 1966; Hale and Delia 1976) have found that adults vary considerably in their ability to devise and make use of communicative strategies that are appropriate to different situations and effective in achieving their desired goals. The ability to adapt one's language to changing interpersonal conditions appears to depend not only on one's knowledge of the applicable linguistic and sociocultural rules for language usage, but also on one's ability to take the perspective of the other person and "read" the requirements of the communicative situation. Even though native speakers are linguistically and sociolinguistically competent, their communicative competence is seen to vary due to differential abilities in these social-cognitive domains.

In keeping with a perspective-taking approach to communicative competence, this study will define L2 communicative competence as constructive language use. To be truly communicatively competent in an L2, an individual must "construct" utterances, taking into account the other's perspective, situational requirements, and cultural norms. The emphasis here is on a speaker's facility in flexibly adapting and managing language productions to changing definitions of the situation, varying role relationships between interlocutors and different interpretations of what the other person means. This conceptualization suggests that the ability to generate multiple perspectives and to entertain a number of possible relationships among these perspectives would be an adaptive advantage for communicating competently.

This study will report on research that seeks to distinguish the abilities that facilitate FL linguistic competence from those that facilitate the development of communicative competence and then place the findings within the perspective of current conceptualizations of the processes of L2 acquisition.

The work applies the framework of Conceptual Systems Theory (Harvey, Hunt, and Schroder 1961) to FL learning. Conceptual Systems Theory is a developmentally founded theory of personality development and organization. Individuals are seen to vary with regard to dimensional and integrative complexity. Dimensional complexity refers to the number of perspectives an individual can generate on a given body of information, while integrative complexity refers to the number and interconnectedness of the rules the individual uses to organize the different perspectives. Dimensional and integrative complexity taken together are referred to as cognitive complexity. These dimensions and rules are said to mediate between environmental stimuli and behavioral performances. The theory postulates that individual conceptual development moves in the direction of increasing dimensional and integrative complexity of the conceptual system. This developmental continuum is often referred to as concrete-abstract.

Gardner and Lambert (1972) have shown a relationship between learner attitudes and L2 achievement; however, the content of the attitudes seems to vary with the context of the language-learning situation. The attitudinal complex associated with increasing abstractness suggests an individual who is generally open to acquiring an L2 and the associated cultural knowledge. More abstract individuals show low use of stereotypes, low authoritarianism, low dogmatism, and low identification with normative American values (Harvey 1967; Schroder 1971).

L2 researchers have suggested that empathy (Guiora, Brannon, and Dull 1972; Horwitz and Horwitz 1977), creativity (Bartz 1974), tolerance of ambiguity and risktaking (Naiman, Fröhlich, and Stern 1975) are related to the development of L2 communicative competence. These same characteristics have also been shown to be behavioral correlates of increasing complexity (Harvey 1967; Schroder, Driver, and Streufert 1967).

Hunt (1971) has applied Conceptual Systems Theory to the educational context. His measure of conceptual development, known as conceptual level (CL), indexes both cognitive complexity and interpersonal maturity. Four developmental stages are postulated below.

Stage 0: The dominant individual characteristic is self-centeredness. The individual does not take into account the thoughts and feelings of others. Typical reactions are impulsive, in a "negative unsocialized manner," or defensive.

Stage 1: The dominant concern is with social acceptability. The individual conceptualizes the world in simple dichotomous terms (e.g., right-wrong, good-bad), and "is sensitive to authority figures (teachers, parents) and how they would behave or what they would expect of him in different situations."

Stage 2: The individual is more open to other people's ideas and is more tolerant of uncertainty, ambiguity, and differences of opinion. Although more aware of outside perspectives, he makes no attempt to integrate them into his own decision making. The individual "is very much concerned with his own thoughts and is striving of independence."

Stage 3: The individual incorporates varying perspectives when seeking a solution to a problem because of his "concern for his own and others' ideas and feelings, and about the possible consequences of his decision." He is independent, but seeks compromises to problems if they do not compromise his principles and independence. He accepts full responsibility for his actions, "is aware of himself, of his relationship with others and how they view him." (Stages adapted from Hunt, Butler, Noy and Rosser 1978, 5)

The purpose of this study was to determine if the social cognitive abilities associated with conceptual level contribute to competence in an FL. It was hypothesized that higher conceptual level would be positively related to communicative competence while traditional FL aptitude measures would be positively related to linguistic competence.

METHOD

SUBJECTS

Female students attending five second year French classes in four secondary schools from a large Southwestern school district served as research subjects (n = 61). The subjects ranged in age from fourteen to eighteen (median age was 15;11), from ninth to twelfth grade.

The five classes used in the study were chosen after a period of classroom observation and teacher interviews confirmed that creative language use was a functioning instructional goal. All of the classes devoted approximately one-third of class time to oral-communication activities during the three observation visits, although the oral activities themselves took a variety of forms. All of the classes followed closely the sequence and activities set out in the textbook, *Son et Sens Level I*, (Valdman, Belasco, and Steiner 1972). The classes were in the last quarter of the book when the study was undertaken. The four teachers involved had from three to twenty-three years of teaching experience. Two held master's degrees and the other two were engaged in graduate study. One teacher was a native speaker of French (she was French-Canadian) and another had lived in France. All four of the teachers used French frequently in the classroom for giving directions and for spontaneous role-playing and conversations.

INSTRUMENTATION

Conceptual level was assessed by the Paragraph Completion Method (PCM) (Hunt, Butler, Noy and Rosser 1978). The PCM is a semiprojective instrument that consists of six incomplete sentences. The incomplete sentences were designed to assess how a person deals with conflict or uncertainty ("Criticism," "Not sure," or "Don't agree") and how he or she thinks about rule structure and authority relations ("Rules," "Parents," or "Told"). Subjects are told that they have three minutes to add at least three sentences to each stimulus. Scoring was performed by an experienced rater trained by one of the authors of the PCM. Based on the underlying structure, a score of 0 to 3 was assigned to each response. A higher score reflected a more integrated response, with multiple perspectives on the stimulus, while a lower score reflected a less integrated response, with fewer perspectives. (Sample responses are included in the Appendix.) The conceptual level score is the average of the three highest scores. Interrater reliability on the PCM typically exceeds $r = .85$.

FL aptitude was assessed by the short form of the Modern Language Aptitude Test (MLAT) (Carroll and Sapon 1959). The short form includes three multiple choice subtests: Phonetic Encoding, Grammatical Sensitivity, and Rote Memory for Foreign Language Vocabulary. The Phonetic Encoding subtest calls on the subject to decipher an English word that has been written phonetically and then to choose the word's synonym from among five words. In the Grammatical Sensitivity subtest, the subject reads a sentence with one underlined word. The subject's task is to choose from among five underlined words in another sentence the word that has the same grammatical function (role in the sentence) as the underlined word in the model sentence. In the Rote Memory subtest, the subject is given four minutes to memorize a list of Kurdish words and their English equivalents. Without looking back at the list, the subject must then choose the English equivalent of each Kurdish word from a list of five words. Scoring was performed by the experimenter in accordance with the protocol provided in the test manual.

The Pimsleur Writing Test, French Level 1 (PFWT) (Pimsleur 1967) was used to assess linguistic competence. This is a standardized discrete-point test of French grammar. Scoring was performed by the experimenter in accordance with the test manual. Level 1 was selected because the grammatical concepts tested corresponded the closest to the grammatical concepts presented during the first two years of French study in this school system.

Three oral French Tasks, adapted from Bartz (1974), were used to assess communicative competence. In the first oral task (paragraph task), the subjects were asked to relate in French the information from a paragraph that they had read in English. In the second task (picture task), the subjects were shown picture 13B of the Thematic Apperception Test ("Young Mr. Lincoln"). The black and white picture shows a boy sitting in front of an ambiguous wooden structure. They were asked to talk about the picture first in English and then in French. The subjects were told that they could say anything they wanted about the picture. They could describe it, tell the story behind it, give their feelings, and so forth. In the third task (interview task), the subjects were asked ten questions about themselves in French. Five questions had been taken from oral exercises included in their textbook and five were created for the experimental task, using vocabulary and structures that they had studied. Scoring of the three tasks was performed on number-coded audio tapes by the experimenter, who was blind to the subjects' scores on the other measures. First, the experimenter listened to the entire set of protocols to identify the range of subject performance. A global score of from 1 to 5 was assigned to the subject's performance on each task. A score of 1 indicated that the subject had communicated essentially nothing in French, and a score of 5 indicated that the subject's performance was outstanding within the range of the group. The experimenter concentrated on amount of communication, fluency (speed and lack of hesitation), ability to incorporate experimenter cues, and complexity and length of the structures used. A total communicative competence score was computed for each subject by totaling the scores on the three oral tasks. A reliability check on a random sample of twenty-five tapes was independently performed by a second rater after she listened to a training tape to familiarize herself with the general scoring criteria and the range of the sample. The interrater reliability of $r = .81$, $p < .001$ was considered quite acceptable, considering that the rater training had been minimal.

PROCEDURE

The PCM, MLAT, and PFWT were administered by the experimenter to the individual classes as a group. The oral protocols were administered individually by the experimenter outside of the classrooms during the subject's regular French period and were audio recorded. When the subjects arrived, the experimenter attempted to put them at ease by engaging in casual conversation.

During the first two tasks (relating information about a paragraph, and talking about a picture), the experimenter attempted to facilitate response by smiling, nodding, laughing appropriately, looking interested, and helping to formulate words. After each subject completed the first task, the experimenter said, "That was real good; that's not easy to do." By pretending to speak and understand only French, the experimenter did somewhat less to facilitate response during the third task (interview), although an attempt was made to help the subjects to understand with gestures and examples. A friendly demeanor was retained.

Data analysis was performed using version 6.50 of the *Statistical Package for the Social Sciences* (Nie, Hull, Jenkins, Steinbrenner, and Bent 1975). Pearson product-moment correlations were computed among the aptitude variables and the tests of linguistic and communicative competence. Two-tailed tests of significance were applied in all of the statistical analyses.

RESULTS

The means and standard deviations for the aptitude and achievement variables are presented in Table 10-1. Table 10.2 is a correlation matrix for the correlations among the various criterion measures.

As can be seen in Table 10-2, a highly significant relationship ($r = .54, p < .001$) is found between conceptual level and communicative competence. This finding indicates that more abstract individuals tend to display higher levels of communicative competence. The results also show a significant positive correlation between aptitude and linguistic competence ($r = .41, p < .01$). In other words, higher levels of aptitude are associated with greater linguistic competence. Grammatical sensitivity appears to be primarily responsible for the relationship between aptitude and linguistic competence ($r = ,49, p < .001$ between grammatical sensitivity and linguistic competence), as neither phonetic encoding nor rote

TABLE 10-1 Means and Standard Deviations of Aptitude and Achievement Variables

	CL	MLAT3	MLAT4	MLAT5	MLATTOT	CC	PIMTOT
M	1.56	18.46	20.55	17.70	56.86	8.47	34.37
SD	.33	7.55	8.02	5.24	14.63	2.85	13.03

CL = Conceptual Level; MLAT3 = Phonetic Encoding; MLAT4 = Grammatical Sensitivity; MLAT5 = Rote Memory for Foreign Language Material; MLATTOT = MLAT Total Score; CC = Communicative Competence; PIMTOT = Pimsleur Writing Test Total Score.

TABLE 10-2 Intercorrelations of Aptitude and Achievement Variables

	MLAT3	MLAT4	MLAT5	MLATTOT	CC	PIMTOT
CL	.27*	.57***	.24	.54***	.54***	.48***
	(59)	(60)	(60)	(59)	(55)	(59)
MLAT3		.32**	.04	.71***	.19	.12
		(59)	(59)	(59)	(55)	(58)
MLAT4			.26*	.81***	.46***	.49***
			(60)	(59)	(55)	(59)
MLAT5				.52***	.15	.23
				(59)	(55)	(58)
MLATTOT					.40**	.41**
					(55)	(58)
CC						.73***
						(55)

CL = Conceptual Level; MLAT3 = Phonetic Encoding; MLAT4 = Grammatical Sensitivity; MLAT5 = Rote Memory for Foreign Language Vocabulary; MLATTOT = MLAT Total Score; CC = Communicative Competence; PIMTOT = Pimsleur Writing Test Total Score; numbers in parentheses refer to number of subjects.
*$p < .05$ **$p < .01$ ***$p < .001$

memory for foreign vocabulary is significantly related to linguistic competence ($r = .12, p < .38; r = .23, p < .07$).

Table 10-2 also shows a significant relationship between conceptual level and aptitude ($r = .54, p < .001$). Since both conceptual level and foreign language aptitude appear to contribute significantly to both communicative competence and linguistic competence, partial correlation coefficients were computed. The partial correlation coefficients permit an assessment of each aptitude's contribution to achievement without the confounding effect of the other. With foreign language aptitude controlled, conceptual level is significantly related to communicative competence ($r = .42, p < .002$, two-tailed test). This finding indicates that conceptual level and communicative competence are associated independent of foreign language aptitude. Controlling for conceptual level, foreign language aptitude and linguistic competence are not significantly related ($r = .20, p < .135$, two-tailed test), suggesting that the relationship between foreign language aptitude and linguistic competence is not independent of conceptual level.

In order to specify more clearly the functioning of the aptitude variables in the development of linguistic and communicative competence, commonality analyses were performed to examine the unique and common contributions of CL and Grammatical Sensitivity to French achievement (see Kerlinger and Pedhazur 1973, 297-305, for a description of the commonality analysis procedure). As seen in Table 10-3, CL and Grammatical Sensitivity together account for 32 percent of the variance in the communicative competence score. Of this 32 percent, 11 percent is attributable to the unique contribution of CL, 3 percent to Grammatical Sensitivity, and 18 percent to their joint contribution. For linguistic competence,

TABLE 10-3 Commonality Analyses

Criterion	R^2	Uniqueness	Uniqueness	Joint
		CL	MLAT4	
CCTOT	.32	.11	.03	.18
PIMTOT	.30	.05	.07	.18

CL = Conceptual Level; MLAT4 = Grammatical Sensitivity; CCTOT = Total Communicative Competence Score; PIMTOT = Pimsleur Writing Test Total Score.

18 percent of the variance is again attributable to the joint contribution of CL and Grammatical Sensitivity, with an additional 5 percent attributable to CL and 7 percent to Grammatical Sensitivity. These results indicate that most of the apportioned variance in both communicative and linguistic competence is due to the shared variance of CL and Grammatical Sensitivity. However, over a third of the apportioned variance in communicative competence is attributable to the unique contribution of CL. The level of linguistic competence seems to be mainly dependent on elements that CL and Grammatical Sensitivity share. While the shared elements play the largest role in communicative competence, there also appears to be a factor unique to CL.

DISCUSSION AND CONCLUSION

Results from previous research on L2 learning and from the present study suggest that several specific components of CL either individually or in conjunction are responsible for the relationship between CL and French achievement. Positive attitudes toward other culture groups, low ethnocentrism and low authoritarianism, empathy, tolerance of ambiguity, and field independence, variables that have shown previous relationships with L2 learning, are also associated with increasing cognitive complexity and interpersonal maturity. Conceptual level appears to encompass aspects of these characteristics, which probably accounts for part of its relationship with French achievement.

How these component variables facilitate FL learning performance can be suggested. Since high CL individuals are able to reorganize information in different ways with high levels of self-awareness, the self-monitoring process advanced by Krashen (1981) would appear to be aided. Moreover, the high CL individual is more of a risk taker, who is willing to experiment with new language structures; the high CL individual views language production errors as incorrect guesses rather than as a source of personal embarrassment. In this sense, the high CL individual approximates what Krashen has called the Super Monitor User (1982). Finally, perhaps one of the most important assets of the high CL individual in FL learning is the ability to generate rules from examples. No language class can present the entire corpus of a language or its entire set of rules. At some point, students must be able to generate their own rules through contact with the target language. In addition to the ability to generate their own rules, high CL individuals are better able to deal with the low structure and the high information load of the FL communication situation.

It was argued that two types of foreign language achievement, linguistic competence and communicative competence, were facilitated by two types of foreign language aptitude. The hypotheses stated that the cognitive abilities associated with the Modern Language Aptitude Test (Phonetic Encoding, Grammatical Sensitivity, and Rote Memory for Foreign Language Vocabulary) would primarily associate with linguistic competence, while the cognitive and social-psychological abilities associated with conceptual level (integrative complexity and interpersonal maturity) would primarily associate with communicative competence. Although there was support for these aptitude-achievement relationships, the picture of foreign language aptitude which emerges from the data appears more complex than these hypotheses suggest.

Of primary importance is the high intercorrelation among all variables. Since linguistic and communicative competence were found to be strongly related, it appears that the development of communicative competence in French is accompanied by a corresponding development of linguistic competence where communicative competence is clearly a focus of classroom activities. The two aptitude variables were also highly related. Commonality analysis indicated that most of the variance accounted for in the criterion measures was due to the joint contribution of conceptual level and the Grammatical Sensitivity subtest of the MLAT. In addition, Grammatical Sensitivity was the only MLAT section that achieved consistent positive significant correlations with the criterion measures. (The only other significant correlation for an MLAT subtest was the relationship $r = .33$, $p < .012$ between Rote Memory for Foreign Language Vocabulary and Part 3 of the PFWT.) In fact, the addition of Rote Memory and Phonetic Encoding to form a total foreign language aptitude score attenuated the relationships between Grammatical Sensitivity and French achievement. Grammatical Sensitivity is also the subtest that achieved the highest correlation with CL ($r = .57$, $p < .001$). This subtest calls on the student to read a model sentence with an underlined word and then to find a word in another sentence which performs the same grammatical function as the underlined word. Although grammatical terms are avoided, knowledge of grammatical categories and the function of words in sentences is required. The student must induce the grammatical rule from the example and then identify another example of that rule.

When linguistic competence is the criterion, almost all of the apportioned variance is attributable to the joint contribution of Grammatical Sensitivity and CL. Inductive reasoning would seem to be one of the abilities that is common to the Grammatical Sensitivity, CL, and linguistic competence tasks. Tomlinson and Hunt (1972) found that high CL students were better able than low CL students to induce rules from examples and then to apply the induced rules. At least three of the four sections on the PFhr WT also appear to require inductive reasoning ability. The student must decide which grammatical rules pertain and then apply them.

On the other hand, when communicative competence is the criterion, commonality analysis indicates that CL uniquely contributes one-third of the variance. It appears that inductive reasoning abilities are not sufficient in performing the communicative tasks. During the oral testing, the student has little time to consciously seek out and apply linguistic rules. Krashen (1981) argues that oral testing reaches an individual's underlying language competence without resort to a conscious application of rules, which he calls a monitor. This underlying competence is primarily developed through the language-acquisition experiences of listening and reading. He believes that individual cognitive differences primarily affect the development of the monitor through language learning but that they have little effect on the language-acquisition process. Individual differences in language acquisition are due to the amount of comprehensible input an individual has. Affective differences can, on the other hand, predispose an individual to interacting with the necessary language input. The social-psychological characteristics associated with CL—tolerance of ambiguity, empathy, interpersonal maturity, low ethnocentrism, low authoritarianism—suggest a person open to the acquisition experiences afforded in the observed classes. Although the evidence presented here is admittedly speculative, there is preliminary evidence to suggest that the cognitive abilities associated with CL, especially inductive reasoning, contributed to the development of linguistic competence, while the interpersonal factors contributed to the development of communicative competence.

NOTES

1. This is a revised and expanded version of a paper that originally appeared in *Studies in Second Language Acquisition* 5 (1982).

REFERENCES

Bartz, W. H. 1974. A study of the relationship of certain learner factors with the ability to communicate in a second language (German) for the development of measures of communicative competence. Ph.D. dissertation, Ohio State University.
Carroll, J. B., and S. M. Sapon. 1959. *Modern Language Aptitude Test, MLAT Manual*. New York: The Psychological Corporation.
Feffer, M., and L. Schotliff. 1966. Decenter implications of social interactions. *Journal of Personality and Social Psychology* 4:415-422.
Flavell, H. H., P. I. Botkin, C. C. Fry, J. W. Wright, and P. G. Jarvis. 1968. *The Development of Role-Taking and Communicative Skills in Children*. New York: John Wiley and Sons.
Gardner, R. C., and W. E. Lambert. 1972. *Attitudes and Motivation in Second Language Learning*. Rowley, MA: Newbury House.
Glucksberg, S., R. M. Krauss, and T. Higgins. 1975. The development of communication skills in children. In *Review of Child Development Research* vol. 4, F. Horwitz (ed.), 305-345. Chicago: University Chicago Press.
Guiora, A. Z., R. C. L. Brannon, and C. Y. Dull. 1972. Empathy and second language learn-

ing. *Language Learning* 22 (1): 111-130.
Hale, C. L. and J. G. Delia. 1976. Cognitive complexity and social perspective taking. *Communications Monographs* 43: 195-203.
Harvey, O. J. 1967. Conceptual systems and attitude change. In *Attitude, Ego Involvement, and Change*, C.W. Sherif and M. Sherif (eds.), 201-226. New York: John Wiley and Sons.
Harvey, O. J., D. E. Hunt, and H. M. Schroder. 1961. *Conceptual Systems and Personality Organization.* New York: John Wiley and Sons.
Horwitz, E. K., and M. B. Horwitz. 1977. Bridging individual differences: empathy and communicative competence. In *Personalizing Foreign Language Instruction: Learning Styles and Teaching Options*, R. A. Schultz (ed.), 109-118. Skokie: National Textbook Company.
Hunt, D. E. 1971. *Matching Models in Education: The Coordination of Teaching Methods with Student Characteristics.* Toronto: The Ontario Institute for Studies in Education.
Hunt, D. E., L. F. Butler, J. E. Noy, and M. E. Rosser. 1978. *Assessing Conceptual Level by the Paragraph Completion Method.* Toronto: The Ontario Institute for Studies in Education.
Kerlinger, F. N., and E. J. Pedhazur. 1973. *Multiple Regression in Behavioral Research.* New York: Holt, Rinehart, and Winston.
Krashen, S. D. 1981. *Second Language Acquisition and Second Language Learning.* Oxford: Pergamon Press.
Krashen, S. D. 1982. *Principles and Practice in Second Language Acquisition.* Oxford: Pergamon Press.
Naiman, N., M. Fröhlich and H. H. Stern. 1975. *The Good Language Learner.* Toronto: The Ontario Institute for Studies in Education.
Nie, N. H., C. H. Hull, J. G. Jenkins, K. L. Steinbrenner, and D. H. Bent. 1975. *Statistical Package for the Social Sciences (SPSS)*, 2nd ed. New York: McGraw-Hill.
Pimsleur, P. 1967. *Pimsleur French Writing Test: Level 1, Manual.* New York: The Psychological Corporation.
Savignon, S. J. 1978. Teaching for communication. In *Voix et visage de la France - Level 1: Teacher's Edition.* R. Coulombe, J. C. Barre, C. Frostle, N. Poulin, S. J. Papalia (eds.) Chicago: Rand McNally.
Schroder, H. M. 1971. Conceptual complexity and personality organization. In *Personality Theory and Information Processing*, H. M. Schroder and P. Suedfeld (eds.), 240-273. New York: Ronald Press.
Schroder, H. M., M. J. Driver, and S. Streufert. 1967. *Human Information Processing.* New York: Holt, Rinehart, and Winston.
Tomlinson, P. D., and D. E. Hunt. 1972. Differential effects of rule-example order as a function of learner conceptual level. *Canadian Journal of Behavioural Science* 3:237-245.
Valdman, A., S. Belasco, and F. Steiner. 1972. *Son et Sens, Level 1.* Glenview, IL: Scott, Foresman, and Company.

APPENDIX

Sample Responses to Two Paragraph Completion Stems
What I think about rules...

I don't like them. Rules are made to break. I feel they are also made to get you into trouble.
Score 0

Rules are good. They teach us different things. Some rules I don't like because they are too strict. Some rules need to be stricter.
Score 1

I think some rules are very good but some of them are a little over done. They don't give you a free will to do some things you want to or have to do, to do your best. Some are very useful to us too.
Score 2

Rules, if they're not too restrictive of my abilities to make my own judgments when the situation warrants it, are okay. I don't need rules for every detail of my life.
Score 3

When I am criticized...

When I am criticized, I will criticize them about something because I don't like to be criticized.
Score 0

If someone tells me I am doing something wrong I guess I would try to correct myself or if I think I was not I would fight back. I don't think I would get mad at him or her. I would just try to do better.
Score 1

I usually take what that person has told me and use it for improving what I did or do wrong. Some criticism that is just meant to hurt, I ignore.
Score 2

I look at myself and wonder if this is constructive criticism. I also look at the person who criticized me and how qualified he/she is to make the statement. Then I weigh all the sides and decide how valuable the criticism is.
Score 3

CHAPTER 11
The Linguistic and Communicative Functions of Foreign Language Teacher Talk

Barbara H. Wing
University of New Hampshire

INTRODUCTION

As Kelly noted in 1969, the question of using the target language as the teaching vehicle is the subject of continuing vigorous debate. In the late nineteenth and early twentieth centuries, advocates of the Direct and of the Natural methods rejected the use of the native language, as well as the traditional instructional techniques of translation and rule learning, in favor of extensive conversational practice. De Sauzé, for example, reported that "classes in which the foreign language was used exclusively as the medium for instruction were showing appreciably better results than others in which English was used for part of the time" (1929, 18).

The debate has been revived recently by the introduction of the construct of "intake," a term first used by Corder (1967) to describe the "input" that is understood and enables a person to acquire more language. Researchers such as Ellis (1981), Gaies (1979), Krashen (1981, 1982), Leemann (1982), and Newport, Gleitman, and Gleitman (1977) have analyzed the learner input of caretakers, teachers, and native speakers. Their results reveal communicative patterns that foster involvement on the part of the listener/learner. They provide support for the contention that teacher talk in the target language, when tailored appropriately to the situation, provides an environment in which students can make significant progress toward proficiency in that language. (See also Brooks 1964; Chastain 1976; Rivers, Azevedo, Heflin, and Opler 1974; Moskowitz 1976.)

Teacher talk in the foreign language (FL) classroom is a critical variable of significant importance and complexity. The active use of two languages, native and target, and the dual instructional objectives of linguistic and communicative competence create a unique educational setting. Systematic investigation of how teachers function in this bilingual, bifunctional environment can provide information about the nature of input in this specialized classroom setting. This information is necessary for an understanding of how learning occurs in FL classes.

BACKGROUND

During the past two decades, researchers in education, linguistics, and logic have analyzed classroom communication to identify patterns of language use that transcend idiosyncratic behavior (Bellack, Hyman, Smith, and Kliebard 1966; Hough and Duncan 1970; Flanders 1970; Lofflin, Biddle, Barron, and Marlin 1973; Smith and Meux 1962). According to Dunkin and Biddle's (1974) comprehensive analysis of research on teaching, these investigations have the potential for making a major impact on education.

Researchers in foreign language education have likewise examined oral communication as it occurs in FL classrooms. Wing (1981) identified three types of observational systems: (1) adaptations by Moskowitz (1971), Rothfarb (1970), and Wragg (1970) of Flanders' Interaction Analysis Categories system (FIAC) (1970); (2) instruments specifically designed to investigate verbal behaviors characteristic of FL classrooms, such as those designed by Fanselow (1977), Jarvis (1968), and Omaggio (1982); and (3) open-ended systems (Bailey 1977) in which the researcher chooses the particular variables to be studied.

As might be expected, the behavioral and attitudinal categories used in these observational systems vary according to the type of system. Those instruments based on Flander's FIAC (1970) reflect concern for describing direct and indirect teacher influence by means of generic teacher behaviors as well as by means of behaviors specific to the FL classroom (e.g., "Models," "Directs Pattern Drill," "Choral," "Uses English"). Instruments designed specifically to analyze behaviors generally found only in FL classrooms (e.g., Jarvis 1968) include behaviors that distinguish between "real" (e.g., "Evoking student response,""Information explanation") and "drill" (e.g.,"Repetition reinforcement," "Modeling or correcting") use of the target language. Bailey's example of an open-ended system includes categories such as "Teacher Questions" and "Teacher English"; however, it is possible to designate any variable of interest to the researcher.

The fundamental difference between the analysis presented in this study and other studies of FL teacher talk is the conceptual framework that underlies the study. This framework, which attempts to deal with the complexity of the variable of language use from a functional perspective, postulates that all teacher talk can be described in terms of linguistic and communicative functions.

The complexity of the language use variable is characterized by the simultaneous interaction of three distinct components of FL teaching:

1. the presence and active use of two languages, the native and target, in the course of instruction;
2. the dual nature, expressed in terms of linguistic and communicative competence, of the goals of language instruction;
3. the patterns of verbal behavior, called "rules of the classroom game" by Wittgenstein (1958), used by teachers and students in classroom situations, regardless of the subject matter under consideration

The following research questions guide the study: What patterns of target language use, expressed in terms of linguistic and communicative functions, do FL teachers exhibit in the classroom? What kinds of FL teachers, as identified by specific variables associated with teacher formative experiences and teacher properties are (1) high, average, and low users of the target language, and (2) high, average, and low target language communicators?

METHODS AND PROCEDURES

The sample for the study consisted of fifteen self-selected teachers of second year Spanish classes in eleven secondary schools in New Hampshire. The data, generated from audio tape recordings of three class sessions of each of the fifteen teachers over a four-month period, provided the basis for analysis.

RESEARCH INSTRUMENT

The three components of the language use variable mentioned above form the basis for the development of the observational system described in this study. The rationale for the development of the system takes into account important developments in FL teaching in the last decade.

The definition of the constructs of linguistic competence and communicative competence represented the major development in FL education in the 1970s. Linguistic competence refers to the ability to comprehend and produce the discrete phonological, morphological, syntactical, and lexical elements of a language (Hymes 1971, Clark 1972, Savignon 1972). Examples of linguistic competence include identifying target language sounds in minimal pairs, being able to provide the appropriate verb form to complete a sentence, or supplying the appropriate relative pronoun to combine two simple sentences. It implies a conscious knowledge of the rules of the target language as well as the ability to apply those rules in what might be called "microlinguistic" tasks. Communicative competence, on the other hand, is the capacity to send and receive messages (oral and written) in the target language as demonstrated by tests designed to measure comprehensibility and appropriateness (Savignon 1972, Schultz and Bartz 1975). Examples of communicative competence include being able to locate sites on a map by means of verbal instructions in the target language, providing appropriate information in response to a request, or expressing an idea or opinion not known to the listener or reader. It implies a more global approach to language use that focuses on the messages being transmitted rather than on the specific forms that are used in the transmission (Clark 1972).

Activities and materials for developing linguistic competence tended to dominate both the grammar-translation and audiolingual approaches to FL teaching in the 1970s. The classroom manifestation of the new construct of communicative competence was the development and implementation of meaningful exercises, simulated testing situations, and small-group communicative activities. These individual components of an overall approach to developing the students' communicative competence have been shown by Joiner (1977), Savignon (1972), and Schulz (1977) to be related to increased student performance and more positive attitudes toward language learning. All too often, these communicative activities have been added to an already full curriculum at a cost of extra time and effort on the part of the teacher.

At the same time, the potential for natural communicative exchanges between teacher and students and among students has been overlooked. Realization of that potential depends upon the teacher. Specifically, it depends upon teacher talk, the predominant activity in the classroom and the primary source of input and intake. Teacher talk is a manifestation of the teacher's linguistic and communicative competencies in the target language. It is competence realized in functional performance in the classroom, analysis of which reveals how teachers use their own linguistic and communicative competencies.

The vehicle for the analysis of these functions is the Linguistic/Communicative Functions Analysis System (L/C-FAS). In this system, functions are operationally defined for the purpose of analyzing teacher verbal behavior in the FL classroom. These functions, like the competencies, can be described in linguistic and communicative dimensions.

By definition, linguistic functions constitute the use of language as a system composed of forms. The objective is to concentrate on the linguistic elements of the language. The primary purposes of teacher talk in this function are to demonstrate, elicit practice of, and reinforce responses in the phonological, morphological, syntactical, and lexical systems of the language. Teacher behaviors characteristic of this function are Modeling, Cueing, and Reinforcing. In each case, the function of the teacher talk is to call attention to the forms that comprise the systems of the language.

Communicative functions, on the other hand, constitute the use of language as a vehicle for sending messages. The objective is to express ideas, feelings, desires, and opinions. The primary intent of teacher talk in this function is to convey meaningful messages in the target language. Teacher behaviors characteristic of this function, which were adapted from a system developed by Bellack et al. (1966), are Structuring, Soliciting, Responding, and Reacting. In each case, the function of the teacher talk is to transmit information to the students in the target language.

A detailed description of the Linguistic/Communicative Functions Analysis System is found in the Appendix. The focal point of the system is the Protocol Analysis Instrument (PAI), which is given in Figure 11-1. As seen in the figure, teacher talk is categorized in terms of Function, (linguistic or communicative), Behavior (verbal moves the teacher is making), Content (what the teacher is talking about), Language (native or target), and Duration (number of words in each utterance). This instrument was refined in a series of pilot studies in FL classes at the secondary and university level. It was then subjected to a reliability test to determine if it was sufficiently explicit and discriminatory to permit trained raters to agree, within an acceptable range, on an analysis of a specific speech sample. Because of the nature of the word utterance as defined in the system (see the Appendix), the critical analytical elements were the identification of utterances, the number of utterances in the Function category, and the number of words in the Function category.

Since utterances may appear in several possible forms, it is crucial that coders, working independently, achieve a high level of agreement on the identification of utterances. A reliability coefficient of .89 at the .05 level was obtained in the reliability test. This degree of concordance was deemed sufficiently strong to say that the instrument provides appropriate guidelines for coders to recognize utterances.

Equally important is the coders' ability to assign utterances to either the Linguistic or Communicative Function category. Since these constructs constitute the primary divisions of the system, it is essential that coders recognize the distinctions between categories. The number of utterances in the Function category serves as one quantifiable index for tallying purposes. The other is the number of words contained in those utterances since the data are quantified in terms of numbers of words. The obtained reliabilities of .85 and .83, respectively, were considered sufficiently strong to attest to the clarity and discriminatory qualities of the instrument.

Data for analysis were obtained from coded protocols (see Figure 11-2). In the example given in Figure 11-2, the protocol represents a transcription of a recorded

Function	Behavior	Content			Language N/T	Duration
L	Linguistic Functions				C	
	MOD	Modeling				
		po	phonological/orthographical items			
		mo	morphological elements			
		sy	syntactical patterns			
		su	semantic units			
	CUE	Cueing				
		op	oral practice			
		wp	written practice			
		pr	prompts response			
		cl	linguistic element			
	REI	Reinforcing				
		rv	repeats student utterance verbatim			
		rc	repeats student utterance with correction			
		rm	restates student utterance with modification			
		rt	restates student utterance in translation			
C	Communicative Functions					
	STR	Structuring with utterances that				
		cp	relate to classroom procedure			
		lc	explain linguistic content			
		sm	explain subject matter content			
		pt	personalize topic			
	SOL	Soliciting with utterances that				
		cp	relate to classroom procedure			
		lc	explain linguistic content			
		sm	explain subject matter content			
		pt	personalize topic			
	RES	Responding with utterances that				
		cp	relate to classroom procedure			
		lc	relate to linguistic content			
		sm	relate to subject matter content			
		pt	personalize topic			
	REA	Reacting by acknowledging (a) or modifying (m) with utterances that		a m		
		cp	relate to classroom procedure			
		lc	relate to linguistic content			
		sm	relate to subject matter content			
		pt	personalize topic			

NOC Noncodable utterance
ITE Idiosyncratic Teacher Expression

Language: N native
T target
C combination

Figure 11.1 Protocol Analysis Instrument (PAI)

sample from a second year Spanish class at the secondary school level.

The transcription, which consists of teacher and student speeches, occupies the center of the page. Teacher speeches are numbered in both margins. Using the

Protocol Number __J-1(b)__ Page __1__

Date transcribed __2/9/80__ SS/6

Date coded _____ Coder _____

Nuestro Mund.

(Correcting homework. Verb chart on board. Includes colgar, equivocarse, componer.)

1. T. Subjuntivo, Esperanza. (T)
   S. Colgué
2. T. Cuel . . .
   S. Cuelgue
3. T. Cuelgue,/sf./Pretérito, Ana. (T)
   S. Colgaba.
4. T. No, pretérito./Imperfecto es/colgaba./El pretérito.
   S. Colgué.
5. T. Colgué./Clase, perfecto./I have hung./ Silvia (T)
   S. He estado colgado.
6. T. Uh,/colgado./Repita, clase:/He colgado.
   SS. He colgado.
7. T. Pluscuamperfecto:/I had hung./Adela. (T)
   S. Había colgado.
8. T. Excelente, si,/pues./He/y/había colgado./ El participio pasivo./Repitan:/he colgado.
   SS. He colgado.
9. T. Había colgado.
   SS. Había colgado.
10. T. El otro verbo, pues, ahora:/componer./ (Forma see next page)

1. C/SOL/lc/T/1
   C/SOL/cp/T/1
2. L/REI/rc/T/1
3. L/REI/rv/T/1
   C/REIa/lc/T/1
   C/SOL/lc/T/1
   C/SOL/cp/T/1
4. C/REAa/lc/T/2
   C/REAm/lc/T/2
   L/MOD/mo/T/1
   C/SOL/lc/T/2
5. L/REI/rv/T/1
   C/SOL/lc/T/2
   L/CUE/op/N/3
   C/SOL/cp/T/1
6. L/REI/rm/T/1
   C/SOL/CP/T/2
   L/CUE/op/T/2
7. C/SOL/lc/T/1
   L/CUE/op/N/3
   C/SOL/cp/T/1
8. C/REAa/lc/T/2
   ITE/T/1
   L/REI/rm/T/3
   C/REAm/lc/T/1
   C/REAm/lc/T/3
   C/SOL/cp/T/1
   L/CUE/op/T/2
9. L/CUE/op/T/
10. C/SOL/lc/T/4
    ITE/T/1
    L/CUE/op/T/1

Figure 11.2. Coded Protocol

definition of utterance (see the Appendix), each teacher speech is divided by slashes into one or more utterances. These utterances are coded, using abbreviations for each of the category designations. For example, the first speech contains two utterances that are coded, respectively, as (1) C/SOL/1c/T/1 and (2) C/SOL/cp/T/1, representing (1) Communicative Function, Solicitation, linguistic content, Target language, 1 word, and (2) Communicative Function, Solicitation, classroom procedure, Target language, 1 word. Some speeches represent one utterance and are relatively easy to code (see speech 2 in Figure 11-2). Others, such as speech 8, represent seven utterances and contain a mixture of linguistic and communicative utterances.

RESULTS

The primary objective of this study was to determine what kinds of FL teachers use what mix of native and target languages for what linguistic and communicative functions in the classroom.

The question of patterns of language use was treated from two perspectives. First, the data were analyzed in order to identify patterns of verbal behavior characteristic of the average teacher, that is, the hypothetical teacher who represents the statistical mean of the sample. This average teacher was found to

1. use the native language 46 percent of the time and the target language 54 percent of the time;

2. use the Linguistic Function 26 percent of the time and the Communicative Function 74 percent of the time;

3. use the native language 52 percent of the time and the target language 48 percent of the time when speaking in the Communicative Function;

4. cue 41 percent of the time, model 35 percent, and reinforce 24 percent when using the Linguistic Function (two-thirds to three-quarters of this talk is in the target language);

5. react 40 percent of the time, solicit 37 percent, structure 21 percent, and respond 2 percent when using the Communicative Function (when soliciting, two-thirds of this talk is in the target language, and in the other categories, slightly more than one-third of the talk is in the target language), and

6. discuss Linguistic Content 43 percent of the time, Classroom Procedures 27 percent, Subject Matter Content 16 percent, and Personalized Topic 14 percent when using the Communicative Function (the percentage of target language use varies from 32 percent for Linguistic Content to 83 percent for Subject Matter Content).

These results indicate that the average FL teacher uses the target language slightly more than half of the time and the Communicative Function almost three-quarters of the time while teaching. Half of the teacher talk in the Communicative Function is carried on in the target language. In the Linguistic Function, two-thirds to three-quarters of the talk is in the target language. In this function,

Cueing is more frequent than Modeling or Reinforcing. With regard to use of the native language for Linguistic Functions, the data indicate that teachers are using the native language one-quarter to one-third of the time, presumably for making comparisons with the target language.

In the Communicative Function, Reacting to student utterances and Soliciting student responses are the primary teacher Behaviors, with Responding accounting for only 2 percent of the teacher talk. Students in these classes obviously did not ask many questions. In fact, they asked fewer questions than did students in Problems of American Democracy classes, where teachers responded 7 percent of the time (Bellack et al. 1966).

The most-often discussed Content is Linguistic—not a surprising finding in a second year language class, despite the current emphasis on communicative activities. Considerable variability was found in the percentage of target language use in this area.

The second perspective for analysis was more specific, and involved dividing the fifteen subjects into three groups based on percentage of target language use in the classroom. This provided a means for determining whether functional language use varied with amount of target language use.

When grouped according to percentage of target language use, a relatively balanced distribution of the fifteen teachers was observed in the three levels of low, average, and high target language. On the total target language use variable, four subjects fell in the low target language user group(0 to 33 percent of talk), five in the average group (34 percent to 67 percent of talk) and six in the high group (68 percent to 100 percent of talk). On the target language use for Communicative Functions varaible (in which subjects were referred to as Target Language Communicators), the distribution was five low target language communicators (0 to 33 percent of communicative talk in the target language), four average (33 percent to 67 percent) and six high (68 percent to 100 percent). All of the four low target language users were also low target language communicators, five of the six high target language users were high target language communicators, and three of the five average target language users were average target language communicators.

The primary findings in this analysis of grouped teachers were the following:

1. Patterns of total target language use and target language use for Communicative Functions are almost identical in individual teachers.

2. Low target language communicators devote substantially more communicative talk to Linguistic Content than do high and average target language communicators. Conversely, they devote substantially less communicative talk to Subject Matter Content than do high and average target language communicators.

3. Average target language communicators show considerable variability in choice of language in the four Content subcategories.

As noted above, it was found that individual teachers are quite consistent in their use of the target language. A high target language user is almost always a high target language communicator; conversely, a low target language user is almost always a low target language communicator. Low target language communicators devoted substantially more communicative talk to Linguistic Content than did their average and high target language communicator colleagues. A logical inference is that they talked more about grammar and that they did this talking in the L1.

Also of interest is the considerable variability that average target language communicators exhibit when talking about the four Content subcategories of the Communicative Function. They tend to use more L1 when discussing Linguistic Content and more target language talk when discussing Subject Matter Content. This indicates that, for average target language communicators, Content is a definite factor in the choice of language. Content is not a factor for high or low target language communicators since they tend to use the target or native language, respectively, for all content categories.

The question of what kinds of teachers use what mix of language was designed to identify teacher qualities and experiences that might be related to how the teacher uses the native and target languages for linguistic and communicative functions in the classroom. The analysis was designed to identify, for purposes of selection and pre- and inservice training, the variables associated with patterns of input.

To provide data for this part of the study, the teachers completed a 48-item self-report questionnaire. Tests for correlations between the 53 predictor variables and the 2 observed variables of target language use and target language use for Communicative Functions yielded the following results:

1. The amount of target language use in the classroom correlated positively with postgraduate travel and residence in a target country (.05).
2. The amount of target language use in the classroom for Communicative Functions correlated positively with length of teaching experience in the classroom (.05).
3. The amount of target language use was not related to such variables as sex, age, reason for learning Spanish, contact with native speakers, aspects of pre- and inservice training, professional affiliation, or any of the other variables tested.

DISCUSSION AND CONCLUSION

In this study, teacher classroom talk, the primary source of input in the FL classroom, was analyzed, using the Linguistic/Communicative Functions Analysis System (L/C-FAS), a multidimensional observational system that focuses on the linguistic and communicative dimensions of teacher classroom talk. The principal objectives were to discover patterns of verbal behavior and relationships between selected teacher characteristics and the identified behaviors.

The results indicated that some teachers were high and consistent suppliers of target language input to their students, regardless of the content of the messages being conveyed. At the other end of the scale, an equally large group of teachers were low and consistent nonsuppliers of target language input, regardless of content. The "average" FL teacher, who fell between these two extremes, was observed to provide target language input for certain linguistic and communicative functions during half of the total time spent with students in the classroom.

The attempt to find relationships between teacher characteristics and patterns of target language use for linguistic and communicative functions was predicated on the assumption that knowledge of what kinds of teachers are high target language communicators, that is, high suppliers of target language input, is useful in selecting and educating teachers. Among the 48 predictor variables investigated, only 2 (postgraduate travel/residence in a target country and length of teaching experience) yielded positive correlations. Of these two, the stronger predictor was postgraduate travel and residence in a target country.

In this study, the L/C-FAS provided a useful profile of teacher target language use in the classroom. The limited number of positive correlations between predictor variables and target language use suggests that other factors influence teachers to use or not to use the target language in the instructional process. Investigation of these factors, especially those relating to attitudes and previous classroom experience, are expected to produce other significant results.

Other questions, which were formulated but not answered during the course of the study, merit investigation. Some of these relate to the "rules of the foreign language classroom game," as perceived by both teachers and students. It was found that similarities do exist between verbal moves of FL teachers and those of social studies (Bellack et al. 1966) and mathematics (Fey 1970) teachers. A more definitive statement of these rules is needed to determine what special rules may be operating in the FL class, given the bilingual, bifunctional nature of the teaching/learning situation. Another facet of this investigation is the analysis of (1) the nature and degree of congruence between perceptions of teachers and students with regard to the "rules of the foreign language classroom game" and (2) the perceptions of students regarding differences between the "rules of the game" in the FL class and in their other classes, which are conducted in the native language.

A second group of questions relates to the interaction between teacher and students in the FL classroom. In this study, the L/C-FAS system was used to investigate teacher talk. With minor modifications, it can be expanded to include student utterances, thus facilitating analysis of all classroom discourse in the L1 and the FL, particularly since peer input and interaction has been claimed to be an important variable in language learning (Krashen 1981; Plann 1979; Pica and Doughty 1985; Porter 1986). Such analysis would reveal patterns of teacher-student and student-student interaction. Some questions that might be studied include, for what percentage of the total class time do students use the linguistic and communicative functions in the target language? What roles (Structuring, Soliciting, Responding, Reacting) do students play in the target and native languages? Does extensive use of the target language by the teacher encourage or inhibit participation by the student?

A third group of questions relates to the outcome of instruction in the FL classroom. Use of the L/C-FAS in this study was confined to analysis of the process of teaching. With the addition of student achievement, proficiency, and attitude measures, data can be obtained and analyzed to determine what effects teachers with differentiated target language use profiles have upon students: What relationships exist between (1) process variables of teacher verbal behavior relative to the amount and type of target language use and (2) product variables of student performance? Is the teacher's linguistic and communicative competence, as behaviorally expressed by that teacher's talk for linguistic and communicative functions, related to students' linguistic and communicative competence? Is there a relationship between extent and type of target language used by the teacher and continued foreign language study by students? Empirically derived answers to these questions would be useful in resolving these long-standing dilemmas: How much target language? For what purposes? At what levels? With which students? With what effects?

REFERENCES

Bailey, L. 1977. Observing foreign language teaching: a new method for teachers, researchers and supervisors. *Foreign Language Annals* 10(6):641-648.

Bellack, A. A., R. T. Hyman, F. L. Smith, Jr., and H. M. Kliebard. 1966. *The Language of the Classroom.* New York: Teachers College Press, Columbia University.

Brooks, N. 1964. *Language and Language Learning.* 2nd ed. New York: Harcourt, Brace, and World.

Chastain, K. 1976. *Developing Second Language Skills.* 2nd ed. Chicago: Rand McNally.

Clark, J. L. D. 1972. *Foreign Language Testing: Theory and Practice.* Philadelphia: Center for Curriculum Development.

Corder, S. P. 1967. The significance of learners' errors. *International Review of Applied Linguistics* 5:161-170.

de Sauze, E. B. 1929. *The Cleveland Plan for the Teaching of Foreign Languages.* Philadelphia: John C. Winston.

Dunkin, M. J., and B. J. Biddle. 1974. *The Study of Teaching.* New York: Holt, Rinehart, and Winston.

Ellis, R. 1981. The role of input in second language acquisition: some implications for second language teaching. *Applied Linguistics* 2:70-82.

Fanselow, J. F. 1977. Beyond Rashomon: conceptualizing and describing the teaching act. *TESOL Quarterly* 11(1):17-40.

Fey, J. T. 1970. *Patterns of Verbal Communication in Mathematics Classes.* New York: Teachers College Press, Columbia University.

Flanders, N. A. 1970. *Analyzing Teaching Behavior.* Reading, MA: Addison-Wesley.

Gaies, S. J. 1979. Linguistic input in first and second language learning. In *Studies in First and Second Language Acquisition,* F. Eckman and A. Hastings (eds.), 185-193. Rowley, MA: Newbury House.

Hough, J. B. and J. K. Duncan. 1970. *Teaching: Description and Analysis.* Reading, MA: Addison-Wesley

Hymes, D. 1971. Competence and performance in linguistic theory. In *Language Acquisition: Models and Methods.* R. Huxley and E. Ingram (eds.), 3-28. New York: Academic Press.

Jakobovits, L. A. 1970 *Foreign Language Learning: A Psycholinguistic Analysis of the issues*. Rowley, MA: Newbury House.

Jarvis, G. A. 1968. A behavioral observation system for classroom foreign language skill acquisition activities. *Modern Language Journal* 52(5):335-341.

Joiner, E. 1977. Communicative practice versus non-communicative language practice in the teaching of beginning college French. *Modern Language Journal* 61(5):236-242.

Kelly, L. G. 1969. *25 Centuries of Language Teaching*. Rowley, MA: Newbury House.

Krashen, S. D. 1980. The theoretical and practical relevance of simple codes in second language acquisition. In *Research in Second Language Acquisition*, R. Scarcella and S. D. Krashen (eds.), 7-18. Rowley: Newbury House.

Krashen, S. D. 1981. *Second Language Acquisition and Second Language Learning*. Oxford: Pergamon Press.

Krashen, S. D. 1982. *Principles and Practice in Second Language Acquisition*. Oxford: Pergamon Institute of English.

Leeman, E. 1982. Classroom discourse and linguistic intake. Paper presented at the Goethe Institute 1982 Expertenseminar. New York.

Lofflin, M. D., B. J. Biddle, N. Barron, and M. Marlin. 1973. *Sex, Race, Social Class, and Language in the Classroom*. Technical Report No. 88. Center for Research in Social Behavior, University of Missouri, Columbia, MO.

Moskowitz, G. 1971. Interaction analysis: a new modern language for foreign language supervisors. *Foreign Language Annals* 5(2):211-221.

Moskowitz, G. 1976. The classroom interaction of outstanding foreign language teachers. *Foreign Language Annals* 9(1):135-143, 146-157.

Newport, E., H. Gleitman, and L. Gleitman. 1977. Mother I'd rather do it myself: some effects and non-effects of maternal speech style. In *Talking to Children*. C. Snow and C. Ferguson (eds.), 109-149. Cambridge: Cambridge University Press.

Omaggio, A. 1982. The relationship between personalized classroom talk and teacher effectiveness ratings: some research results. *Foreign Language Annals* 15(4):255-272.

Pica, T., and C. Doughty. 1985. The role of group work in classroom second language acquisition. *Studies in Second Language Acquisition* 7(2):233-248.

Plann, S. 1979. Morphological problems in the acquisition of Spanish in an immersion classroom. In *The Acquisition and Use of Spanish and English as First and Second Languages*, R.W. Andersen (ed.), 119-132. Washington,D.C.: TESOL.

Porter, P. 1986. How learners talk to each other: input and interaction in task centered discussions. In *Talking to Learn: Conversations in Second Language Acquisitions*. R. Day (ed.), 200-222. Rowley, MA: Newbury House.

Rivers, W. M., M. Azevedo, W. Heflin, Jr., and Ruth Opler. 1976. *A Practical Guide to the Teaching of Spanish*. New York: Oxford University Press.

Rothfarb, S. 1970. Teacher-pupil interaction in the FLES class. *Hispania* 53(2):256-263.

Savignon, S. J. 1972. *Communicative Competence: An Experiment in Foreign Language Teaching*. Philadelphia: Center for Curriculum Development.

Schulz, R. A. W. 1977. Discrete-point versus simulated communication testing. *Modern Language Journal* 61(3):94-100.

Schulz, R. A. W., and W. H. Bartz. 1975. Free to communicate. In *Perspectives: A New Freedom*, G. A. Jarvis (ed.), 47-92. ACTFL Review of Foreign Language Education, vol. 7. Skokie, IL: National Textbook Company.

Smith, B. O., and M. O. Meux. 1962. *A Study of the Logic of Teaching*. Urbana, IL: University of Illinois Press.

Strevens, P. 1978. The nature of language teaching. In *Understanding Second and Foreign Language Learning: Issues and Approaches*. J. C. Richards (ed.), 179-203. Rowley, MA: Newbury House.

Wing, B. H. 1978. The languages of the foreign language classroom. Ph.D. dissertation, Ohio State University.

Wittgenstein, L. 1958. *Philosophical Investigations.* Oxford: Basil Blackwell.
Wragg, E. C. 1970. Interaction analysis in the foreign language classroom. *Modern Language Journal* 54(1):116-120.

APPENDIX

The Linguistic/Communicative Functions Analysis System

The Linguistic/Communicative Functions Analysis System is an observational procedure that consists of a data collection phase and a data analysis phase. In the first phase, a series of audio tape protocols is obtained from ongoing classes. In the second phase, these protocols are transcribed, coded by trained coders, and subsequently analyzed to reveal patterns of teacher verbal behavior. This procedure is similar to that used by Bellack et al. (1966) in their study, *The Language of the Classroom.*

The focal point of the Linguistic/Communicative Functions Analysis System is the Protocol Analysis Instrument (PAI). This instrument is a multiple-category coding system designed to describe all teacher talk in the FL classroom. It is an all-inclusive system, composed of mutually exclusive categories, that yields a profile of teacher talk in both qualitative and quantitative terms. The function of native or target language use by the teacher serves as the qualitative dimension of the category instrument. Within that dimension, the constructs of Linguistic and Communicative Functions, and their respective subdivisions, describe teacher utterances. The amount of native or target language use by the teacher in each of the functional categories is the quantitative dimension of the category instrument.

As seen in Figure 11-1, the Protocol Analysis Instrument (PAI) contains five categories that describe teacher use of the native and target languages:

1. Function. As defined in the PAI, Function is the purpose for which the native and target languages are used by the teacher in the classroom. Two functions are recognized in the system: Linguistic and Communicative. The Linguistic Function is defined as use of language for its own sake when the purpose is to concentrate on the linguistic elements of the language—specifically, phonology, morphology, syntax, and lexicon. In contrast, the Communicative Function is defined as use of language as a tool for sending and receiving meaningful messages. The purpose is to concentrate on the ideas, feelings, desires, and opinions being transmitted and received. It is a given of the system that all teacher talk in the FL classroom can be assigned to either the Linguistic or Communicative Function.

These two functions each contain subdivisions that serve the purpose of explicating the functions. The subdivisions refer to the type of verbal Behavior exhibited by the teacher in a particular utterance. Because the Linguistic and Communicative Functions are used for different purposes, the types of Behavior found in the functions are different.

2. Behavior. In the Linguistic Function, as seen in Figure 11-1, the three Behaviors characteristic of and unique to the FL class are Modeling, Cueing, and Reinforcing. Modeling is providing an oral model so that students may hear how a word is pronounced, how conjugations are formed, or how phrases and sentences are constructed. Students are expected to listen and to attend to the linguistic characteristics of what is being modeled. No overt student behavior is expected. Cueing is supplying an oral stimulus that shapes a student response. This stimulus serves as a linguistic cue to assist the student in the formulation of a response. Reinforcing occurs when the teacher provides an oral reinforcement of a student response. This reinforcement takes the form of several types of teacher repetition of the student responses.

In the Communicative Function, the teacher employs four types of Behavior that have been found to describe teacher talk in classrooms, regardless of discipline. The four Behaviors in the PAI, Structuring, Soliciting, Responding, and Reacting, are adapted from the system designed by Bellack and his colleagues (1966) in their study of talk in classes studying Problems of American Democracy. These categories represent pedagogical "moves" or "plays" in the classroom "game." Adaptation of these constructs to the FL classroom is based in part on the proposition by Bellack et al. (1966) that they are a potentially useful technique for the investigation of classroom teaching of high school subjects such as English, social studies, mathematics, and science. This study represents the second utilization of the "pedagogical moves" for research purposes, the first being a system designed and validated by Fey (1970) to analyze teacher talk in mathematics classes. Fanselow (1977) also includes these "pedagogical moves" in FOCUS, a multidimensional observational system.

The first of the four Behaviors, Structuring, sets the context for subsequent behavior by initiating, or halting or excluding, interactions between students and teacher. These statements do not, in themselves, elicit a response, nor are they made in response to one of the other moves. They are an expression of what the teacher thinks should be said or taught at that moment. Soliciting elicits a verbal or nonverbal response on the part of students. The solicitation may be a command, a question or a statement that implies a command. Responding occurs in relation to Soliciting moves on the part of students and serves as the fulfillment of the solicitation. Responses begin as answers to questions or requests for information and assistance but may be expanded by the teacher to the giving of new information that is related to the solicitation. Reacting occurs in relation to a Structuring, Soliciting, Responding, or Reacting move on the part of a student but is not elicited directly by them. Reactions acknowledge (through praise, criticism, or nonjudgmental comment) or modify (through clarification, synthesis, or expansion) the move that prompted them.

3. Content. Like the Function category, Behavior is also subdivided to provide further differentiation and specification of verbal utterances. The subdivisions in Behavior describe the Content of utterances. Content is defined as the substantive matter that the teacher deals with in each Behavior.

The three Behaviors of the Linguistic Function, as seen in Figure 11-1, each have four subdivisions that describe specific aspects of the Content included in the particular Behavior. Modeling behavior consists of modeling (1) phonological or orthographical items, (2) morphological elements, (3) syntactical patterns, and (4) semantic units. In Cueing behavior, the teacher has recourse to four Content areas, all of which are related to providing a cue consisting of (1) an oral stimulus in those exercises generally associated with oral practice, (2) an oral stimulus in those exercises generally associated with written practice, (3) the linguistic framework for a student response by prompting the first word or words of the answer, and (4) a linguistic element within a communicative context. In the last Behavior of the Linguistic Function, Reinforcing, the teacher repeats a student utterance in a variety of forms: (1) verbatim, (2) with correction, (3) with modification, or (4) in translation.

Within the Communicative Function, the four Content subdivisions pertain to four basic topics of conversation in the FL classroom. These subdivisions, which are the same for each of the four Communicative Behaviors, are (1) classroom procedures (talk pertaining to classroom routines, materials, and activities), (2) linguistic content (talk pertaining to the analytical study of language), (3) subject matter content (talk pertaining to the nonlinguistic substantive content being discussed), and (4) personalized content (talk that personalizes the topic and relates directly to student involvement with what is happening inside or outside of the classroom).

These three levels of the PAI, Function, Behavior, and Content, are interrelated, since Content is nested in Behavior, which, in turn, is nested in Function. The two remaining categories of the PAI, Language and Duration, are independent and apply to all of the three nested categories. In the analysis, they are determined by a verbal unit that is called an utterance.

In the PAI, the utterance is the basic unit of talk. It can be a complete sentence, a clause in a sentence, a self-contained phrase, a single word, or even a syllable or a letter. An utterance is expressed entirely in the native or target language, with one exception (see below). The boundaries of the utterance are determined by a change of language and or a change of function or both within one of the languages.

4. Language. This category of the PAI identifies the language used by the teacher in the utterance, thus permitting an analysis of target/native language use by the teacher. It is possible to designate native language use (N), target language use (T), o, in exceptional cases, a combination of the two (C). C is used as a subscript to N or T in those instances where the teacher mixes the native and target languages arbitrarily in the same utterance for purposes not recognized by the functional categories of the system. In Spanish, for example, such an utterance would be: "If I giver señor Jones un punazo en la cara, he's going to get red or angry rapidamente."

5. Duration. The final category of the PAI is the number of words or letters (if the teacher is focusing on spelling) in the utterance. This category is the quantifying element that provides data for determining ratios of teacher talk in each of the several categories of the coding system as well as ratios of native and target language talk.

Two additional coding entries are included to designate noncodable utterances (NOC) or Idiosyncratic Teacher Expressions (ITE). The former are used primarily to designate unintelligible utterances while the latter refer to utterances such as "uh," or "pues" that the teacher uses periodically for functions that are not recognized by the system.

Closing Remarks

CLOSING REMARKS

The primary goal of this volume has been to focus attention on the foreign language (FL) learner, on context and on learning process. Although, in many ways studies here can be considered only exploratory, they represent important steps in constructing a more complete understanding of each of these aspects and in suggesting answers to some of the questions raised in the introduction to this volume. Is language acquisition possible when the classroom is the sole source of target language input? Is there a FL learning process that all classroom learners share? Is it the same process that is shared by second language (L2) learners? To what extent does the experience of FL learners suggest the use of universal strategies for comprehension and production?

The studies in the first section clearly support the idea that FL learners internalize language in ways that are not explained by classroom materials or instruction. There is evidence that FL learners progress through transitional stages of competence. Both the structure of those stages and the shape of the errors that learners make along the way strongly suggest the use of strategies that are similar to those documented for both L1 and L2 learners. The studies in the second section suggest that FL learners, like L2 learners, rely on both L1 skills and universal strategies in developing certain skills for language comprehension and production. While the FL learner and learning processes are thus shown to have much in common with their L2 counterparts, the studies in the third section and others elsewhere in the volume indicate that the impact of the classroom context needs to be considered in any explanation of the eventual success of FL learning, and indeed in any account of the strategies and processes involved in that learning.

Although problems relating to teaching methodology have purposely not been addressed here, all of the authors are themselves FL teachers, and the reader will have noticed that almost every study reveals a concern for the implications of the research findings for FL instruction. Looked at from the perspective of these concerns, the findings can be summarized as follows:

1. Instruction, considered as the sequencing and presentation of grammatical information and the variety of classroom practice that students receive, does not seem to be directly responsible either for the interim forms that students use as they progress toward the acquisition of a particular structure or for the order in which those forms emerge. (Eubank, Terrell, VanPatten, Kaplan).

2. The process of language learning itself triggers the use of strategies that FL learners share with others (i.e., children acquiring L1 and L2 learners) involved in language learning (LoCoco, VanPatten, Kaplan).

3. The context of instruction that is shaped by teacher input (Wing, Eubank) and by certain classroom demands (Eubank) may be responsible for some strategies (Eubank, Frantzen and Rissel) that affect the progress or direction or both of FL learning.

4. Development of skill in language use involves abilities other than those used in improving grammatical proficiency (Dvorak, Lee and Ballman, Frantzen and Rissel, Horwitz), but not all abilities or characteristics will necessarily have an impact on early-stage learners (Bacon).

Whether or not the evidence summarized in points 1 and 2 justifies redoing the FL syllabus to make it correspond to a more "natural sequence" of grammar development (e.g., avoid early emphasis of late-acquired forms, teach certain items only when learners are ready for them—the pros and cons of which have been argued for some time in L2 research (cf. Krashen, Madden and Bailey 1975, Krashen 1982, as well as the 1985 volume edited by Hyltenstam and Pienemann), there can be no doubt of its importance in providing language teachers and language learners with needed insights regarding the interpretation of learner difficulties and the setting of achievable classroom goals (see VanPatten 1986 for some discussion of how learners may benefit by "being in on" the findings of FL/L2 research).

The findings have two important implications for FL instruction. First, if points 1 and 2 above lead one to the conclusion that methodology has relatively little to do with the way that foreign languages are internalized, points 3 and 4 suggest that methods comparisons may still be worthwhile with regard to the development of skills for language use— reading comprehension, writing, conversational management and survival strategies, proofreading and self—correction—and positive, productive attitudes toward the language learning process. In a sense, the message is that teachers may not have to worry about teaching grammar in order for students to absorb it, but that without explicit teacher help in the development of effective "usage skills," students are unlikely to be able to develop them on their own. Second, since these usage skills appear to have little direct relationship to the students' linguistic competence, the traditional placement of reading and writing late in the instructional sequence needs reexamination.

As is often the case, in looking for an answer to one question, each of the studies included here has uncovered a number of new issues for further investigation. The editors find that the questions raised by the studies collected here are as important as they are interesting. It is our hope that this volume will encourage the research necessary to find their answers.

REFERENCES

Hyltenstam, K., and M. Pienemann (eds.). 1985. *Modelling and Assessing Second Language Acquisition*. San Diego: College Hill Press.

Krashen, S. D. 1982. *Principles and Practice in Second Language Acquisition*. Oxford: Pergamon Press.

Krashen, S. D., C. Madden, and N. Bailey. 1975. Theoretical aspects of grammatical sequencing. In *New Directions in Second Language Learning, Teaching, and Bilingual Education*, M. Burt and H. Dulay (eds.), 44-54. Washington, D.C.: TESOL.

VanPatten, B. 1986. Second language acquisition research and the teaching/learning of Spanish: some research findings and implications. *Hispania* 69:202-216.